AFGHANISTAN FROM DAIRUS TO AMANULLAH

AFGHANISTAN FROM DAIRUS TO AMANULLAH

GEORGE MACMUNN

GYAN

Published by

GYAN

Gyan Publishing House
5, Ansari Road
Daryaganj, New Delhi-110002
Phone: 011-47034999, 9811692060
E-mail: books@gyanbooks.com

Distribution Network
gyanbooks.com
India, USA, Canada, UK, Australia

ISBN: 978-93-7014-015-8 (PB)
First Published, 1929

2nd Impression 2025

Printed at: Gyan Press, Delhi.

AFGHANISTAN FROM DAIRUS TO AMANULLAH
Author: GEORGE MACMUNN

AFGHANISTAN

From a photo by Fry of Lucknow

Amir Abdurrahman

Amir el Kebir

AFGHANISTAN

FROM DARIUS TO AMANULLAH

BY

LT. GENERAL SIR GEORGE MACMUNN

K.C.B., K.C.S.I., D.S.O.

COLONEL COMMANDANT THE ROYAL ARTILLERY

CONTENTS

ILLUSTRATIONS

OUTLINE MAPS

COLOURED MAP

NOTE ON SPELLING

So far as possible the system adopted is, with certain notable exceptions, that laid down by the Permanent Committee on Geographical Names.

The General Staff Map, from which the main map in the book is taken, spells on some other system, for in truth there is no system as yet universal, and there probably never can be. That adopted here is the one that meets to-day with most agreement and is that used in the British official histories of the World War.

For certain Indian and Afghan names that are household words in their unscientific transliteration it would be affectation to spell more correctly. For instance, *Mirath* for Meerut would be unthinkable, or *Dehli* for Delhi. Nor can the " q " convention be entirely accepted, that useful arrangement whereby the " q " without the " u " is used to represent the second " k " in Arabic, often called the " round " or " Arabic ' k,' " with pronunciation verging on the " g." It would be pedantic to write Qandahar for Kandahar, even though it be nearer Gandara; Qalat-i-Ghilzai is printed Kelat-i-Ghilzie, because the regiment of that name and the British Medal spell it so, and it is a household phrase also. Among the difficulties of spelling is the change in pronunciation in India which has taken place in the last hundred years in the forgetting, except in Kashmir, of the deep, long " a " and " o " of the Afghani Persian. In the days of our grandfathers Cawnpore did give the correct pronunciation, and Ali Cawn or Lol Singh, for what the modern transliteration now spells and pronounces Khanpur, Ali Khan, Lal Singh. But in Kashmir, where the deep " o " is still a joy to hear, it is Lol Mandi, not Lal, and everyone talks of the mulberry season as "*Job* (not *jab*) *molberi hoega,*" " when the mulberries are in," the mulberries that incidentally are eaten in that happy season by fish and bears, by ox and by ass, by dogs and fowls, and all the humans of the valley.

Therefore it is to be hoped that the reader will bear with the anomalies for the reasons explained.

In the spelling of personal names the *Cambridge History* has for the most part been taken as a guide, except that the awkward inverted comma denoting the Arabic " a " has been omitted.

Certain names, such as Abdurrahman, Shujah, etc., have been spelt in the manner which has become familiar by frequent repetition.

INTRODUCTION

THERE are books without end which deal with some phase or other of the British connection with Afghanistan, and there are many histories which, making use of the work of the Muhammadan historians, tell in considerable detail the story of the Afghan invasions of India during the last thousand years. But there is no book that gives any presentment of the romantic and often terrible story as a whole, that pictures the great uplands into which the earth between the Oxus and the Indus has been thrown, or that tells us of the strange medley of ancient races that fill the pockets among the mountains, or shows us the panorama from Darius to Amanullah. Most important of all to the understanding of the modern problem, the inseparable connection geographically, politically, and ethnologically between Afghanistan and India has never been emphasised, yet neither the public sense behind statesmen nor statesmen themselves can deal with the future without some grasp thereof.

This book has therefore been written in the hope of presenting the story in all its absorbing interest to those who would view it from the comfort of the easy-chair.

But romantic as is the coming of the Aryan waves through the Afghan passes to India and Mother Ganges, stirring as is the march of the Macedonians, ruthless the Afghan massacres and conversions, magnificent the Empire of Mogul Delhi and pitiable its fall, yet it is in the world of to-day that interest must centre. What can the modern world expect to see this museum of past tragedies evolve?

The Victorian historian in his smugness has failed to do justice to the steady purpose of Britain towards the various portions of that Mogul Empire to which fate made her the heir-at-law. The progress suited to the people which a young man in his haste has for the moment put an end to, has been the result of a steady, helpful,

British policy, hesitating and mistaken in some of its methods, but perfectly consistent in its major aims.

It is hoped that the story has now been set forth in the greater justice to ourselves and to the better understanding of the material which Afghan rulers and leaders have to handle would they bring the valuable constituents in the national make-up to the culmination of some fair edifice.

CHAPTER I

THE GEOGRAPHY AND EARLY HISTORY OF AFGHANISTAN

Popular Conceptions · The Geography of Afghanistan Afghan Turkistan and Kafiristan · Afghanistan through the Mist of Ages · The Coming of Alexander · The Rise of Islam · The Roadways of Afghanistan · The Way of the Invaders

Popular Conceptions

ERRATUM

Page 337, line 22, and page 343, line 6 of Envoi, *for* "nephew" *read* "step-brother."

numerable were very familiar with the country and its people, but because disaster and contumely attended our policy, despite the brilliant military retrievement, and because scalded dogs fear cold water, it seems to have disappeared behind the black entrance to the Khaibar and the great curtain of the Mountains of Solomon. For three years, from 1878 to 1881, once again was the purdah lifted from our imagination, and the British Army and the British public, through the far more modern war correspondents, did for a short time have some familiarity with that romantic and in many ways still savage country.

Yet again, in 1882, the fog of oblivion descended, and we have till the last year or so still looked on the country somewhat as Alice in Wonderland looked through the small door in the hall to the Duchess' garden beyond.

This point of view, and the conception of aloofness engendered, reflects the wrong light in which to study either the past or the future. As a matter of fact, Afghanistan as now known to us has not only been concerned with Indian affairs from north to south, but has from almost prehistoric times been an integral part of India, taking that term in its widest conception as the country of the Hindus and those who once were Hindus. Geographically, racially, and politically India and Afghanistan have been one. And based on that aspect, the principle underlying the British policy of 1837–38 was a correct one.

To arrive at a wide and true conception of the story it is necessary to turn to very early times and then follow the history of Afghanistan and both Hindu and Moslem India up to the present day. For our convenience the term Afghanistan and Afghan must often be used long before that term came to be applied to the provinces of Delhi west of the Indus, and when Kabulistan and Zabulistan or Khurasan were the terms in general use for the northern and southern portions of that country.

Seated as it is where the valleys of Asia surge up into great mountain barriers, leaving here and there more accessible ways, not only does it contain sheltered pockets of overwhelmed ancient peoples, but it is the most remarkable storehouse of antiquities. Owing to the persistent endurance of savagery and the uncertain safety for travellers, these have hardly yet been touched by the hand of modern science. Not only are the relics of Græco-Bactrian rule and Buddhist settlements numerous, in addition to the famous caves and rock-cut figure at Bamian north of Ghuzni, but there are pre-Buddhist Hindu remains and monasteries in many valleys both in North and South Afghanistan and in the border hills west of the Indus. The passes near Landi Kotal contain ruins of great fortresses [1] whose lofty walls still frown down on the caravan, which must have existed when Alexander's legions marched into Swat to avoid, no doubt, both them and the marauding Aprœtæ who dwelt there then as they do now.

[1] See p. 16.

In spite of the fact that the site of the rock of Aornos, which Alexander stormed on the way to his crossing of the Indus at Amb, is most circumstantially described and of the most romantic interest, it had never been located, and it was not till a couple of years ago that the tribesmen in the hills were sufficiently civilised to allow Sir Aurel Stein to make a journey of discovery which has at last settled this absorbing mystery and controversy.

There is no limit to what a period of careful exploration may not reveal, and just as in India the last few years have taken us far from Buddhist and Bactrian days to Sumerian times, so in Afghanistan there are certain to be missing links of earlier knowledge to be laid bare. The French archæological mission in Afghanistan during the last two or three years has discovered Buddhist and Hindu paintings which vie with the remarkable discoveries of the same kind in India; indeed nowhere else in the world does so romantic a storehouse still await the unveiling and unearthing.

The Geography of Afghanistan

The modern Afghanistan, the name which has gradually taken the place of Khurasan, though natives of India still use the latter for the southern portion, has an area of some 250,000 square miles, and is therefore appreciably larger than France with its 212,000. The north and east consist of strange tumbled mountain systems, which emanate from the gigantic tablelands of the Pamirs, and trend south and south-west till they die away in the deserts and swamps of the Hamuns on the Persian border, and the inland sumphs to which the Helmand group of rivers flow. If we imagine the letter V so suspended that its sharp end is up in the north-east and its legs pointing west and south-west, we shall get into our minds the principal trend of the system. The upper leg of the > would thus be lying horizontal, and would represent the range of the Hindu Kush, or Paropamisus, with its extremity at Herat, while the lower leg would represent the mountains of the Kunar River, the Safed Koh, and the Sulaiman Range, with the extremity at

Sibi, at the Indian end of the Bolan Pass. Near the top of the >, midway between the legs, would be Kabul. Parallel to and outside the lower leg runs the mighty Indus, the river of Sind, while between the Indus and the leg of the > there lies the country of Ruh, the ancient name for the hills of the Pathan tribes, whence came the Rohillas, and which is now for the most part the British tribal tracts on the north-west frontier. North of the upper leg, between it and the river Oxus, lies the province of Afghan

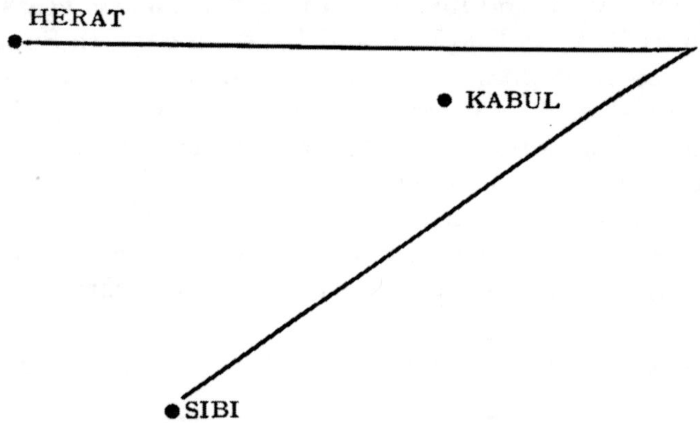

Turkistan, of which Balkh is the principal town. Between the legs run parallel ranges of hills, while close to Kabul itself rises the Helmand River, which flows south-west into the Registan deserts and flats, between Kandahar and the Persian border, much of which, in the days before Chingiz Khan and his Tatars lived to make the world a desert, was a thickly populated area.

If the reader will draw the > as described and fill in the points mentioned, he will have a very clear idea of the general trend and shape of Afghanistan, to which may now be added a few more details.

Between the Helmand and the upper leg lie the Hazara highlands, inhabited by a group of Turki tribes resembling greatly the Anatolian Turks, and south of the Hazaras the hills of Zamindawar, the home of the Abdali or Durani, the Afghan proper. Between Kandahar and Kabul lies the Ghilzai country, with Kelat-i-Ghilzie, and Ghuzni, the road so often traversed by armies on the march to Kabul, by Alexander of Macedon, and in our own times by Sir John Keane in 1839, by Sir William Nott in 1842, by Sir Donald Stewart in the spring of 1880, and downwards by Sir Frederick Roberts in the autumn.

The plateaux and mountains of Afghanistan drain their waters in three directions: north of the > to the Oxus or the exitless oases such as Merv, east of it to the Indus, and between the legs down to the swamps and Hamuns of Seistan. To understand the geography and water systems of the country it must be realised that there lies on the borders of Persia and Afghanistan, in the centre of Khurasan, a vast basin with a level of some 1600 feet above sea-level, into which drain the waters, the snows, and the rains from the mountains round, and from which there is no exit to the sea, and which constitute the Hamuns aforesaid.

Down the space between the legs of the > run many parallel chains of hills, and between them parallel rivers. The greatest is the Helmand, and east of it run the Tarnak and the Arghandab, with several others. These others eventually join the Arghandab, which itself flows into the Helmand at Qala Bist, eight miles west of Kandahar, and the joint waters thence hurry down to the swamps and the Hamuns.

Kandahar stands almost on the edge of the basin close on 3500 feet above the sea. From it along the old strategic road to Kabul the marching columns rose 2000 feet to Kelat-i-Ghilzie, nearly 2000 more to Ghuzni, which stands over 7200 feet; but still higher runs the marching road, crossing the Wardak hills at Sheikhabad, 10,600 feet above the sea, thence dipping to the Kabul basin, at head of which stands Kabul city, 5700 feet above the sea.

Out of the Sulaiman mountains and Kabul hills run the main stream of the Kabul River with the conjoint waters of the Kunar River to the Indus just above Attock, the Kurram, and the Gumal. But neither of the latter bring much water down, it all being taken off to the myriad hillside fields, except in times of great snow-melting and spate. Into the Gumal flow the Zhob and the Kundar, with little final result, so sought after and so diligently used is the normal flow. All the waters between the > go to the Hamuns of Seistan, while north of the Hindu Kush the streams all flow to the Oxus, or, like the Murghab which rises near Herat, into an oasis, and never reach even an inland sea.

Afghan Turkistan and Kafiristan

The northern leg of the > runs west to Herat, and the distant province of Afghan Turkistan between it and the Oxus only after 1850 became definitely part of the kingdom of Dost Muhammad. It runs down from the Hindu Kush with its 16,000-foot peaks to the Oxus, at a level of 900 feet above the sea, in many bastioned spurs that finally die away to rich and fertile plains. Here for the most part the inhabitants are no longer Ghilzai or Abdali or Pathan, but of Turki or Persian origin, the lords of Turan. In the east of the land lies most mountainous Badakhshan, and all along the cis-Oxus plains are wealthy trading towns—Kunduz and Mazar-i-Sharif, Tashqurghan, Balkh, and Andkhui — till we come to the westerly district of Badghis, where the evil cold wind blows, which lies just north of Herat. That city of great contentions lies snug on the hitherside of the Paropamisus, which is the end of the Hindu Kush.

From Herat, which stands at 3000 feet, the road curls round the end of the basins which drain down to the Hamuns, by Sabzawar and Farah to Kandahar.

Sixty-five miles west of Herat the Persian frontier lies from Zulfiqar in the north to Koh-i-Malik Siah in the south —close on 400 miles; while west from Herat runs the time-honoured road to holy Meshed, up which have marched Persian armies to this key town since Time was.

One more district remains to be described, and that is the country lying north of the Kabul River—the inaccessible valleys of Kafiristan which were long unknown to the outer world, and which legend filled with a Greek-descended, marooned people. These deep valleys, amid lofty hills trending up to the highest peaks and uplands of the Hindu Kush and the Pamirs, were opened out for the first time by Abdurrahman in 1896 and the unfortunate inhabitants converted to Islam.[1] Centuries before, Timur Lang had poked his nose up them and been stung for his pains; and in the early nineties Sir George Scott Robertson from Gilgit had penetrated there too, and dissipated the Greek legend, that legend which Rudyard Kipling has told of in the fascinating tale of *The Man who would be King*.

Robertson found the people to be just one of the pockets of ancient Dardic races as in Gilgit and Punnial who had fled away from Aryan invaders, but who had kept their ancient pagan faith and evaded Islam.

Afghanistan through the Mist of Ages

From the earliest times the way to India from Central Asia by land has been from the north-west. The great barrier of the Himalayas, though it has admitted invasions by China at the expense of years of preparation, has done so in but a feeble streamlet. Here and there some earlier Mongolian or Tatar race has slowly infiltered, but the open road to migrating races and marching armies has been from the north-west alone. The great wall of the Himalaya has shut off the Tatar and his derivatives from the east in anything greater than a trickle.

The Arabs have come by way of the sea, but Aryan, Turk, Tatar, Mogul, Afghan, Scythian, whatever that may mean, the lord of Iran and the lord of Turan, have come from Khurasan—from Herat and Kandahar—through what we now call British Baluchistan, or from Balkh and Kabul by the Kabul River and its adjacent debouches. When the Aryan race started moving from the Central Asian steppes, impelled perhaps by Tatar pressure, and split into the three streams of accepted theory, the stream that came toward India crossed the Oxus and inhabited for many hundred

[1] See p. 24.

years the plains and fertile valleys between the Paropamisus and that mighty river, and then pushed on down any promising valley towards the Punjab, filling up those that were worth filling and passing the stream on, as lava flows down the mountain-side.

It must have been a leisurely stream, occupying many a hundred year in the coming, and enduring long as a force

on the Indian side of the Oxus, building at Balkh a great fortress city that for many generations was the bulwark of Iran against Turan. It buttressed the Aryan against the horses of Togomar, against the Turk, the Tatar, the Mongol, and all those races which flowed from that extinct crucible which is now the desert of Gobi, before that crucible was smothered by the rotting of sand mountains. When therefrom poured forth that strange stream of almond-eyed races which some say are the descendants of Cain and carry his brand of the Mongol fold to this day, it was this Balkh on the far side of the Hindu Kush, bastioned and turreted when the Babylon of Nebuchadnezzar had not yet risen from its earlier ruins, that kept the Tatar waves from Ariana.

Many centuries even before our era the dominion of Persia extended into parts of what is now Afghanistan, for Darius brought under his dominion Herat, Kandahar, and Kabul. The heritage of this tradition lasted well into the Victorian age, and is even much concerned with the story of the British in Afghanistan. It was just before this that the Persian Empire brought Indian soldiers to fight the Greeks in Europe, at the Battle of Platæa in B.C. 479—a service not repeated till 1914. It was somewhere about 500 B.C. that Kabul and the Indus valley became a Persian satrapy; and we know how Skylax, the Persian admiral, presumably after the Persian advent into the great valley of the Indus, sailed down to the sea as Alexander did after him.

We may feel sure that there was then no great divergence of habits and ideas between the Aryans of Persia and those of Bactria and the Kabul valleys, and we know that Zoroaster (Zarathustra) himself was a native of Balkh, the capital of Bactria.

The Coming of Alexander

It was probably the story of the easy conquest of Darius over Northern India that first fired the Western Aryan Alexander with the desire to make his move on India, after finding his march through Persia no great matter. Once he had beaten the Persians, who like the Babylonians employed many Greeks, he probably found Greek merchants, traders, and even officials installed along the great Persian highways. He marched to Kandahar, which some men say still bears his name, and thence to Kabul, up the parallel valleys of the Helmand tributaries, and over the Paropamisus or Hindu Kush to Balkh, and made Bactria his own before moving through Kabul to India. He found ordered Persian provinces, and the people he met with were the Aryans of India, the subjects of Hindu kings and themselves Hindus. They submitted fairly readily, as one Aryan to another, when the difference between Eastern and Western Aryans was less marked than now, and his young Westerns organised and trained the Eastern Aryans to serve as his auxiliary soldiers exactly as young British officers have done in modern times. And here it may be remarked that it is better for Aryan India to be led and developed by people of their own race than to cower, as they had done for a thousand years before the British came, under the Tatar and Semite races, whose first strangle-hold of India began before the days of the Norman conquest. But that is by the way.

With the death of Alexander, the break-up of his empire among his generals naturally applied to his Indian territories. Bactria became a kingdom under Satrap Philip, Kabul, Ghuzni, and perhaps Kandahar, another under Starsanor and Sibertius, while India was left to Oxyartes, a father-in-law of Alexander. And thus the provinces of the land showed this age-old fissiparous tendency, as we shall see recurring constantly in later days and as, in January 1929, they have again exhibited.

The quarrelling and fighting were prolonged, and it was not for several years that Seleucus emerged as emperor of the country from the Euphrates to the Oxus and Indus. He it was who was persuaded to give up the valleys of Ghor and Panjshahr to the Indians and forgo that great strategic possibilities of highway. But when Seleucus died these provinces broke away again, and from the immense number of coins found, the sovereigns, many of them gaining ascendancy for short periods but all eagerly exercising their prerogative to mint, must have numbered legion. Their cities were very large, for at Begram [1] alone, outside Kabul, are immense ruins which it is said yield perhaps thousands of coins a year to those who potter and dig in the vicinity. All this points to an immense population and great trading centres; but the mass of the people were

[1] Probably the Nicæa of Alexandrine history.

Buddhist figures in the rock at Bamian

evidently Hindu or Aryan who, after the rise of Asoka, became Buddhists. These varied Hellenic kings seemed to have ruled for perhaps 140 years—viz. to 120 B.C.—when invading Scythian hordes, possibly Jāts not un-akin to the Aryans, drove them forth towards India, where they established Hellenic kingdoms on the Indus which lasted for many years more. The earlier dominions in the Punjab, the province governed by Oxyartes, must have passed very quickly, as the comparatively small number of what in these days we should call "C 3" men left by Alexander, were soon swallowed up, overwhelmed, and perhaps absorbed.

We may feel certain that Hindus did inhabit the Afghan valley as the principal subjects of the Hellenic kings for many centuries after Alexander, and became Buddhist when King Asoka forsook the older gods and turned to the pure philosophy that Sakya Muni the Buddha had preached centuries before.

During the first century of our era the Scythian races who had pushed out the Hellenic rule were in their turn overcome by the Yeuchi, a Tatar horde from Central Asia who settled in Bactria and some of the Kabul country, adopting the prevalent Buddhism; and here the Chinese pilgrim Hiuen-Tsiang found them in the seventh century, still Buddhists.

But even with this come and go of races many of the valleys, and especially those of the country east of Kabul, retained for the great part their Hindu hillmen. In fact, Kabul, Kandahar, Gandara, the Kurram, the Derajat, and Yusufzai were all integral parts of Hellenic or Indian kingdoms, and occupied by the same people as held the Punjab and the Gangetic plain—viz. the earlier Aryan invaders from across the Oxus.

The Rise of Islam

So for the first centuries of our era it would seem that Ariana and Khurasan continued under their Græco-Bactrian and Hindu, and later under Tatar, rulers in varying proportions. Nor were they uncivilised, so far at any rate as the plains and cities went. Some remnant of the rule of Persia, and " the grandeur that was Greece," must have remained in their cities and in their culture, at any rate until the rise of Islam in the seventh century, which was to bring a considerable change over the whole face of the country and its relations to the people of the South.

The first generation after Muhammad saw the Arab wave of conquest pass over the middle east in a remarkable manner. It spread to Khurasan, and many of the Aryan race accepted the new faith—some from the glamour of the sword, and some because neither Buddhism nor Hinduism had enough to give. The simple, straightforward, monotheistic appeal, backed by the glamour of conquest, was irresistible to many.

From the conquering hordes of the Caliphs some remained and settled, especially from the tribe of the family of the Prophet himself. From these come the Sayyid people and those who, rightly or no, claim such descent and are to be found in small patches all over Afghanistan, and who later came to India. In the eighth century, too, came by sea the Arab conquerors of Hindu Sind, leaving an Arab population, which is this day most marked in the Indus boatmen. It was about the time of the Arab conquest that the Afghan proper, the *Ben-i-Israel*, claiming Mosaic origin, came to Southern Khurasan, and also sent streams and pockets to lodge among the Aryan converts to the faith the length and breadth of the land. The Islamic stream met the Tatar stream about the banks of the Oxus, and an agelong feud commenced, which but partly ended when the Tatar races of the trans-Oxus gradually embraced, somewhat half heartedly, the faith of "the Submission," abandoning their paganism and reluctantly, perhaps, their Buddhism ; for it is among the Mongol races that Buddhism seems to have its real home.

When the great Caliphate at Bagdad fell from its high estate the Arab power over Khurasan failed, and Kabul and Kandahar developed a separate existence, though Herat remained a great centre of the original Islamic culture and learning, as developed by the Arab leaders who came there. For that reason the mosques and religious buildings of that ancient city are of great beauty. Dilapidated and ill-cared for as many are, there is nevertheless an air of culture here which is not to be found elsewhere in Islamic Afghanistan.

The Roadways of Afghanistan

The roads in Afghanistan run much the same now as in the days of Alexander, and are little better, save that of recent years a few good motor roads have been made, while British campaigns have improved the gradients for gun-wheels.

The conformation of the country and the lie of the mountains mean that for all time the general trend must remain the same, though modern engineering and explosives will find a better alignment. But so long as the main means of transport is the camel and the pack-horse, so long is there little to be gained by improvement. Pack-tracks are countless, but few are open all the year round.

From Afghanistan to India there are but two groups of roads: those from Southern Afghanistan, which leave Kandahar and penetrate, not through the Bolan Pass as people often think, but through the parallel valleys of Baluchistan via Pishin, to emerge all along the Derajat by various openings in the Sulaiman hills. Here ancient Bactrian forts barred the defiles, as British posts bar them now, and on the larger of them, as at Harrand, Mangrota, and one or two other defiles, huge fortresses still stand. This group of passes, coming out sometimes by the Gumal, sometimes by the Vihoa or by Harrand or the Sakhi Sarwar, converge for the most part on Multan, which from time immemorial has been the strategic point of the lower Indus, and one which bulked very large to British strategical thought a generation ago. The other group, which comes from Ghuzni and Kabul, may be divided into two sections, the southern entering the upper Derajat and Bannu by the Gumal and Tochi valleys, the northern coming over the

THE INVADERS' WAYS TO INDIA

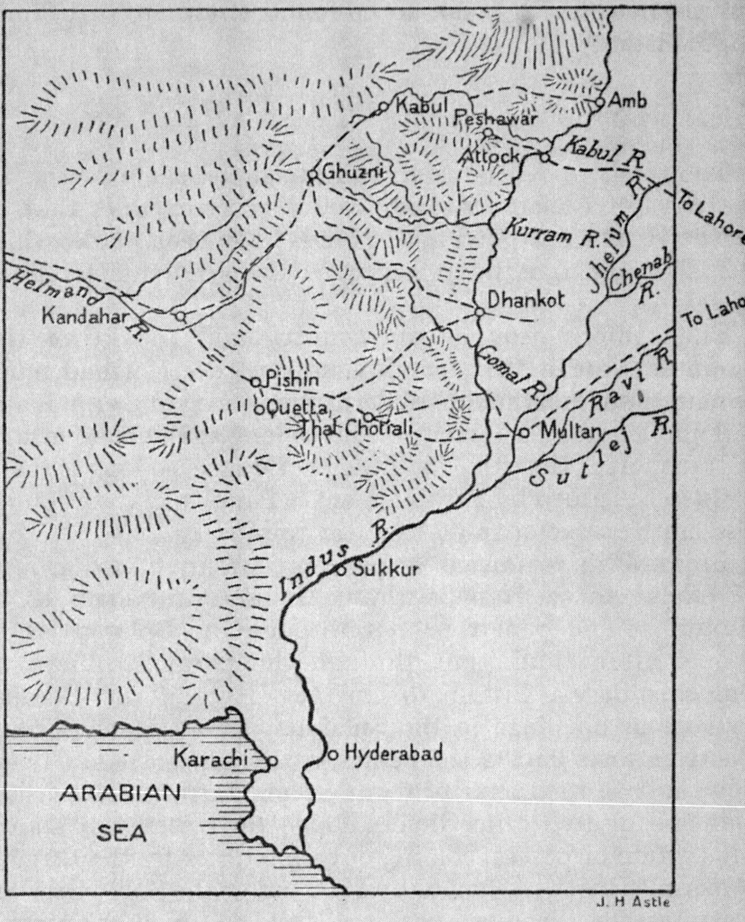

Kurram from Kabul or down via Jalalabad. From the latter the usual route did not lie, in earlier times, as people often imagine, by the Khaibar Pass and the wasps' nests that border it, but crossed the Kabul River and came into Peshawar valley by the easier routes which run between the Kabul River and the old Græco-Buddhist road over the Malakand. It was by one of these routes that Alexander came. Looking westward from India, by whichever route you enter Afghanistan you must climb. The most southerly route of all, viz. that by the Bolan Pass, did not bring the invaders into a fertile and prosperous India—at least in historic times. But whether you enter the Baluchistan hills by the Derajat passes or whether you go by the Bolan, you converge on Pishin, and you climb from the 300 or 400 feet above the sea of the Indus *kachhi* up to close on 6000 feet, and then, crossing the Khwaja Amran range 1000 feet higher, descend to the 3500 feet of the Kandahar plateau on the edge of the drainage basins. If you would go by the Gumal valley or the Tochi you climb by way of rising gorges and widening *kach* to the high Ghilzai hills and valleys and the pastures of the Powindahs, and do not again descend as to Kandahar. From the Kurram valley, the Paiwar Kotal, and the pass of the Shutur-Gardan, or Camel's-neck, over 10,000 feet must be passed, and thence to Kabul by the Logar valley; but if you go from Peshawar, then you must also climb to Kabul either via the Khaibar or the passes north of it, descending from Landi Kotal down to Jalalabad, and then up again to some 7000 feet and down again to Kabul. From Gandamak run two routes: one by the Kabul River for a bit and then up to Lataband and Butkhak, or the more southerly one up the valley of Surkhab, via the pass of Jagdalak and the Khurd Kabul defile. Both are well known to the British, but the latter is the scene of evil memory of the struggles of the Kabul force in the winter of 1841 in the grip of the snow and the Ghilzai tribesmen.

The great arterial road of Eastern Afghanistan lies from Kabul to Kandahar, and from Kandahar the road runs with no great difficulty north-west to Herat into the valley of the

Hari Rud, which drains away to the Caspian. Out from Kabul run great caravan routes to the Oxus, which cross passes that are over 10,000 feet and snow-bound for many months, while down the valley of the Hari Rud run groups of roads from Kabul and Ghuzni to Herat.

Roads, in their modern sense, are discussed later in connection with trade and progress in the twentieth century.

The Way of the Invaders

Much has been written, and often loosely written, of the routes taken by the long vista of invaders and their armies who have poured into India through the ages, and the "gloomy portals of the Khaibar" has been a favourite theme. But as a matter of hard fact the Khaibar from time immemorial has not been a highway for the armies of the past. It has always been too difficult to force, too easy for defenders to hold, and too haunted and infested by the Aprœtæ or Afridi, the Khyberree [1] of the Victorian writers, to make it a popular or tactical route.

Alexander crossed the Kabul River near Jalalabad, and came down into the Peshawar valley out of Swat and crossed the Indus above Attock. When Mahmud of Ghuzni started on his career, Kabul, as in the days of the Macedonians, was India and part of the kingdom of Rajah Jaipal. But we may be sure that his troops preferred to go through Swat and the Kunar valley rather than brave the Khyberrees. Traders, of course, could in normal times get through if they paid fair robber's cess; but that is another matter. To this day vast castles of great antiquity overhang the road, and probably were there in Alexander's time. Whether they barred or protected the road it is not possible to say. They are but known as the *Kafir Kots* (the Castles of the Unbelievers), which is the term that uninquisitive Islam has for all that is before the age of the Prophet.

From Ghuzni the great route came down the Gumal and led to the Tangdarra Pass, where the Kurram River cuts

[1] The earlier English spelling of Khaibar and its denizens.

through the low line of conglomerate which separates it from the Indus, and thence to the historic ford of Dhankot, which is now Mari-Kalabagh ferry; [1] or else went down the Derajat, the "country of the people who live in tents," to one of the crossings that lead to Mankera or Multan. There were the alternative routes from Ghuzni, just described, that made either for Bannu and Dhankot or, in earlier times, for Peshawar by the Kohat Pass. Among the several, that of the Tochi is the best known, and by all these routes the different clans of the Sulaiman Khel come down each year to the Indus *kachhi* for winter grazing—each pass for each clan, by tribal custom of ancient date. Those who came by way of Kandahar came also into the lower Derajat by way of Pishin and Thal Chotiali, and several alternative debouchments through the Sulaiman mountains, as already described. Chingiz Khan never crossed the Indus, though he chased Jalal Sultan's army from Ghuzni to the Dhankot ferry. Timur Lang came down by that ferry *en route* to Delhi by way of Bannu, turning aside, as the British might, to punish some tribes in the Tochi who had looted a convoy. Nadir Shah, it is true, came from Kabul by the Khaibar, but that was after the Moguls had made it a road *de luxe* for bullock-carts, and taken every stone and bush from out the roadway. Akbar had made it a supreme highway, though every spring the stones had again to be removed and the scrub cleared.

[1] Or perhaps opposite Mianwali, once a cantonment, now a civil station by the Kot of Raja Til.

CHAPTER II

RACIAL DIVISIONS, AND THE CONFLICT OF MOSLEM WITH HINDU

The Races of Afghanistan · The Ghilzais · The Pathan Races · The Kafirs of Kafiristan · The Tatars and Turkomans of Turkistan · The Persian Races · The First Moves from Afghanistan into India · Mahmud of Ghuzni · The Turki Dynasty of Ghuzni and Ghor

The Races of Afghanistan

It is pertinent to a study of Afghanistan to understand what we mean by that name and by the term Afghan. Afghanistan is, naturally enough, to be interpreted the country of the Afghans, from which it derives its name; but that only brings us to the more intimate question, What do we mean by Afghan? It is not a term of antiquity, nor at any rate till quite recently has it been used of the people to denote their own country. We only move round in a circle if we say that we mean the inhabitants of Afghanistan, or if we do intend that, we should be prepared to say definitely why. But if we turn to the word England we shall perhaps get a fair analogy, with the difference, that the races in Afghanistan have not blended. England is the country of the Angles, and the people they subdued or who came with them, though even that name takes no ken of the question of the Normans. Afghanistan may perhaps best be defined as the country in which a portion of the inhabitants and the dominating and dynastic race is Afghan. Accepting this, we may now ask, Who are this dominating and dynastic race?

Some time before the coming of the Arabs to the plains of Seistan and Gandara, and before the spread of the Arab conquest, and with that conquest, of the faith of Islam, "the Submission," there came into these regions a virile Semitic race. This race claims that it is descended from Saul by a grandson Afghana, said to have been Solomon's Commander-in-Chief, through one Kish or Kais, eighteenth in descent from the first King of Israel. There is no direct evidence in support of this claim. The extremely Jewish appearance of many of the true Afghan tribes—that is to say, those who belong to the race of the Abdalis whose home is in Zamindawar—their Jewish names, and many of their customs, have been brought forward as proof. But the Afghans came to notice at a time when the "Lost Tribes" and the prophecies were very much in British minds, and when speculation as to the whereabouts of the tribes was very rife. The fact that the Afghans claim to be the Ben-i-Israel, viz. the Children of Israel, appealed widely. But their physiognomy would point much more to Judah than to Israel; for it is Judah that had acquired the Hittite nose as the guerdon of their commerce with Moab, while the rest of Israel, as are many Hebrew to this day, especially those of Syria and Iraq, were probably a straight-nosed, blue-eyed, and sometimes red-haired people. The Jewish names, Ibrahim, Musa (Moses), Isa (Jesus), Yusuf, and the like, are but the names of Arabia and Islam and not necessarily of Israel. But of course the "trek" from somewhere near the upper waters of the Tigris and Euphrates, or from North Persia, would have been nothing at all. There is every possibility that the Afghans or Aoghans, that is to say the Abdalis, are of Hebrew origin; but as yet there is very little in the way of evidence.

However, Hebrew or no, it is these strange, fierce Semite people to whom we must admit that the name Afghan really applies. They share the provinces of Kandahar, Ghuzni, and Kabul with the Ghilzais and the Pathan tribes, whose origin will be discussed later, of whom the larger portion are the tribes who inhabit the Sulaiman mountains and the hills east of the Safed Koh, and who speak with the Afghans the language Pashtu or Packhtu,[1] a tongue derived chiefly from Sanskrit. The Pathan is the speaker of Packhtu,

[1] The soft or hard centre of the word is used in different parts.

or Pashtu, probably the Pactyæ of the Alexandrine historian, and it would appear that the Afghans acquired this tongue because they settled among a Pashtu-speaking race who had come from Yusufzai. In a linguistic sense all Afghans who are not of Perso-Turki origin are Pathans; but ethnologically, all Pathans are not Afghans.

The conquest of India by the races of, or coming by way of, Afghanistan, and the overruling, oppressing, slaughtering of India due to these invaders and settlers, have probably caused the Indian historian to call them all Afghans, whatever their ethnic origin, whether Persian, Semite, or Turk, in the same way as all who followed the fortunes of the Mogul were often spoken of as Moguls.

However that may be, the Afghan proper, the Abdali, Durani, or Ben-i-Israel, inhabit the country of Zamindawar north of Kandahar, and round Kandahar and towards Herat, and have flowed into many a valley in the country round for many miles It is they who have dominated the country since the days of Ahmad Shah.

In the modern conception of the word it is probably correct to say that the Afghan nation consists of three great branches of people who live on the east of the Hindu Kush and Paropamisus, viz. the Abdali, or, as we call them in future, the Durani, the Ghilzais, and the Pathans; while among them, though not of them, in this area are the Turki Hazaras who inhabit the highlands north of Zamindawar. North of the Hindu Kush and Paropamisus we have the races of Afghan Turkistan, a district which comprises at least a third of the whole area; in this are tribes who are largely of Tatar origin, the Turkomans, the group often referred to as the Char Aimak, the Usbegs, and the Tajiks. The latter are an Aryan folk from Persia. It is these three races, Turkomans, Usbegs, and Tajiks, for whom the Oxus is not a boundary, and who dwell in Russian Turkistan also. The inwardness of this geographical division is a prominent question in the relationships of the Soviets with Afghanistan, and will be discussed hereafter.

The Ghilzais[1]

The second great division of the Afghan people are the Ghilzais, who have ever regarded the Duranis with jealousy, and are far too powerful a group of chiefs and clans to be held in anything except respectful alliance. They are said to be of Turkish origin, and to derive their name from the word *kalij*, a sword, but judging from their appearance, tall men of aquiline countenance, they show no trace of Turkish origin, which is so marked in the Hazaras. It would seem probable that they were either Aryan hill folks conquered by some Turkish overlords who settled among them as Norman barons among the Saxons, with sufficient of their own men at arms to compel obedience, or they were led into the country by Turkish adventurers from elsewhere. It is very doubtful if more will ever be known. They followed, of course, the conquerors of many races to India, acquired lands and settled. From them came a dynasty that sat a while on the throne of Delhi—that of the Lodis, often somewhat loosely termed Lodi Pathans.[2]

They have long been in the habit of coming down with the whole of their belongings—their ox and their ass, their camels and their families—into the Derajat, leaving their arms in the British frontier constabulary lock-ups; and after settling their families in camp about the Indus, proceed far and wide, trading and working over the length and breadth of India, even to Australia, where they introduced the camels that are so much used in the goldfields. Now and again some returning Ghilzai has even brought back an Australian wife.

During the Afghan wars they have done much carrying for the British, and have been by no means loath to assist in the discomfiture of the Durani. From their spending half the year in British India, it is almost possible to say that they are in some sort British subjects, and by arrange-

[1] Thus the usual spelling. The pronunciation locally is Ghulzai, with a very guttural "Gh."

[2] The Lodis are a Ghilzai clan, after which is named the Indian town of Lodianah, now usually spelt Ludhiana.

ment with their headmen the British have always expected to enrol many camel corps if and when the British Army were called on to enter Afghanistan for the defence of the country against Russian aggression. The principal tribes known to the British from their migration under the generic name of Powindahs, are the Lodis, a big group of the Sulaiman Khel, Kairotis, and Nasirs. In the past some of them have settled permanently in the Derajat, and have been British subjects for many generations. Of such are the small tribes of Gandapurs, Babars, Chaudwans, and the like, on the line of the Powindah routes to India.

The Pathan Races

The third main division of the Afghan people are the Pathan or Pakhtan people, the tribesmen of Ruh—that is to say, the hills immediately west of the Indus, the Sulaiman mountains, and the Kunar valley. They for many generations have tacked themselves on, with the assistance of the genealogy mongers, to the Ben-i-Israel, and thus claim descent from the mythical Kais, and therefore from Afghana. A very large portion of the Pathan tribes are now within the British border, and some on both sides, as for instance the Mohmands and Wazirs, while the Shinwaris are entirely on the Afghan side. Almost all these tribes are believed to be Aryan, but there is no means of saying whether or no some of the divisions are Duranis who have edged their way into the valleys of Ruh. In India all are known equally as Afghans and Rohillas. But since Kabul was a Hindu and an Aryan province till the days even of Mahmud of Ghuzni, in spite of its admixture of Tatar settlers from the conquests of Kanishka, it seems very probable that many of the Kohistani tribes also—viz. those of the valleys around and especially north and west of Kabul—are also Pathan rather than Durani. Nor, as has been said, can the Turkish origin be accepted for the mass of the Ghilzais, who would appear to be in some cases Pathan and in some perhaps Afghan—viz. Durani, or Arab.

The Pathan tribes who are admittedly such, that are within our border or influence, are the Yusufzai, Mohmand, tribes of Swat and Bajaur, Afridi, Orakzai, Darwesh Khel, Mahsud, Sheranni, Bhitanni, etc.; though here again among them may be Durani clans and bits of clans, and the Yusufzai, originally Aryans from the Peshawar neighbourhood, have been away for many generations in the Kandahar region, and have returned later with no one knows what Afghan admixture.

Then we know not what Macedonian strains there may not be in the baking. Certain it is that a young lad from Ruh, a recruit, for instance, for the Indian Army, has often enough the purest Grecian profile, and is on all counts a choice young man to boot.

In fact, for the ethnologist, the anthropologist, and the mendelist, the tribes and races of Afghanistan, of the Sulaimans and the Indus valley, offer a most fruitful and fascinating study.

The Kafirs of Kafiristan

Among the interesting races, though not among those that count in the make-up of the country, are the *Kafirs*, the "Unbelievers," which is the same word as that of "Caffre" that we have used so much in South Africa. Kafiristan lies in the high, inaccessible, shadow-ridden mountain valleys that trend down towards the Kabul and the Kunar Rivers from where the Hindu Kush surges into the vast peaks in the neighbourhood of the Pamirs. It is a country which lay for generations untouched by the outer world, and around which legend and romance had arisen, as has been described in the last chapter.[1] The people, who were believed at one time to be the stranded relic of a white, viz. a Macedonian, race, have been known these last forty years to be but pockets of an earlier folk crowded into the hills by the Aryans and kept there by Islam. Their actual affinities are not very clear, and they speak several languages, which differ considerably

[1] See p. 6.

as between one valley and another. Dard, Dravidian like the Brahui, or something similar, they are now often enough to be seen in Kabul as labourers, and in 1896 their isolation was ended for ever on their ruthless conquest and conversion to Islam, carried out by Abdurrahman. There is still much to be learned of them, when circumstances permit a fuller study by some careful German student of languages, customs, and folklore long extinct elsewhere. Forty years ago, when Sir George Scott Robertson penetrated into their valleys, they were virgin soil for research, and only Timur Beg had dared peep into their fastness.

The Tatars and Turkomans of Turkistan

Afghan Turkistan, or simply Turkistan, as the people themselves call it, forms a very large portion of Afghanistan, and has already been described. Its inhabitants are largely of Turkish or Tatar origin, and speak various dialects of the Turki language. The people generally are Tajiks,[1] Turkomans, and Usbegs, with several lesser divisions. The Oxus is not their ethnological nor linguistic boundary, for people of the same races lie on the other side in what were the khanates of Khiva, Bukhara, Khoqand, etc., and which, after being for many years Russian Turkistan, now form a group of soviets—Turkmenistan, Usbegistan, Tajikistan, and Qara Qirghiz. The tribes and peoples themselves vary considerably, having come in with many different waves of Tatar and Mongolian invasion, often separated by many centuries.

The Usbegs, who form the larger portion of the Turki or Tatar peoples, are for the most part descended from the early Turki race of Uighars, that word of terror which in the Turkish comings to Europe in early times produced its terrifying derivative "ogre"; and their principal statelets are Maimana, Andkhui, Sar-i-Pul, Shibarghan, Balkh, Khulm, Kunduz, and Badakhshan. They have practically only been subject to any part of modern Afghanistan

[1] See p. 26.

E. N. A.

Afghan traders

E. N. A.

Tribal khassadars (levies)

since late in the sixties, though the Dost had conquered several of them somewhat earlier. The principal towns of those states, which for the most part bear the same name, are large and thriving commercial cities intent on trade trans-Oxus, and it cannot be denied that the Turki folk in these parts are far more civilised than the Abdali Afghan, who from all times has been an idler, a swashbuckler, and a destroyer, with nothing creative to his credit.

But there is another Tatar race that is of great importance, and who have little enough sympathy with the Abdali or Durani, and that is the Hazara. Their origin is a little uncertain, but they are believed to have been planted in the great uplands between Ghuzni, Kandahar, and Herat as a military colony by Chingiz Khan. They are of the Shiah branch of Islam, and now speak Persian and not Turki, and are very well known to the British, in whose regiments they serve.[1]

In the neighbourhood of Herat the Turki tribes are often described as the Char Aimak, the Jamshidis planted by the Seljuk Turks, the Firozkni by the Mongols, and the Taimuris by the Turko Tatars of Timur's day. But any discussion of the origins and interminglings of the Tatar, Turki, Mongol, and other waves of this description opens up a vast and puzzling subject. For practical purposes it is a useful classification to say that Turki peoples are Moslems and Mongol folk are Buddhists; but when we peer back into history we find that even this distinction grows faint, for the Turks and Mongols pouring into India were pagan, and then adopted Islam whatever their previous faith. Nevertheless the numbers of the Mongol branch of the Tatar race who profess Buddhism are very great, and as the Turks themselves are rarely as ardent and fanatical in their faith as the Semite Moslems, it has been said, and probably rightly, that Buddhism is what suits the psychology of all who have the "Mongol fold," as the almond eye is termed, and that Islam is the true faith for the Semite and not for the Tatar.

[1] Hazaras and Kizil-bash belong to the Shiah branch of Islam.

The Persian Races

There are, too, a good many people of Persian origin in the land, some of very distant coming, others of recent planting. For instance, in Kabul is a large community known as the Kizil-bash (or "Red-head"), who are Persian Turks settled there by Nadir Shah, differing, however, in every way except religious affinity from such people as the Hazaras.[1] Their sympathies in days gone by were not Afghan, and they have always been ready to assist the British, though they are of course part of the regular warp and weft of the countryside.

But in Afghan Turkistan, and also in the Kandahar province and in Herat, are many Persians of Aryan or earlier stock, who have come in to work on irrigated lands both near the Oxus and towards Seistan, being more than expert in the ways of putting water on to alluvial lands. Those of Persian as distinct from Perso-Turki stock are known as Tajiks, though curiously enough that word in Persia belongs to those of Arab origin. Indeed the term may be but a reference to the Arab settlers who came to Meshed and Herat in the early days of the Islamic portent. The Soviets have a republic known as Tajikistan on the Oxus, and would absorb the Afghan Tajik too. But the Tajik is a quiet, industrious creature, not anxious to ride any political storm.[2]

The First Moves from Afghanistan into India

The invasion of India from Afghanistan became possible as the latter country generally became Moslem, when Kabul ceased to be a Hindu province, and the Indus became for a while the barrier between that faith and Hinduism, and the country was as it were broken off from India. With the dying away of the universality of the Arab Empire,

[1] Broadfoot's sappers, famous in 1839–42, were largely Hazaras.

[2] He is largely enlisted into the Afghan Army, being more bidable and less efficient than the Afghan clansman.

an empire far greater than that of Alexander, the outlying provinces fell away. In Khurasan and trans-Oxania separate rulers and sultans came into power, warring, of course, the one with the other, much as Afghanistan has broken into pieces in 1929. The various dynasties that prevailed—Tahirites, Sofarides, Samanids, and the like—are of no very great importance, and throw no particular light on the practical story of Afghanistan in its relation to India, until we come to the days of the kingdom of Ghuzni. In 903 there had arisen in Central Asia a dynasty known as the Samanid, which existed for a hundred and twenty years. The fifth prince of this dynasty, one Abdul Malik, possessed a Turki slave, Alptigin (*tigin* indicating slave origin), who was Governor of Khurasan. On the death of his patron the latter lost favour with the successor, fled to Ghuzni with a small following, and established himself among the Sulaiman mountains. About 976 he died, and was succeeded by another slave, Sabuktigin, who had married his daughter, as Alptigin's own son had died without issue.

The "slave" status of these stories needs some explanation, for it is to be noticed how much the "slave" takes prominence in Eastern dynasties, as with the slave kings of Delhi, the Mamelukes of Egypt, and the Janissaries of Constantinople. The custom of bringing captive boys away from their parents and bringing them up in a military cadet service did not of necessity postulate slavery in the usually accepted sense of the word, and was the product of a desire of the great conquerors to surround themselves with soldiers and officers of no nationality and no family ties, who could be trained from early days to arms and to devote themselves to the fortunes of their masters, and from among whom they could select officers and even successors. It also put at their disposal the special qualities that might be inherent in any particular race, should such be evinced by any of the slave protégés.

Sabuktigin, who was believed to be of illustrious descent, displayed early military qualities, conquered Kandahar and most of the Indian tribes on the Khurasan side of the

Indus. Anxious to conquer the Punjab and Kashmir, he crossed the Indus, but returned to Ghuzni with much booty, without leaving any enduring conquest behind him. But Jaipal, the Rajput king of the Punjab and Kabul, had no intention of sitting down under such aggression, and by no means regarding the Afghan hills as close country, marched in a large force to Lumghan across the Indus. Overcome by severe weather, however, the Hindus surrendered their elephants to Sabuktigin, and engaged to accept the envoys of Ghuzni at their court of Lahore. Jaipal Singh, once safely home from the snows, repudiated his treaty engagements and gathered about him all the forces of Ajmere, Delhi, Kalinga, and Kanauj to resist the advance of the now enraged Sabuktigin. A Moslem victory took place, but the Ghuznivide contented himself with retaining Lumghan and the Peshawar valley, which we shall see later in Victorian times to be still the bone of contention between Moslem Afghanistan and Hindu India. This brought the Afghan frontier to the Indus, and marked, practically for the first time, a division in what had for ages been Hindu or Aryan country, to the far west of Kabul and the Hindu Kush.

As in the Afghan invasion of India in the eighteenth and nineteenth centuries, the invader's attention was then called off to his Bactrian provinces, which we in modern times should speak of as Afghan Turkistan, and the Indus had peace for a while. But we can here clearly see how Islam had torn in two the Hindu and Buddhist homogeneity of the previous centuries.

Sabuktigin now passed away about 997 at Termez, and was brought home to Ghuzni, in the twenty-first year of his reign and the fifty-seventh of his age. He had nominated his second son Ismail as heir, but Mahmud, the eldest, said to have been illegitimate, claimed the Ghuzni-Indus throne and offered to share the easterly provinces with Ismail. Negotiation failing, Mahmud defeated Ismail and interned him for life, apparently in honour and without the destruction of eyesight, which became so popular a concomitant of such struggles in later years.

Mahmud of Ghuzni

Mahmud, the famous Sultan of Ghuzni, the *But-shikan*, or "Idol-breaker," he who made the inpouring to India a habit of the north, was thirty years of age when he came to the throne, and was a Turk—that is to say, descendant of a Turki slave. Trained to war by Sabuktigin from earliest times, he was a leader of great experience. His first step was to offer allegiance to the royal house of the Samanids at Samarqand. When this was rejected, Mahmud not only maintained his position, but when the Samanid ruler, Mansur II, was deposed and blinded, declared his independence, marrying the daughter of Ilak Khan, the usurper of the Samanid dynasty. This practically left Ilak Khan master of trans-Oxania, and the Ghuznivide of all that lay between the Oxus and the Indus.

Mahmud was now free to pursue his design on India, and also to develop his capital in the magnificent upland valley at Ghuzni. He too was a Moslem zealot, and looked with unspeakable horror on the idolatry and apparent polytheism of popular Hinduism and the *Mushariks*.[1] This, according to the immemorial custom of early Islam, impelled him to attack and convert his non-Moslem neighbours, the peoples on the east of the Indus.

In August 1001, when the fiercer heat of the Indus plains was abating, he set out from Ghuzni and met the forces of the Hindus in the Peshawar valley, still led by the old opponent of Sabuktigin, the now aged Rajah Jaipal of Lahore, at the head of 12,000 horse and 30,000 foot. The Moslem was victorious and Jaipal was taken prisoner. Mahmud spared the aged king on condition of an annual tribute. Jaipal, however, abdicated in favour of Anandpal his son, and burnt himself on a funeral pyre. Three years later, the Hindu tribute not being paid in full, Mahmud returned, and fell on those princes whose contribution was in defect. Baji Rai of Bhatiya was the principal opponent, and he was defeated and his kingdom annexed. A Ghilzai

[1] Lit. "the Sharers," those who parcel out their worship to many gods.

chief who ruled Multan had joined the Hindus against Mahmud, and the latter brought that city and district low and added it to his tributary dominions.

Once again came the relief from the north, as Ilak Khan now invaded his son-in-law's territories. But Mahmud marched across the land as Harold of England a few years later marched from London to York, and back again to Senlac, met his invaders at Balkh and disposed of them, and flew back to meet a vast Hindu gathering in the Peshawar valley. All northern Hinduism realised the issue at stake, and had sent their chivalry to join Anandpal, the women stripping themselves of their jewels to provide the needed monies. But the die was cast irrevocably in favour of Islam for many a hundred year. The Hindu Rajputs, the descendants of kings, were defeated, and the Ghuznivide sent home to his mountain capital huge stores of Hindu treasure, and also for the first time commenced his fervid work of idol-breaking, the results of which are to be seen far and wide in Northern India to this day.

Anandpal, however, must have been retained in some tributary position, for in 1011 Mahmud, by agreement, passed through his territory on his way to dominate Thanesar, near Delhi. Anandpal, however, appealed for the sparing of holy Thanesar itself. Mahmud replied, relentless, that by the Grace of God he would root out idol-worship from all India and proclaim the faith in God and his Prophet. Hindu opinion was too feeble to again rise *en masse* in a national campaign. Thanesar was captured, its idols destroyed and its treasure carried off, but with Anandpal doubtful in his rear, Mahmud then returned to Ghuzni, taking with him, it is said, 200,000 captives.

It was not till 1017 that Mahmud was fain to continue his idol-breaking, and appeared in India with a vast force destined to conquer the great Hindu centre of Kanauj. The Rajah, quite unprepared, submitted, and Mahmud passed on to Meerut and to Muttra. At Muttra, the holiest of cities, were the magnificent shrines of Krishna with temples and wealth galore. Terrible destruction of these homes of idolatry ensued, and Mahmud returned in religious triumph to Ghuzni with more slaves and more treasure, after falling on many Rajput princes on his return journey, when the latter, sacrificing their women after the Rajput custom, themselves died in despairing resistance.

And so it was that Mahmud sowed the seeds of the hatred that lasts so bitterly to this day, and which breaks out at any moment and occasion, let drawing-room politicians preach of goodwill and amity never so sweetly.

Mahmud, however, was a man of culture and a patron of literature and arts, and when not idol-breaking was encouraging art at Ghuzni, where also he set out to emulate Hindu religious building by erecting a mosque which he called "The Celestial Bride," and he made his city a magnificent and abiding capital.

It is not possible to follow here in detail all the invasions of India by this relentless Turk. Farther and farther into India did he push his crescentades, till finally in September 1024 he penetrated to the famous super-holy and super-wealthy Hindu temples at Somnath in Kathiawar, on the western coasts of India. It was a place of pilgrimage for Hindus from all over India, and therefore well worthy of his destructive attention.

Moving from Multan to Ajmere Mahmud crossed Gujarat, and after three days' assault took the temple fortress from its Rajput defenders, putting five thousand to the sword, to find before him the magnificence of the great temple. In vain the Brahmins prayed for the preservation of their great sacred figure in return for large sums. Mahmud, declaring that he was "an idol-breaker and not an idol-seller," struck it with his mace and had it broken to pieces, when an immense store of jewels was found in the interior. Among the treasures that he removed were the celebrated sandalwood gates which were to figure so much in the story of Victorian times.

But Mahmud's course was now nearly run. After a campaign against the Jāts of the Indus, who had molested his return march from Somnath, he passed away in the year 1030 at the age of sixty-three, having reigned thirty-three years.

His character, and his fame, and his patronage of the

arts are all favourite themes to the Moslem historian, but it cannot be said that he really founded the Turkish empires of Delhi. The destruction of idols, the collection of wealth, and then the leaving of the Hindu rulers as tributaries, often merely nominal, to recover wealth as best they could, was his policy. As Turkish conquerors went, he was on the whole humane, and his inroads were not characterised by those orgies of slaughter which stained the work of Hun and Turkish hordes of other world-compellers. His unquenchable thirst for plunder was his worst characteristic. Had the Hindu chivalry combined against him more thoroughly and been moved by energy rather than feebleness, he could not have achieved the victories that he did. It was by his successors in the long line of Sultans which he founded, and by the cognate dynasty of Ghor, that the true conquest of India by the peoples of Afghanistan was to be carried out, which was to join once again the lands of Ariana to Northern India in a union destined to endure till the end of the eighteenth century.

The Turki Dynasty of Ghuzni and Ghor

Mahmud left behind him two sons, Muhammad and Masud, who battled for the succession till the former was conquered and deprived of his sight, when Masud became Sultan. For the first two years the Seljuk Turks impinged on his borders, but in 1033 he was free to return to the family habit of invading India. For three years he pursued his conquests and conquered Lahore and the country near to Delhi on more permanent lines than those adopted by his father. But after nine years his army mutinied, bringing the blind Muhammad back to the throne, after which Masud himself was made away with. His son Maudud, however, the Governor of Balkh, immediately moved south, put Muhammad and all those who had supported him to death, and ascended his father's throne.

The old Afghan story repeats itself with wearying insistence, and it is astoundingly like the events seven hundred years later in the time of Ahmad Shah. The reappearance of the Seljuk Turks recalled Maudud, and while he was away the Hindu kings rose against his overlordship. A desperate siege of Lahore followed, at which the Moslem garrison was eventually successful. Kings of this dynasty now came and went, and ere long Lahore grew to be the capital of the Ghuznivide dynasty and kingdom, which included Balkh, Kabul, Ghuzni, Kandahar, Sind, and the Punjab, and was pretty much the same in extent as the Aryan kingdom of the north before Darius and Alexander appeared on the scene. Masud III of this dynasty had married into the house of the Seljuk Sultan, and the latter in 1118 interfered in one of the disputed successions. The house of Ghuzni was now near its end, leaving but the fame of having founded the first of the great Moslem empires of Northern India. The last of the dynasty murdered his son-in-law, a prince of Ghor, in the Afghan mountains north of Kandahar, and this brought that savage principality out in enmity. The brother of the murdered prince, Ala-ud-din, Sultan of Ghor, now conquered Ghuzni, and burnt most of its beautiful buildings, earning for himself in the history of the East the epithet of *Jahan-suz*, the "World-burner."

The Punjab portion of the original Ghuznivide kingdom remained for two lives in the hands of Mahmud's descendants, but in 1180 was once more concentrated in the hands of the Ghorids by Shahab-ud-din Muhammad Ghori, nephew of Ala-ud-din, more usually known by the second name, through treachery. Sultan Khusrav, the last of the Ghuznivides, was sent prisoner to Ghuzni, though history does not record his further fate; and thus the great Ghuznivide dynasty of Afghanistan and Northern India came to an end in the year 1180 after 234 years, of which, however, the last thirty years was limited to the Punjab.

Muhammad Ghori now continued the Moslem conquest of India under far more difficult conditions than Sultan Mahmud had encountered. Mahmud's invasions were the first that the Hindus had had to face for many a century, and they were quite unprepared; but now the whole chivalry of the Rajputs was on the alert and trained to serious war. Advancing into India, Muhammad was badly defeated by a vast body of Rajput horse on the holy Saraswati River. Returning to Ghor to lick his wounds, he collected a large force and re-entered the Punjab by way of Peshawar. The rival confederations met again on the old battle-ground of the Saraswati, and this time the Hindus were utterly defeated. Prithvi Rai of Ajmere was captured and put to death, and Rajah Chawund Rai of Delhi fell on the field, together with many another of the flower of Rajput chivalry. It was just such a battle as that of the last Battle of Panipat when Ahmad Shah, the Durani, destroyed the Marathas in 1761, and it virtually decided the fate of India.

The victory was stained, as was that of Panipat, by massacres after the battle, and Muhammad left Qutb-ud-din Aibak, his slave, as his deputy in India, who in 1193 took Delhi, and for the first time made that imperial site the headquarters of Moslem dominion in India.

While Muhammad was back on his western frontier, fighting the King of Khwarazm, Qutb-ud-din was carrying on the subjection of the Hindus in the Ganges valley and Gujarat. Between Delhi and the Indus, however, the formidable clans of the Gukkurs about the Jhelum had risen against Muhammad, and in subsequent operations they surprised the Sultan in his tents and killed him. Thus ended the Ghorid dynasty of Afghanistan and Delhi in 1205, after enduring for fifty-one years, of which, however, only twenty-five years covered the possession of the cis-Indus as well as the trans-Indus territory of the Ghuznivides. Short as was its space, it had been pregnant with the fate of India.

CHAPTER III

THE AFGHANS IN INDIA

The Turkish Slave Kings of Delhi · The Four Classes of Indian Moslems · Turk and Turanian, Tatar and Mogul · The Ghilzai, Tugluq, and Lodi Dynasties · The Mogul Period · The Rohillas

THE TURKISH SLAVE KINGS OF DELHI

WITH the death of Muhammad Ghori began the dynasty of the Turkish slave kings at Delhi, which, however, took some time to consolidate. Muhammad Ghori had no issue, and three Turki slaves governed the principal provinces of Ghuzni and India. Qutb-ud-din Aibak (the moon-lord), Governor of Delhi for the Ghori succession, eventually gained the upper hand and instituted the Slave dynasty. Even then for a while the story of the Afghan dominion of India is confined to a great extent to India herself, for the fissiparous properties of the Afghan provinces prevailed. Ghuzni, Kabul, and Kandahar only at times recognised the supremacy of Delhi. To grasp this feature it is necessary to understand the procedure of the formation of the agglutinative Eastern empires. There arises from some small section a man and a leader of men, gathering to himself, as a born leader always does, hosts of those who follow but cannot lead, and a kingdom is built up. As each province is overcome, the conqueror either establishes one of his own followers as governor or viceroy, or else leaves the original ruler in a tributary position.

The terms on which the province is held are those of tribute or revenue contribution to the central power, with liability for military support. This, of course, postulates loyalty, which may be rendered so long as the prestige of the central power is maintained. If it be dimmed, the provincial governor may try and set up "on his own," or offer allegiance to some stronger group. When the central ruler dies or is deposed, the provincial governor, if he deem it expedient, sends his homage to the successor, or attends to pay it, and is careful to see that any arrears of revenue are paid up. When the converse exists, and the successor is not to be feared, then the fissiparous tendency comes into play. It is such conditions that we see at work in the central power of Ghuzni or Delhi, now controlling a vast number of provinces, now with power dwindling to only those within the reach of its feebler grasp.

The slave kings seemed to have had little to say to their outlying western provinces of the Ghuznivide dynasties, and to have concentrated on the conquest of India. Both under Muhammad Ghori and the succeeding kings Afghan governors were set up far and wide, supported by Afghan troops and mercenary leaders who had come to carve out a patrimony. Far down the Ganges to Bengal the Afghan rule extended, and before long Gujarat, Malwa, Khandesh, Jaunpur, Multan, Sind, and even the Deccan became Moslem, which meant that Afghan rule took root, and in time the Moslem Afghan settlers and retainers were increased by those of the Hindu races who accepted Islam. Farther south, Islam came as Christianity had first come—a means of uplift and a sense of a personal place in the scheme of the world for the slave and the humble.

The Four Classes of Indian Moslems

It is important to dwell at some length on the wide colonisation and settlement of Afghans in India, because it emphasises the inseparable connection between India and what is called Afghanistan which is so often overlooked. Indeed the history of Islam in India is the history of Afghan invasion and land-seizure, for the Arab coming to Sind in the seventh century did little to spread the faith.

The Moslems of India by common consent and phrase are divided into four classes: Sheikh, Sayyid, Mogul, Pathan. The former two are memories of the Arab coming to Sind and Khurasan, for a Sheikh is the descendant of an Arab generally, a Sayyid of the family of the Prophet, who may have come via the invasion of Sind, or through the settlement of priestly families in the Afghan hills before they came to India. The term Sheikh, however, has in fact a far wider meaning, for in the euphuistic custom of the East it is largely used to denote those inhabitants of India who have been converted to Islam, as distinct from those who were of that faith before coming in from outside. It may be remarked by the way that there need not be very much in this distinction, for many of the invaders themselves, especially among the Turkish races, were of very recent conversion. Nevertheless these terms are very well understood and are quite distinct from the Mogul, viz. Moslems of Turkish or Tatar blood, and the Pathan or speakers of Packhtu or Pashtu, be they Afghan in the sense already described, or Aryan Pathan from the mountains west of the Indus.

Turk and Turanian, Tatar and Mogul

We have seen that from the days of Mahmud of Ghuzni, and his successors in that dynasty, under the Ghorids and under the slave kings, the curious fact remains that the rulers of India have been of Turki extraction, whatever were the hordes of horse that they brought with them. And indeed this same Turki obsession lasted till the coming of the British.

During the rule of the slave kings a new peril, of Turkish origin at source, threatened India. In 1217 the Mongols, or Moguls, under Chingiz Khan, began to sweep the world, and actually penetrated through Ghuzni to the Indus. From this time on the waves beat on the Sulaimans and swept through them for several generations. The Moguls came to loot as pagan invaders, but softened towards Moslems as they gradually adopted that faith. Finally large bodies of them came to serve the Afghan leaders and rulers in India, eventually settling in the land. But wherever they went in their first coming it was for loot and loot only, accompanied by the most wholesale slaughter for slaughter's sake. Indeed to this day Seistan, to the south of Kandahar, displays the ruins of countless towns and villages destroyed by Mongol invasions.

The term Turk, as explained in the previous chapter, is wide in its interpretation, and setting aside the now obsolete term "Turanian," we may use it to cover all those races who before miscegenation with Aryan or aboriginal stocks displayed in some degree the Mongol fold, which gives the almond eye, and who speak in some form the agglutinative Turki language so different in every way from those of Sanskrit origin. The term, in fact, would embrace Tatar and Mogul, which is but another word for Mongol.

It is indeed an interesting fact for those who would follow the wanderings and ramifications of these mysterious peoples, to reflect that for many generations Asia has been quartered by four Tatar crowns from the Pacific to the Black Sea: the Manchus at Pekin, the Moguls at Delhi, the Kajiars at Teheran, and the Osmanli at Constantinople. Their rule lasted to the World War, with the exception of the Mogul throne, which was rescued, blind and impotent, from a conqueror's grasp by the British in 1803, the first to vanish from its earthly splendour, while now—none so poor to do them reverence!

But though the conquerors of India were Turks, yet they came from Afghanistan, and with them rode thousands of Afghan and Pathan horse, as well as the hordes from Central Asia, by way of the Afghan passes, so that, regardless of ethnological exactitude, we often find the phrase Afghan covering the whole. Later on will be related a new coming of Afghan proper and Pathan to whom the term Rohilla is applied.

The Ghilzai, Tugluq, and Lodi Dynasties

With the termination of the Slave dynasty the Afghanisation of India may be said to have been completed, and the Qutb Minar erected at Delhi by their first king serves to keep green the memory of the Slaves for all time. Their doings and those of their successors are crowded with interest, but for the purposes of a study of Afghanistan and the Afghans the details must be resisted. With "The Slaves" also died the regular connection with Ghuzni and Kandahar or Kabul, though the young men from those provinces still flocked to the spoil and the colonisation of Hindustan.

The last of the slave kings was succeeded by a king of Ghilzai, and therefore more definitely of Afghan [1] origin, and endured for thirty-three years, going down in 1321, when Ghazi Tugluq Beg, Viceroy of Lahore, was called to the throne, popular as one who had administered a heavy defeat to the Mogul hordes on the Indus.

The dynasty of the Tugluqs [2] did much for India, the rule of Firuz Tugluq being specially enlightened, and famed as putting a stop to the ferocious code of mutilation and punishment with which the Afghan overlords kept their Hindu subjects in order. But by the end of the fourteenth century the dynasty was in great disorder, and involved in quarrels and uprisings, of which the news filtered through the western Afghan provinces to far Samarqand, where the great Tamerlane or Timur Lang, the Lame Tatar, was at the height of his power. The provinces west of the Indus—Ghuzni, Kabul, and Kandahar—had already been overrun by his Tatars and Moguls, and on 12th September 1398 the mighty conqueror and destroyer crossed the Indus *en route* for Delhi and the golden south. Approaching Delhi, Timur, it is said, slaughtered 100,000 captives who were an encumbrance. The forces of Delhi were defeated outside the walls of the city, and the king fled. In Delhi squabbles in the city led to a great slaughter, like to that in the days of Nadir Shah, and Timur returned north with immense booty, leaving no governors behind, but appointing as his deputy one Sayyid Khizr Khan, the Tugluq Viceroy of Lahore. There now ceased to be any kings

[1] Though possibly of early Turkish descent.
[2] Who still were Turkish in origin.

of Delhi, and the great provinces of India, governed by Afghan governors, broke away, as the Mogul provinces did in the eighteenth century, and became independent kingdoms—Malwa, Gujarat, Khandesh, and Bengal, Oudh, Lahore, Multan, and the like. Four Sayyids in succession ruled, nominally on behalf of Timur and his successors at Lahore, from 1416 to 1478, and then another Afghan dynasty arose at Delhi, that of the Lodis, in the person of one Buhlul Lodi, descended from a rich Afghan merchant, and probably also of Ghilzai extraction. Under the Lodis some control was recovered over the seceded Moslem kingdoms that were nearest to Delhi, and the dynasty lasted till 1526, when there appeared on the scene, again from Afghanistan, a conqueror of an entirely new type, Babur, the first of the Great Moguls who were to change life at Delhi from that of rule by conquest to something like a national rule.

The Mogul Period

From the first invasion of India by Mahmud from Ghuzni to the coming of Babur from Kabul, always from the north-west and from Afghanistan—from 1001 to 1526—was 525 years, but up to the reign of Muhammad Ghori, 200 years later, these invasions were little more than raids for slaves and treasure. Hence it is better to date the real Muhammadan government of India by dynasties and mercenaries from Afghanistan from the Battle of Narain in 1193, when Qutb-ud-din (the moon-lord), the first slave king, broke the last of the Hindu armies.

The period of 333 years which ensued was that of the pre-Mogul Moslem rule, which gradually spread and spread, west and south, enduring practically as long as from the reign of Queen Elizabeth to the end of that of Queen Victoria. It was a period in which every endeavour was made to extirpate Hinduism, when tens of thousands of temples were destroyed and millions of Hindus butchered, proceedings at which the Moslem historians write in undisguised exultation.

Yet though the Hindus apparently had to live under Moslem laws, nevertheless Hindus alone could carry on the revenue work, the trading, and the manufactories. The conquerors were landowners and soldiers, who lived at ease where others sowed. Moslem merchants and Moslem artificers were few and far between, just as to this day it is the Hindus who do the bill-broking and the banking in Afghanistan and far into Turkistan.

The old Hindu life was alive under the Afghan surface, and ripe to blossom into prosperity if someone would give a rule of security and some semblance of a human government. Curiously enough it was an empire bearing the terrifying name of Mogul that was destined for a while to give this more human rule.

But the name of fear by which this Turkish Empire of Delhi is known is itself a misnomer, for Babur and the most of his followers were Turks or Tatars. He and his successors apparently adopted the term because of the great fear that the word Mogul, or Mongol,[1] had spread for several centuries, and possibly because there were a number of the old Moguls settled and attached to many of the Indian courts. In Northern India itself the name Mogul is not in frequent use with reference to this period, but rather the more accurate word of Jagatai or Chaghatai. Chaghatai was one of the sons of Chingiz Khan, to whom fell on his father's death the rule of all the Turki tribes and clans, of which Samarqand and Bukhara were the centres. Babur was sixth in descent from Timur Beg or Tamerlane,[2] who was himself a Chaghatai Turk born in Bukhara, and Babur's grandfather, Abu Said, had put his son, Umar Sheikh Mirza, in charge of Kabul. Babur was himself born at Ferghana in Turkistan. His mother was, it is true, a Mogul and a descendant of Chingiz Khan, but it is recorded that he had an antipathy to all the Mogul race, who though Tatar too, in the wider sense, were separated by long centuries from the more civilised and developed Turki and Tatar tribes of Turkistan. Babur's dynasty was essentially Tatar. His early adventures,

[1] Lit. "The Brave."

[2] Also Timur Lang, *i.e.* "The Lame."

thrilling though they are, are not Afghan history, and it suffices to say that by fifteen he had gained possession of his ancestors' capital of Samarqand, but by his twenty-third year had been driven out of all his possessions trans-Oxus, and had possessed himself of Kabul, where he dwelt in a constant state of watchfulness and warfare. By 1511 he had again taken Samarqand, but a combination of Usbeg Tatars and Persians drove him from all his dominions except Bactria, *i.e.* the provinces of Kabul and Balkh. Lahore still owned some fealty to the house of Timur, and from its viceroy came news of all the quarrels and futilities of Delhi, and Babur conceived the idea of basing a claim for the Empire of India on Timur's conquest.

So forth he rode on the great magic quest, as had so many men of Kabul before him. His first step was to demand of the Emperor Ibrahim Lodi a recognition of the fact that Lahore and the Punjab belonged to him as the successor of Timur. With many crossings and recrossings of the Indus, it was not till 1525 that he was able to pass it for good, and was eventually joined by the Viceroy of Lahore.

From all sides now came invitations and offers of support as Babur rode south, till on 10th May 1526 the Indian-bred Afghans and Turks were defeated on the battlefield of Panipat. The Emperor Ibrahim Lodi was killed, Babur entered Delhi, and was proclaimed Emperor in his stead. India, however, was even less homogeneous than Babur had been led to expect, and after four years of warring with fissiparous Afghan princes, he died in the year 1530 in the fiftieth year of his age. Nevertheless the empire that he left behind him ran from the Oxus to Oudh at least. He was succeeded by his eldest son Humayun, and the old story of seceding provinces began again. Humayun was driven from India within two years by Sher Khan, an Afghan chief of Chunar, on the lower Ganges, who established what is known as the Sur dynasty—almost the first that can be called pure Afghan—becoming Emperor of Delhi and its nearer provinces in 1540 under the title of Sher Shah. The new Shah's family claimed descent from Ghor, and hailed from near Peshawar, where it had always been looked on as illustrious. Sher Shah had steadily come to the front by a long chain of circumstances, and had always treasured the idea of setting up an Afghan dynasty. In 1545, however, he lost his life from the bursting of a shell. His ineffective successors in the dynasty were quite incapable of controlling the rival Afghan chiefs, and in 1556 the Mogul Humayun, who had regained Kabul and Kandahar, re-entered India after fifteen years' absence with a strong body of Turks and Afghans, and destroyed the Indo-Afghan Army, to find the throne of Delhi at his feet. A few months later he died from the effects of a fall, and his son Akbar succeeded him to inaugurate one of the most brilliant periods in Indian and Afghan history. It was not till 1559, however, that he was able to crush the warring Afghan elements and to inaugurate that reign of organisation and understanding for which he is so justly famous. So far as Afghanistan itself went, after some trouble at Kabul it settled down, at any rate for a while, to be a definite and ordered part of the Delhi Empire. In its great cities then as now were the administrative and intelligent classes, inherited perhaps from the days of the Persian and Bactrian rule, who, as in India, were competent to provide a machinery of administration as soon as the war lords were properly restrained.

It is interesting to note, as illustrative of the homogeneity which to some extent still existed over the whole of Afghanistan and Northern India, that Rajput troops under Akbar's generals readily entered Afghanistan to subdue risings there as they had done in the days of Rajah Jaipal, and no word was heard of any caste-breaking at crossing the Indus, as our Hindustani soldiers tried to urge in 1842.[1] As a matter of fact, Akbar's Rajput troops under Rajah Birbal Singh were very severely handled in trying to subdue Bajaur and Yusufzai, the Rajah with 8000 troops being destroyed by the tribesmen.

[1] For those who moralise on such things it may be noted that when affairs gang agley religious objections to any course arise readily in Eastern climes, and caste-objections to enter Khurasan were prominent in 1842, much as in 1916 Bagdad became too holy for Moslem troops to go near when Kut was being besieged.

We need not follow in detail the rise of the fortunes of this amazing Turkish Empire, the curbing of the Afghan war lords in India itself, and the establishment of the most brilliant court that India has ever seen, nor the production of the *Ayin Akbari*, the "Code of Akbar," which, like the Code Napoleon, stands as a model of wise empire planning and administration. Suffice it perhaps here to say that this empire lasted in some sort till 1803, if only in the form of puppetdom, and even then some slight shadow still survived till 1857, when the King of Delhi, whose writ but ran within the walls of the rose-red palace fortress of Shah Jahanabad—the modern Delhi built by Shah Jahan—lost even that by allowing himself to be the puppet of the mutinous and largely Hindu army of Bengal.[1]

Akbar, as all the world knows, had three great successors, Jahangir, Shah Jahan, and Aurangzib Alamgir, sonorous titles which sing themselves as they go; after whom the great fabric toppled of its own weight as feebler hands took the reins, and the Afghan princes and nobles and the rising Marathas commenced to fight for their own hand. The policy of Aurangzib, of destroying the power of the Afghan-descended princes who ruled in the south and west, hitherto independent of Delhi, and who were a great counterweight to the rising power of the Marathas, contributed very considerably to the break-up of the empire. Kabul and Kandahar still remained provinces of Delhi, but in 1621 the Persians conquered Kandahar, and succeeded in holding it for several years against the attempt made by the Emperor Jahangir to recover it. Although the complete *rapprochement* with the Hindu elements that Akbar had so aimed at was waning, nevertheless in 1644 we again find a force of 14,000 Rajputs across even the snowy passes of the Hindu Kush in Afghanistan, with Rajah Jaswant Singh, assisting the Moguls to reconquer Babur's territory in Afghan Turkistan, the Rajah himself being later Commandant of Kabul. But Shah Jahan, who was now on

[1] Bengal was misapplied by the British to all the country ruled by the Presidency of Calcutta as far as the Sutlej, and its army recruited from Beher and Oudh was miscalled the Bengal Army.

the throne, himself went to Kabul, and fearing the strain of holding Balkh, withdrew the troops to the hither side of the Hindu Kush.

In 1668 the Persians again captured Kandahar, and though Prince Aurangzib, and also Prince Dara Shikoh, the eldest son, was sent against it, they failed to regain it, and from henceforward it remained in Persian or Afghan hands.

Except for this province, Afghanistan remained with Delhi till the death of Aurangzib, to which date the Mogul Empire in all its glory endured. When it tottered it was not long before fresh Afghan invaders appeared on the scene, and as their story is the story of Afghanistan as it comes into the picture of modern times, it must be told in more detail. As it unrolls before us it will be possible to grasp the astounding tragedy of the collapse of the Mogul Empire, the brilliant rise and somewhat mediocre waning of the Durani Empire of Afghanistan, and the final coming of the *Pax Britannica* to sorely stricken Hindustan.

THE ROHILLAS

A study of the Afghan colonisation of India would not be complete without reference to the Rohillas, and that portion of Hindustan generally spoken of as Rohilkhand, or in the more popular spelling, Rohilcund. This consisted of what is now the Bareilly division, the State of Rampur, and certain tracts at the foot of the Himalayas. Rohilla or Rohela means a hillman, from the Pashtu word *Rohu*, a hill. The term *Ruh* or *Roh* was formerly applied to Eastern Afghanistan from Swat and Bajaur, down to the mountains of the Derajat, and the Rohillas were therefore, generally speaking, men from those very hill tracts which are now designated as the "frontier tribes" under British political control between our border and the "Durand Line" or Afghan frontier. It was the people from these mountains who flocked as keenly to the forces of the Emperors of Delhi as their descendants to the Indian Army. Indeed many of the Moslem nobles and country magnates even to-day style themselves by the clan names that are so well known on the frontier—Bungash, Orakzai, Yusufzai, Chamkani, and the like. To this day, for instance, the Nawab of Bhopal recognises his descent and connection with the Orakzai clans of the Orakzai Tirah.

Buhlul Lodi, one of the kings of Delhi of the Lodi dynasty, was specially favourable to the men from Roh, and is recorded as having said: "Every Rohilla shall have a jagir [1] more than his deserts."

It would appear, moreover, that a large number of Rohillas moved into Rohilkhand and received jagirs and seized land there when Nadir Shah sacked Delhi. In 1774 Ali Muhammad proclaimed himself chief of Rohilkhand, and it was he, fearful of the increasing Maratha power, into whose hands the Mogul had fallen, who had implored Shah Ahmad and his Afghans to come to the rescue of Islam and extract the Mogul from the hands of the Marathas in that invasion which ended in 1761 with the Battle of Panipat.

The term Rohilla, however, has been used generally throughout India in later times to represent the Afghan, for even to-day folk in Khandesh call dacoits from the old Mogul province of Hyderabad "Rohillas." A Pashtu saying illustrated the feeling in *Roh* against the demoralisation that settlement in India wrought in the mountain character: "*Sadik Rohilla yam pa Hindubar Gad.*" "I was a simple mountaineer compelled to live in Hindustan."

The general opinion of Afghans and Rohillas may be gathered from the following quotation from the *Seir Mutaqerin*: "After all, the Rohillas are but the best of a race of men, in whose blood it would be difficult to find one or two single individuals endowed with a good nature and with sentiments of equity. . . . In a word they are Afghans."

During the last stages of the Mogul Empire the hillmen of Roh flocked to India, and this stream of fortune-seekers with a sword to sell is constantly referred to in the histories of the time. The Afghan settlers of early days had also

[1] Jagir=a grant of land in feu.

E. N. A.

Iron man-cage

A warning to evil-doers

Afghan villagers

Differing little from those of the British frontier

constantly recruited their ranks by sending for relatives, and by this means to some extent put off the physical degeneration which seems eventually to overtake those who come down from the north and neither go back nor refresh their blood with marriage. Since the Afghan War of 1842 a good many Afghans have been settled in India when it was necessary for the British to permit those who had supported them in the country, to come away with them to save their lives, while from time to time pretenders to the Afghan throne have escaped, bringing a considerable following to India with them. Some of the best horsemen of the irregular cavalry of the Company's army were drawn from men of recent Afghan descent.

It is not sufficient, however, to refer to the Rohillas without mentioning the Rohilla War undertaken by Warren Hastings, and which has been so curiously and unfairly dealt with by Burke and James Mill, from whose inaccurate pages Macaulay wrote, and from which subsequent writers have drawn material unchecked, so true is it that the original charge so often sticks and the complete refutation is unnoticed.

It was a war to release Hindu peasantry from the most cruel and grasping usurpation of overlordship, as well as to prevent the conversion of more neighbours to a similar condition, by the Rohilla chiefs who had battened on all within their grasp.

For the true facts of the case Sir John Strachey's *The Rohillas* should be studied.

CHAPTER IV

THE DAWN OF MODERN AFGHANISTAN

The Afghan Conquest of Persia · Nadir Shah · The Rise of Ahmad Shah and the Durani Empire · The Barakzais · The Successors to Ahmad Shah

The Afghan Conquest of Persia

Afghanistan as a country, and the Afghans as a separate people, and something more than a part of the kingdom and peoples of the Empire of Delhi, began with the failing of the power of Aurangzib a year or so before his death in 1707. Till then Kabul had been a province of Delhi, but Kandahar had been lost to Persia, while Herat had been part of Persia. Kandahar, however, had repeatedly passed from one to the other—from the control of Delhi to that of Persia and back again, as already related; but in any case, both Kandahar and Herat had nothing but hatred for Persian dominion.

Southern Afghanistan itself had, it is true, been known as part of Khurasan; but never in spirit, for its people looked to Delhi with some affection, since not only had thousands of Turks and Afghans settled in India, but a profitable trade with India had endured for centuries, and Indian bankers largely conducted the financial affairs of Khurasan. The Moslems of India and the majority of those of Southern Afghanistan belonged to the orthodox branch of Islam, while those of Persia were of the hated *Rafzi* or heretic persuasion, the Shiah branch of the "Faith," and between the two there is less love than even between Protestant and Romanist in Ireland.

This quarrel between Persia and Afghanistan, which bulked so large in the nineteenth century, though in some ways in direct sequence of the days when Ariana was a Persian province in the time of Darius, took on its modern form, as aforesaid, with the death of Aurangzib. Between

1545, when Humayun took Kandahar for the Moguls, and the end of the seventeenth century, that city and its province was tossed backwards many times between Persia and Delhi, when the latter held the rest of the provinces of modern Afghanistan, as has been already related. As the century came to an end, both Herat and Kandahar were in the hands of that potentate whom early British writers call "the Persian Sophy." But Kandahar was racially an Afghan province containing largely an Afghan people, and a Ghilzai chief, one Mir Vais or Wais, was its Wali, an office hereditary in his family.

In 1706, a year before the death of Aurangzib, who had often attempted the capture of Kandahar, Mir Wais successfully headed an insurrection against the Persian Governor of the province, Prince Gurgin, and thus commenced an astounding chapter of Perso-Afghan relationship, and of Afghan dominion paralleled only by the subsequent rise of Nadir Shah. Mir Wais killed the Governor of Kandahar and drove out his troops, and for the moment held that province as an independent principality, at a time when the Mogul throne was in disorder. This victory stirred the Afghan imagination and set light to a train that was to inaugurate a long era of Afghan conquest and lead eventually to the modern Afghanistan of to-day, which had not yet been a kingdom by itself. It is curious to note that it was the Ghilzais, and not the Abdalis, who took the leading part at the start.

The Afghans of Herat, however, were not long behind. Herat had always been a stronghold of the Abdali clans, and these now rose against the Persians, under the leadership of Asadullah Khan Saduzai (a clan which eventually became the Royal Clan), and, driving out the Persians, likewise formed an independent province, defeating, with 15,000 Afghans, 30,000 Persians and a large force of Usbegs who attempted to recover it. Thus again was the Perso-Afghan conflict regarding Herat restarted in modern times.

When we reflect on the comparatively recent days when Persian dominion extended too close to the lower Indus, it is possible to understand the attempt of the Amirs of Sind to try and affiliate themselves to Persia, as a means of escape from being reabsorbed into the new Durani Empire of which Shah Shujah and the British dreamed in 1838.

The expelling of the Persians from Kandahar and Herat was soon to be followed first by raids into, and then by a permanent invasion of, Persia. Mir Wais died, and, after a seizure of authority by a brother, his eldest son Mahmud came to power. In 1720 the first great raid into Persia took place, in which Kirman was captured, and, in the next year, the Abdalis from Herat followed the exciting example of the Ghilzais and raided towards Meshed.

In 1722 Mahmud made a more ambitious inroad, and with 20,000 wild Afghans, with nothing of civilisation, and notable only for their swords, their hardy beasts, and their camel guns, or "wasp stings," met all the chivalry of Persia eleven miles from Isfahan on the field of Gulnabad.

But the glory and the manhood of Persian chivalry had long departed; magnificent inlaid armour, gilded spears, and damascened blades, with all the trappings of a rich empire, availed them nothing. They went down before the men of the hills as, centuries before, a similar array had melted before the desert-wizened Tatar savages of the Mongol hosts. Forty thousand Persians fled from 20,000 Afghans before they had lost 2000 men, and left their heavy, cumbrous artillery on the field. Isfahan itself fell, and the Persian "Sophy," Shah Husain himself, surrendered to the Afghans, saying that "since God so wills it, the empire is with you." The Afghans then swept over the country even to far Kazvin.

For a few months Mahmud restrained himself and appeared to deal fairly with the Persians, but, exasperated by attempts to recover independence, Afghan rage and ruthlessness broke out. Two thousand Persian guards were massacred and numbers of the Persian nobles, while the Afghan king even endeavoured to exterminate all those who had in any way served the Persian dynasty. Shiraz was captured shortly after, and before long Mahmud put to death all members of the Persian royal family who had fallen into his hands, with the exception of the ex-Shah

Husain. Especially did he concern himself with an attempt to eradicate the Shiah branch of the faith of Islam and reintroduce that of the orthodox Moslem. In the meantime the Turks had invaded Georgia, and in 1724 had entered into a treaty with Russia for the joint dismemberment of the Persian Empire. It may be put into the other side of the balance in the horrible memory of Afghan dominion in Persia, that they did once and for all prevent this dismemberment. Mahmud died in 1725 and was succeeded by his son Ashraf, who then busied himself with the murder of more Persian nobles.

Soon after his accession the Turks invaded Persia and marched to Isfahan, but were defeated by the Afghans with a loss of 2000 men. Ashraf Khan demanded of the Turkish commander how it was that he, a Moslem of the orthodox faith, could be in arms against fellow-believers of the "sunni" persuasion. To which the Turk replied that he did so by order of the Caliph; whereon 60,000 Turks and seventy guns advanced, only to be again defeated with heavy loss by the Afghans, with the result that a treaty was signed (1727) by which Ashraf Khan acknowledged the overlordship of the head of Islam and remained lord of Persia. Nevertheless this vigorous, protecting, but otherwise ruthless and uncivilised dominion of a far more civilised people was nearing its end. Shah Tahmasp, son of Husain, still maintained himself at Farahabad in Mazanderan, where he was joined by a soldier-adventurer, one Nadir Quli, to whom ere long was given the remains of his forces and the title of Tahmasp Quli Khan, the "Slave of Tahmasp." A general and a leader, Nadir came of one of the many Turki races included in the Persian make-up,[1] and proceeded to put some heart into the remnant of the Persian forces, bringing to their banner many of the Turki tribes, who bore no goodwill to anything Afghan. Ashraf Khan soon marched into Khurasan to deal with Nadir, but was heavily defeated at Mihmandust in 1729, and was compelled to retire on Isfahan. Nadir followed, defeated him again at Murcheh Khur with a loss of 4000 men, and

[1] See p. 53.

then carried Shah Tahmasp back to Isfahan in triumph, only to find that the retreating Afghan *more suo* had slain the aged Shah Husain. In Isfahan Tahmasp found that his own mother had worked as a slave for nine years, sadly waiting for his coming to his own again.

One more victory was yet to come before the Afghan dominion was entirely broken. This took place at Zarqan, twenty miles from Shiraz, whence the Afghans fled in all directions. The remnant in Lar and Kirman were now hunted out, and in 1730 Ashraf Khan, a fugitive on the Dasht-i-Lut, was slain by a Buhluli chief. Such as survived fled to the coast and reached Bahrein, where their descendants are to be found in humble circumstances to this day.

Nadir Quli, now a prince and a ruler, was not to submit long to hold anything but the principal rôle in Persia, and was soon carving out for himself that amazing position and power that enabled him to turn and conquer Afghanistan and ride in ruthless triumph to Delhi. Those who would moralise may dwell on the state in which peasantry and bourgeois found themselves during these long years of misrule, a people too feeble to defend themselves as the burghers of Europe were the better fitted to do, in similar times.

Nadir Shah

No story of Afghanistan can be complete without some longer account of this most wonderful of conquerors, Nadir Shah Quli, *i.e.* Nadir Shah the coolie or slave, who conquered all the provinces of Afghanistan and made the Durani Empire of Ahmad Shah possible. His name means the Slave of the Wonderful, and it admirably suits his career.

Born of the Kukhlu clan of Ashraf Turks, of humble grazier parentage, Nadir on Kupkan kept his father's flocks. At the age of eighteen he and his mother were carried off to Khiva as slaves by Usbeg raiders. But, as we see in all Asiatic history, there was no height to which a sturdy slave, stout in heart and subtle in brain, might not rise. And

Nadir soon showed himself a leader of men, rising to authority in the service of Baba Ali Beg, Governor of Alivard, eventually taking service with that Mahmud who made himself master of holy Meshed. Thence he found himself, as has been related, a general in the service of Shah Tahmasp, to whom he became practically vizier, re-raising Persia against the Afghan dominion and expelling the Afghans from Western Persia and from Khurasan. He then proceeded to rid Persia of the Turkish invaders, who had recovered from their defeat at the hands of the Afghans. After Nadir's successes Shah Tahmasp ventured into the field to lead his armies himself, only to be handsomely beaten. Nadir Quli then deposed him, and placed his infant son on the throne, after which he proceeded to expel the Ottoman Turks from all the provinces of Persia that they had overrun, viz. the provinces of Gilan, Asterabad, and Mazanderan, and also Kars, Erivan, and Armenia, all of which were wrung from them at the Treaty of Resht. The Russian encroachments, made in accordance with the will of Peter the Great, were also regained, including Derbend and Baku. In 1736 the infant Shah died, and Nadir proclaimed himself in the babe's stead.

In 1737–38 he overran the province of Kandahar and expelled therefrom the Ghilzais, deporting a great number, and, after the old Assyrian fashion, planted Persians and Persian Turks in their place. He then turned his attention to Mogul India, marching first by the great road of the armies via Ghuzni to Kabul, whence the Mogul Governor fled before him. His progress to Delhi is described in the next chapter. Like Ashraf Khan the Afghan, his great aim, among other acts of consolidation, was to win back Persia to the orthodox faith, from which she had been led away, and he lost much of his influence thereby. But this did not prevent his victorious progress.

After his return from Delhi he overran Bukhara and Khiva in 1741, but his prolonged successes were too much for his temper, and he became so fiercely tyrannical that the inevitable end came in 1747, when he was assassinated by Salah Beg, the captain of his guard.

The Rise of Ahmad Shah and the Durani Empire

The difficulty has been referred to of saying when the term Afghanistan, for the agglomeration of varying districts and provinces that lay between the Oxus and the Indus, came into general use; but, in any case, it was not till the rise of Ahmad Shah, the Abdali, that it stood for a separate political entity and people. As has been explained, anything like a purely Afghan state flared into being for the first time for a short while with a conquest of Persia from a matrix at Kandahar, but the modern kingdom, or, indeed, any kingdom of Afghanistan, dates from the seizure of certain provinces that had owned the sway of Nadir Shah on the assassination of that great Turkish adventurer in June 1747.

Among his amirs and successful leaders was one, Ahmad Khan, a young man of the Saduzai clan of the tribes of the Abdalis, who, as has already been related, called themselves, as they still do, the Ben-i-Israel, or the Children of Israel. Ahmad Khan, then a young man of twenty-four, had under his control 10,000 effective horse, and what was even more valuable, the treasure of Nadir Shah, which included the Koh-i-nur. This treasure he at once seized—indeed there was perhaps no better owner—and with this and his own personality and prowess, he was able to gain the support of the Abdalis, more especially of the largest group, the Barakzais.

Ahmad now proclaimed himself Shah of all the essential states north of Khurasan, viz. Kabul, Kandahar, Herat, Sind, Multan, Kashmir, the Daman,[1] the Peshawar valley, Hazara, and the like, including four districts cis-Indus that Nadir Shah had annexed.

Ahmad Shah had no great difficulty in winning to his side the governors of Nadir Shah's Afghan provinces, provided as he was with funds and force, though the Governor of Kabul fled to Delhi, to which Kabul had belonged in name before Nadir had arrived. The Shah now proclaimed

[1] *Daman-i-Koh* = the skirts of the hills, usually called the Daman.

The city of Kabul

his kingdom as the Durani Empire, his people to be known henceforth as Duranis, and himself, their emperor, as Dur-i-Duran, the "Pearl of Pearls," or, as it is sometimes translated, the "Pearl of the Age"; and by this name the Abdalis have been known from his time till the final expulsion of Shah Shujah. As soon as the provinces of Kabul, Kandahar, and Herat had recognised his rule, his thoughts turned to India, as the thoughts of all Afghans have always turned before him. Sind and Multan were his, and so were Kashmir and the area of Peshawar, spread somewhat debatedly across the Indus, to, at any rate, Hassan Abdal, and probably down to Sher Shah's ancient fortress at Rohtas, in the hills about Jhelum. He desired at least to make the Sutlej his frontier, if not to acquire the ancient Empire of Delhi, to which his provinces would appear to entitle him, by all the history that had gone before.

He had little difficulty in collecting to his standard large numbers of the hardy horsemen of Central Asia, and advanced in the autumn into the Punjab, after an intrigue with the Mogul Governor of Lahore, who, however, was sufficiently stimulated from Delhi to resist, but without success. The Shah then advanced into Sirhind, where he was defeated in this his first attempt to make good his claim to part of India.[1]

Though the Durani Empire, before the Shah died, stretched from Meshed in Khurasan to Lahore and the Sutlej, it is not to be doubted that the Shah's constant marches into India (and he crossed the Indus eastwards no less than nine times) did result in loss of influence over his Afghan people, and did prepare for that decay which set in under his feeble successors. The Shah, himself the very ideal of the Afghan genius, "hardy and enterprising, fitted for conquest, yet incapable of Empire, seemed but to exist for the sake of losing and recovering provinces." [2] However true that may be, he was a man among men, and he ruled with energy for the twenty-six years of his enthronement. The story of these twenty-six years is intimately mixed up with the last years of the Mogul

[1] See p. 65. [2] See also p. 71.

dynasty, and his attempts to restore the might of Islamic dominion in India as it fell before the rise of the Maratha confederacy and that of the Sikh theocracy. In addition to the strain of Ahmad Shah's incursions on Afghan resources, this newly risen Sikh power was destined to whittle away much of the Durani Empire that he left.

The ultimate relationship of Afghanistan to India, and its position *vis-a-vis* a self-governing India, is so mingled with conditions which, though of the past, yet in many ways belong to the future, that a bowing acquaintance at least is necessary with the involved conditions in Northern India, which both brought about and resulted from the fall of the mighty Mogul Empire. In the next chapter, therefore, it will be desirable to turn aside from the direct narrative of Ahmad Shah and his successors and look at the Afghan invasions as they appeared from India, and to glance, in outline, at the tragedy of a great empire falling by decay, by disease, and by treachery, and disappearing in contumely and dishonour.

The Barakzais

When Ahmad Shah Saduzai, by his prowess as a leader, and by the help of the treasure of Nadir Shah, succeeded in persuading the rest of the Abdalis to accept him as their king, and accord him that style and title, he was specially supported by the chiefs of the most powerful of the clans, that of the Barakzais, the "Sons of Barak" (*i.e.* of Lightning). Indeed, it has been said that the Barakzais somewhat fancied themselves even then as king-makers and protectors of the throne, and that Ahmad Shah was the more acceptable, that his own clan was a small and uninfluential one, and that, at any rate, his descendants would be facile puppets in Barakzai hands. The Eastern views of kingship are best instanced by the game of chess. The piece that we call the Queen is known in the East, where the game had its origin, as the Vizier, the all-powerful minister, who shelters a feeble and haltered crown, steeped in luxury and languor, as at Bagdad in the later caliphs' days, Nepal in recent times, and many another. The King, or Sheikh, with little power or energy, is covered and succoured by his Vizier ("*Sheikh mud*," or *Cheikh* as the French spell it, "The Sheikh is dead," is but our "Checkmate!").

In dwelling on the acceptance or election of Ahmad Shah, Abdurrahman tells how,[1] in the past, Barak and Sado were brothers, so that when Barakzai succeeded to Saduzai the dynasties were really the same.

Be that as it may, it is very probably true that the smallness of the clan of the Saduzais was an attraction to the rest of the Abdalis, who were not prepared to put for too long a halter round their necks. Nevertheless, the prestige of Ahmad Shah, who was a "choice young man and goodly," lay in his own prowess, and in the stores of dollars that had fallen to his hand, to which he was able to add a strong body of horse disciplined by himself—powerful enough claims all the world round. The would-be viziers, therefore, were probably looking to the second and third generations, as events were to prove. At any rate, Sarfraz Khan, whose name was Payindah Khan, head of the Barakzais, supported Ahmad Shah, and we shall see his horde of twenty-one vigorous sons taking a very leading part in the days of the feeble successors to the throne of the Abdali.

Payindah Khan's host of sons between them held all the high offices and provincial governorships under the successors to Ahmad Shah, and so long as they themselves could be controlled by any one of their number, served the Afghan interests as a whole well enough. When this controlling influence failed, as it did on Akram Khan's death in 1827, he then being vizier and one of the brothers, the country fell apart lamentably, until one of the youngest, Dost Muhammad, the son of Payindah Khan by a despised non-Afghan mother, succeeded first to Kabul and later to Kandahar, and eventually to the complete amirship of the country. It was he who established the dynasty from which Amanullah descends, and which has furnished a line of amirs whose history will be related in due course. The

[1] In his autobiography.

Durani Empire failed when Ahmad Shah's line failed in one sense. In another, it still prevailed when Amanullah held the throne, since the Barakzais were equally "Duranis."

THE SUCCESSORS TO AHMAD SHAH

The Durani Empire commenced, as has been said, in 1747 with the rise of Ahmad Shah, who reigned for twenty-six glorious but unsettled years, during which time the Afghan frontier was carried south to the Sutlej River till it joins the Indus, and thence to the sea along that mighty river itself.

In 1773 the conqueror died, and he was succeeded by his son Timur Shah, who reigned for twenty inglorious years on the prestige of his father, to be succeeded by his second son Shah Zaman, under circumstances to be described hereafter.[1] Shah Zaman was not apparently man enough to fill the bill, or was too occupied by his plans for the invasion of India. But in 1803 he was blinded, and succeeded by his half-brother Shah Mahmud, who in turn gave way before his brother Shah Shujah and the might of the king-making Barakzais. In 1809 Shah Shujah was driven out, and succeeded again by Shah Mahmud, who eventually was relegated to a separate throne at Herat, while Akram Khan Barakzai controlled the country under the minor kingship of Shah Ayub, another half-wit of the royal family. By 1827, when Akram Khan died, Afghanistan was the heritage of anyone who could manage it, and to this rose the younger brother Dost Muhammad, who succeeded in carving out a throne which he held till 1863, save for the three years when the British intervened in the endeavour to maintain a better government by the restoration of Shah Shujah. To the Dost succeeded his son Shere Ali, two others for a short while, and then his nephew Abdurrahman, to whom succeeded in 1901 his son Habibullah Khan, and then in 1919 his grandson Amanullah.

Such in outline is the story of the Durani dynasty, of which the events and happenings are now to be detailed at

[1] p. 88.

greater length from the long-drawn-out agonies of the dying Moguls to the struggles of the Dost, the endeavours of the British to obtain a strong and peaceful Afghanistan, the success of their policy for so many years, and its collapse when they had allowed the young man Amanullah to try his own hand in empire-breaking. It is a long and interesting story, full of much incident and romance, and many lessons for those who put their trust in princes. The doings of Ahmad Shah's successors will be more fully described in the next chapter, which deals with the continued Durani invasions of India.

CHAPTER V

THE INVASIONS AND CONQUEST OF INDIA BY THE DURANIS

The Crumbling of the Mogul Empire · Nadir Shah at Delhi · Ahmad Shah in India · The Afghans crush the Marathas at the last Battle of Panipat · After Panipat · The Afghan Victory over the Sikhs · The Successors of Ahmad Shah in India

THE CRUMBLING OF THE MOGUL EMPIRE

THE crumbling and decay of the Mogul Empire, apart from the effeteness of its later holders, and weakness inherent in size, distances, and heterogeneous composition, must largely be attributed to the Afghan influence. Even the bond of Islam could not weld or mend the disruptive and selfish tendencies inherent in its members, and no doubt the subconscious antagonism between natures born of Semite and Aryan stock towards those of the entirely different Mongol stock and proclivities contributed.

When Aurangzib Alamgir, the last of the great Moguls, died in 1707 in his ninetieth year, after a reign of fifty years, there ensued a scramble amid his feeble descendants and their ambitious supporters that defies description. Murder, treachery, rapine, the popular sport of emperor-blinding, were paralleled only in the days of Ahmad Shah's equally worthless descendants.

Here in England, it is true, we went through a similar time of removals in high places immediately before the Elizabethan days; but royalties and great personages then sent each other decently to the block, without involving Merry England in civil wars and mass slaughterings. In India the unfortunate peasant and trader paid with their lives and prosperity the quarrels of the pillars of the State.

Aurangzib was succeeded by his eldest son Muazzim, Governor of Kabul. It is the tragedy of long reigns, especially in dynasties where monarchs must rule as well as reign, that sons come to the throne at an advanced age. Muazzim was approaching seventy when he ascended the Peacock Throne and assumed the title of Bahadur Shah. Two brothers defied his authority, but were defeated and slain, and he then reigned for five years, a kindly but ineffective personality, under the shadow of his father's prestige, dying at Lahore in 1712. Then commenced a generation when the Imperial throne fell into the hands of a succession of king-makers. Supported by Zulfiqar Khan, one of the ablest of Aurangzib's generals, the eldest son of Bahadur Shah was proclaimed Emperor with the high-sounding if pitiful title of Jahandar Shah, the "Possessor of the World." Anxious to profit by his father's experience, he put to death all the accessible males of the Imperial house. But it profited him little enough. His action stirred and shocked the supporters of the House of Timur, and the famous Sayyid brothers proclaimed Farrukhsiyar, a nephew of Bahadur Shah who had escaped the sword, as Emperor, the vast army of Jahandar Shah being defeated at Agra within the year. Farrukhsiyar and his supporters then seized Delhi, the able Zulfiqar was cruelly murdered, and with him his protégé, Jahandar Shah, while Farrukhsiyar ascended the ill-fated throne. The story of the Sayyid brothers and all their doings, a story of Eastern empires, is outside the immediate scope of the Afghan legend, and ended as such stories do. The unfortunate Farrukhsiyar, intriguing to escape from their influence, did not long enjoy his throne, for in 1719 the king-makers first blinded and then strangled him for his pains. They then tried in quick succession two other weakly sprigs of the house, who ascended but to die of consumption within the year. The choice now fell on Roshan Akhtar, the grandson of Bahadur Shah, who dared aspire to be the great Mogul, and was seated on the throne amid scenes of great splendour with the title of Muhammad Shah, his succession being dated to the sending of Imperial Farrukhsiyar to a better world.

These troubles gave an opportunity for the rising military sect of the Sikhs, whose later story was so fatal to Afghan pretensions, and most bitter struggles ensued in the country between Delhi and Lahore. Mosques were destroyed wherever possible, and in return massacres of Sikhs took place, their leader Bunda, the successor to the great Guru Govind, being forced to slay his own son before being torn to death with hot pincers. The memory of these and subsequent struggles produced an enmity between Sikh and Afghan or Sikh and Moslem which has not died even to this day, and which breaks out in all frontier wars unless forcibly restrained by the British officers.

During this period the great Turk Chilliq Khan, who became Viceroy of the Deccan with the titles of Nizam-ul-mulk and Asaf Jah—long known by the latter—came into power, and the story of Muhammad Shah's reign is largely the story of the removal of the Sayyid brothers and of the struggle between the Viceroy of the Deccan and the Viceroy of Oudh to control the person of the new Emperor, whose long but feeble reign ended in the rise of Marathas to power, and the practical independence of the three great Moslem provinces of Bengal, Oudh, and Hyderabad. The rise of the Marathas and that of the Sikhs are the two features of this time which affect the story of the new Afghan kingdom that was about to come into being on the Mogul ruins.

The Maratha policy was entirely a predatory one: they wanted authority from the Emperor and from his governors to levy *chouth*, or the fourth part of the revenue, from certain provinces. If they were given the right, they, with their hordes of horsemen, would collect it for themselves, and if they were not given the right, they would nevertheless collect it wherever they could. They got this preposterous right by fair means and by foul for certain provinces, and they eventually extended their demands to the greater part of India. Such a nefarious and impudent system of piracy has rarely been paralleled, and the story of the empire and the reign of Muhammad Shah is largely the story of the triple struggle—that is to say of Oudh and

Hyderabad, to control the Emperor as its minister, and of the Marathas to gain the *chouth* of the empire—a claim only vitiated by the fact that the British had the *diwani* or right to collect the revenue in Bengal, and were a far tougher nut for Maratha freebooters than any of the Mogul viceroys.

Many books of wonders and evils have been written, and might still be written, of this astounding disease in the bowels and the extremities of the Turkish Empire of Delhi, of surpassing interest to all historians and to all students of Oriental psychology.

It must here suffice to record that the Marathas had appeared in arms up to the very gates of the Imperial city itself, when the catastrophe occurred which disposed for all time of the prestige of the Mogul Empire and the future of the House of Timur.

Nadir Shah at Delhi

Nadir Shah, the Perso-Turkish soldier of fortune, swept into Afghanistan in 1737, as has been related, after seizing the Persian crown and expelling therefrom the Afghan king, and occupied Kandahar and Kabul, the erstwhile provinces of the Delhi throne. Muhammad Shah at Delhi was too involved in the anxieties of the Maratha menace to take effective notice of the loss of Kabul, and the Persian Shah advanced in a leisurely manner and by easy stages through the Khaibar and the Punjab, crossing the Indus in November 1738 and entering Delhi on the 14th of February 1739, barely a hundred years before the accession of Queen Victoria.[1] The Imperial armies had given way as he advanced, and had assembled at Karnal but to endure defeat. The Emperor went out to meet the conqueror, and together they entered Delhi. The latter no doubt intended as bloodless a squeeze as possible, but there ensued by ill chance those terrible riots and massacres,

[1] As an instance of the communications of the world in those days, the arrival of Nadir at Delhi in February 1739 was not known in London till 1st October.

followed by a sack and extortions which left the empire prostrate and devoid both of wealth and of its remaining prestige.[1] Nadir Shah, in withdrawing with the Peacock Throne and the wealth of which so many conflicting estimates have been made, left the crown in the hands of Muhammad Shah, his "brother Turk," securing for himself Sind, Kabul, and Kandahar, and the four districts of the Punjab adjoining the Indus.

Before going, Nadir Shah also extracted some two millions sterling from Saadat Khan, the Persian-descended Viceroy of Oudh, who in his chagrin and fear eventually took poison.

The coming of Nadir relieved Delhi for the moment of the Maratha menace, though had Baji Rao, the head of the Maratha confederacy, been near, it is probable that he would have rallied his forces for the defence of India and joined hands with the Emperor. The great Asaf Jah was the Imperial Vizier, and largely instrumental in managing the conqueror. He, however, soon returned to his own province of the Deccan, leaving a son, Ghazi-ud-din, in charge of the Vizier's offices.

The next ten years were largely occupied in repressing the rising energies of the Sikhs, who had acquired some wealth in ravaging the stragglers from the retiring Persian Army. A rebellion was terminated by the execution of many of their notables, the scene of the martyrdom being known to this day as "Shahid sarig," "the Place of witnesses"; and the enmity between Sikh and Moslem was proportionately increased thereby.

Ahmad Shah in India

In 1748 Ahmad Shah, as has been related, started off to assert his control of the Indian provinces of Nadir Shah, intent, if possible, on acquiring the whole of the Punjab, and at any rate making good the four districts which

[1] It is said that a fanatical ascetic spread in the bazaars a rumour that Nadir was dead, which stirred the Delhi mob to fall on his followers.

Muhammad Shah had assigned to Nadir. If pretexts were necessary he found two: first, that the Governor of Kabul had rebelled against him and fled to Delhi, where he was sheltered, and secondly, that he had been invited to come by the Mogul Viceroy of the Punjab, one Shah Nawaz, a grandson of Abdul Summad who had destroyed Bunda and his Sikhs, and incidentally had usurped his brother's office and generally weakened the Mogul influence in the Punjab. Ahmad Shah had been eagerly joined by large bodies of hardy Central Asian horsemen, to whom the cry of "Hindustan!" was as the north to the loadstone, and he advanced across the Punjab easily enough. Shah Nawaz, stimulated from Delhi, did put up some unsuccessful show of resistance; but it was not till the Afghans had penetrated to Sirhind that the forces under the Vizier Qamar-ud-din and the heir-apparent were able to defeat them, the Vizier being killed in the hour of victory. Ahmad Shah then found it necessary to return to Afghanistan, harassed by the Sikhs *en route*. The Vizier's son, Mir Manu, who had taken the leading part in the victory, was appointed Mogul Viceroy of the Punjab, which included Lahore and Multan, with the title of Muin-ul-mulk.

The Emperor Muhammad Shah had now reigned for twenty-nine troubled and by no means always dignified years, and overcome by the loss of his minister in the hour of victory, passed away Safdar Jang, son of the Viceroy of Oudh, had now succeeded to the viziership, and placed on the throne Prince Ahmad, the heir-apparent, with the same name and title as the Durani Emperor, viz. Ahmad Shah.

The new Viceroy of the Punjab was able and active, but by no means wrapped up in fidelity to the Mogul throne and the person of the new Mogul. At Delhi the struggle for control of the empire still waged between the Persian party of Oudh and the Mogul party of the Deccan and the followers of the still mighty Asaf Jah, who passed away on the march to Delhi shortly after the Emperor, at the wonderful age of one hundred and four. The struggle between the Lords of Iran and the Lords of Turan, as the

Persian and Turkish parties have been called, was now complicated by the rise to power of an Afghan party, the land-owning Rohilla barons, in the province between Delhi and the Himalaya, who rebelled against the new Emperor, and were only defeated by the help of Jāts and Marathas. At Lahore Mir Manu, anxious to emulate the other great viceroys in freeing himself from the control of Delhi, and perhaps achieving independence, began to intrigue with the Durani, who was at worst a more distant master at Kabul.

Ahmad Shah and his Afghans now returned for their second invasion in 1748, having settled the affairs west of the Indus, and were opposed on the Chenab by the Viceroy of Lahore. Ahmad Shah, the Abdali, had taken a fancy to the young soldier who had contributed to his defeat at Sirhind, and agreed to retire across the Indus if the revenues of the four districts ceded to Nadir Shah were paid to him.

The Mogul authorities at Delhi were pleased enough at this escape, but the Vizier decided to reduce the power of Mir Manu by appointing Shah Nawaz, the former Governor of Lahore, to Multan. This Mir Manu would not stand, and having defeated and slain Shah Nawaz, and being elated by his success, held back the revenues assigned to Kabul. This brought the indignant Ahmad Shah on the scene, for the third time in 1752 to capture Lahore itself. His demand for the entire surrender of the Punjab was granted by the Emperor at Delhi, to the disgust of his Vizier Safdar Jang, who was absent at the time. A quarrel ensued, and Safdar Jang retired to Oudh, to the vice-royalty of which he had succeeded and which became henceforward virtually independent of Delhi. It was now the turn of the Lords of Turan, and young Shahab-ud-din, son of Ghazi-ud-din and grandson of Asaf Jah, was appointed Vizier. Believing that the Emperor Ahmad Shah was still intriguing with Safdar Jang, he deposed him in 1754, and having blinded both him and his mother, placed the former's son on the throne under the high-sounding title of Alamgir II, the "World Grasper," a title fine enough for Aurangzib, but sorry enough for a puppet.

After the cession of the Punjab to the Afghans, Ahmad

Shah, the Durani, appointed the competent Mir Manu as his Viceroy, and once again marched away to the west across the Indus. But the Mir died shortly after, and his widow, endeavouring to hold the balance between Delhi and Kabul and keep the vice-royalty for her son, betrothed her daughter to the Vizier Shahab-ud-din. The Vizier, wishing to recover the lost province for the empire as well as obtain a bride, marched to Lahore, removed his irate mother-in-law, and placed in the vice-royalty Adina Beg, an officer of the Mir Manu's régime. The Afghan Emperor was not likely to rest quiet under this insult, which occurred in 1755. He marched from Kandahar by Baluchistan and the valley of the Indus, entering the Punjab for the fourth time, reassumed control of Lahore, placing his son Timur in the vice-royalty, and annexed Sirhind. He then proceeded to Delhi, which he plundered, with Muttra also, forgiving the Imperial Vizier and his puppet Emperor for their insult, but placed Najib-ud-daulah, the Rohilla chief, as commander-in-chief of the Imperial forces and as custodian of Afghan interests at the Mogul Court, thus bringing the Afghan or Rohilla party still further into prominence. He secured his own son Timur in the vice-royalty of Lahore by marrying him to the daughter of the Great Mogul.

The Afghans crush the Marathas at the last Battle of Panipat

Four times now, between 1748 and 1756, had Ahmad Shah, at the head of his hordes of Afghan horsemen and with long trains of artillery, ridden to India. Four times had he established his rule and returned to the affairs of the northern kingdom, and now was master to the Sutlej in something more than name. India was already deadly sick of these comings and goings, these rapings and lootings and burnings; and all the while the new power of Sikhdom was rising as each come-and-go lessened and weakened the resources of at any rate Moslem Delhi. India knew not where to seek for protection. On the west the great hordes of the Marathas destroyed more than they gave. On the east the Afghan colonist barons thought more of themselves and their aggrandisement than of the country and the Raj, and were tainted with the racialism of the Durani.

At Delhi the Durani nominee, the Rohilla Najib-ud-daulah, had grown intolerable to the court party in his insistence, and the Vizier and Alamgir in despair appealed to the Marathas to rally round the Empire of India as against the rievers from the north. Nothing loath, with their tongues in their cheeks, they rode from Poona, from Malwa, and from Indore and other states of the Deccan. The Sikhs had risen against the Afghans and for a while gained Lahore, and with the Marathas drove the Afghans across the Indus in some hurry, following them to Attock and far Multan. Then it was that for a few weeks the horsemen of the Deccan fulfilled their boast that one day they would water their horses in the Indus. The dreams of controlling the empire which the Peishwa and chiefs of the Maratha Confederacy had long been cherishing seemed now about to be realised, and it is generally believed that if Ahmad Shah had been defeated, it was the intention of Sindia to have seized the throne and declared Wiswas Rao, the Peishwa's son, Emperor of India.

But their triumphs were not for long. Ahmad Shah was little likely to brook the expulsion of his troops from India, and before long appeared on the Indus once again with a larger force and a powerful army of experienced soldiers. The Marathas hastily retired across the Sutlej, and Ahmad Shah swept down in Afghan fury. Nor was he without support in India. The Hindu ascendancy had brought Islam out in arms, and while the Mogul barons at Delhi were for the moment prepared to accept Maratha help as the best for the Empire, the Rohillas were not, and had called on Ahmad Shah to come quickly, promising their support.

The sweep of the Afghans was irresistible. Sindia and Holkar were separately pushed back as Ahmad Shah came up the Indus from Baluchistan again. Delhi was occupied, and Ahmad Shah pressed on down the Ganges to enlist the support of Shujah-ud-daulah, now Nawab of Oudh, in an anti-Hindu campaign.

But while Islam hurried from the north and stirred in the east, up from the south came all the chivalry of Marathadom, and Sudasheo Rao drove the Afghan garrison from Delhi. They came in their thousands to join Sindia and Holkar: "the hawk-winged horse of Damajee, mailed squadrons of the Bhao," and with them the great yellow standard of the Confederacy and the Bhao himself.

But as Ahmad Shah swept down the Punjab plains a great evil had taken place at Delhi. The Vizier Shahab-ud-din, believing that the Emperor was intriguing with the Afghans, as well he might, slew him with contumely.

The accession of strength of the Maratha hordes and their reoccupation of Delhi brought Ahmad Shah and all the Rohillas together to the field in the vicinity of Karnal, while the Marathas had entrenched themselves on the historic field of Panipat.

Then ensued the last great fight on that historic field, known as the "Battle of the Black Mango Tree," by reason of the ancient tree that stood on the plain.

Suraj Mall, the leader of the Jāts, had left the Marathas in disgust when Sudasheo Rao had stripped seventeen lakhs of valuables from the murdered Emperor's palace. His advice had been not to fight the Afghans, but to rely on harassing their supply convoys.

The Maratha leader, however, had great faith in his trained infantry, the latter chiefly the corps of Ibrahim Gardi, so called because of his training with the French guards of the Nizam, and in a large park of artillery. On 5th October 1760 Sudasheo Rao moved with his whole force to the field of Panipat, having for the moment raised to the throne Jawan Bakht, the son of the Prince Imperial Ali Jauhar, who was absent endeavouring to assume the viceroyalty of Bengal, which his father had conferred on him, and having made Shujah-ud-daulah of Oudh the Imperial Vizier in place of Shahab-ud-din, who had murdered the Emperor.

The Afghans crossed the Jumna above Delhi and commenced skirmishing with the Marathas, who had thrown up a wide rampart and ditch round their camp. The

Afghans entrenched also a short distance off, and for two months the two forces watched each other with daily conflicts of varying importance.

The Maratha force numbered 55,000 horse, with 15,000 foot and 300 cannon. The Afghans and Rohillas, 41,800 far superior horse, with 38,000 foot and 70 cannon. The Afghans managed to steal the Maratha rôle, and kept them almost without supplies through the activity of their horse, till at last, driven to desperation, they sallied from their entrenchments—all the chivalry of the entire Maratha Confederacy. They formed into regular line of battle in the early hours of 7th January, and a most desperate fight ensued.[1] After varied fortunes the Afghan reserves of horse charged and completely overthrew the Marathas, who retired broken from the field, and were subjected to a most relentless pursuit. Wiswas Rao, the Peishwa's son, and many other notable chiefs were slain; the slaughter was great, and all male prisoners were beheaded next morning by the Afghans, who made slaves of the numerous women and children within the camp. News of the defeat flashed through India by that mysterious banker's channel, couched in these terms:

"Two pearls have been dissolved, twenty-seven gold mohurs have been lost, and of the silver and copper the total cannot be cast up."

It echoed through India like the news of Flodden Field through Scotland, and the shock killed the Peishwa, who had moved up in support to the Narbada.

The battle has been sung of with all its fierceness, horror, and pathos by Rudyard Kipling in his poem, "With Scindia[2] to Delhi," the story of the fight and Sindia's ride from the field with a woodland girl who had followed him:

"The children of the hills of Khost before our lances ran,
We drove the black Rohillas back as cattle to the pen;
'Twas then we needed Mulhar Rao to end what we began,
A thousand men had saved the charge; he fled the field with ten!

. . . .

[1] Described at length by both Elphinstone and Grant Duff.

[2] Usually written to-day Sindia.

I held by Scindia, my lord, as close as man might hold;
  A Soobah of the Deccan asks no aid to guard his life;
But Holkar's horse were flying and our chiefest chiefs were cold,
  And like a flame among us leapt the long lean Northern knife."

It was many a year before the Confederacy recovered from the great Afghan victory and showed themselves again at Delhi; and there is no doubt that this victory did to a considerable extent change the conditions under which the British gathered up the warring pieces of the Mogul Empire.

After the battle Ahmad Shah entered Delhi and declared Ali Jauhar, the absent heir-apparent, Emperor, with the magnificent title of Shah Alam,[1] instead of his son, the Maratha's nominee, securing to himself again by treaty the whole of the Mogul provinces of Afghanistan and the Punjab, thus leaving to Delhi little but the surrounding districts.

After Panipat. The Afghan Victory over the Sikhs

After Ahmad Shah had returned once again to his own country, the Sikhs, who had been steadily consolidating their confederacy during the decay of Mogul power and the hopeless condition of authority at Delhi, attacked the Afghan Governor of Lahore, driving him within his walls, and also turned against the Governor of Sirhind. This brought the restless Ahmad Shah down post-haste on his sixth incursion into India. Of him at this stage Cunningham writes: "This prince, the very ideal of the Afghan genius, hardy and enterprising, fitted for conquest, yet incapable of empire, seemed but to exist for the sake of losing and recovering provinces."[2]

He was at Lahore by the end of 1762, driving the Sikhs south of the Sutlej, and after two long marches from Lahore by way of Ludhiana came up with them when engaged with the Governor of Sirhind. Bitter was the defeat he inflicted on them on the night of slaughter, a

[1] King of the World.

[2] *History of the Sikhs*, p. 108.

loss which varies in the estimates from 12,000 to 25,000 slain. It is still known in the Punjab as *Ghuloo ghara*, or the "Great disaster."

Here, too, Ahmad Shah interviewed his old Rohilla ally, Najib-ud-daulah. After making a Hindu Governor of Lahore, he flew back again to quell a rising at Kandahar. But before he went he gratified his own resentment and the savage bigotry of his followers by destroying the rebuilt temples of Amritsar "by polluting the pool with slaughtered cows, by encasing numerous pyramids with the heads of decapitated Sikhs, and by cleansing the walls of the desecrated mosques with the blood of his infidel enemies."[1] It may be remarked, however, that the Sikhs had just done much the same with the mosques.

The Sikhs, nevertheless, throve on disaster, and a year later 40,000 defeated and slew the Afghan Governor of Sirhind and became masters of the whole of that province, while Delhi was too feeble to do anything for the defence of Islam. The Sikhs swept down and with the Jāts of Bharatpur besieged Delhi. This joint attack and the loss of Sirhind brought Ahmad Shah back once more, which relieved the pressure on Delhi; but this done, the Afghan king, who had plenty to occupy him in his own mountains, contented himself with appointing a Sikh of the Malwa as governor of the provinces, and marched back.

This seventh coming was in reality of little avail, for the Sikhs soon ejected his Governor from even Lahore, and in 1764 proclaimed their authority up to the Jhelum. For two years Ahmad Shah left them to themselves, but in 1767 back he came, though weakened by disease, and this was his last crossing of the Indus. Avoiding Lahore, he advanced to the Sutlej, and by way of conciliating when he could no longer overcome, made Umar Singh of Patiala Chief of Sirhind. But even Afghans tire of war, and 12,000 of his troops left him and marched towards Kabul, so that he was compelled to follow, the Sikhs yapping at his heels. In 1768 the Sikhs again secured Sher Shah's old fortress of Rohtas on the way from the plains

[1] Cunningham.

to Rawalpindi, and in the succeeding years occupied themselves in subduing all Afghan settlements and areas in the Punjab.

The Successors of Ahmad Shah in India

In 1773 the restless Emperor passed away, a hero to his people, after leading them to plunder and rapine for twenty-six glorious years. His nominal empire still held where his horse had carried it—from the Sutlej to the Oxus and the borders of Khurasan. He was succeeded by his eldest son Timur, a name of great prestige, but who, like so many successors of Eastern conquerors, was feeble and effeminate, much given to pleasure, and quite unfit to handle the team that his father drove so long. Nevertheless, the prestige of the latter kept him on the throne till his death twenty years later, though all and sundry bit off the extremities of the Durani possessions.

A few years after his accession he stirred himself to drive the Sikhs from Multan, which he finally did in person in 1778–79, while fear gripped the hearts of the Punjab lest the days of Ahmad Shah were to return. The Indus, however, was not to see him again, for trouble on the Oxus and his easy nature kept him in Afghanistan itself—a story which belongs to that of Afghanistan rather than to that of the Afghans in India. With the waning of the Afghan influence in the Punjab, Delhi made some attempt to regain the lost Mogul province of Lahore, but with ill success. Old Najib-ud-daulah had passed away, and his son Zabitah Khan headed the Rohillas; but he, in pursuance of one of the many intrigues that were in progress, turned Sikh and assumed a Sikh name for a while, leading Sikhs and Jāts to beleaguer Delhi, after which a welter of Rohilla, Sikh, and Jāt intrigue, with the Marathas again intervening, surrounded the puppet throne.

In 1793 the feeble Timur died, and left six sons and many daughters. Zaman Shah,[1] the second son, supported by

[1] Zaman Shah, called indifferently Shah Zaman.

Payindah Khan, Chief of the Barakzais, seized the throne,[1] and defeated and then blinded Humayun, his elder brother. the Governor of Kandahar. With Zaman Shah on the Afghan throne commenced the phase in which Afghan politics became a definite problem for the British, and in which it was necessary for them to develop some policy in regard thereto—a policy very soon to be complicated with the designs of Russia, which had birth before even the days of Napoleon and his ambitious schemes.

[1] The general ethics of Moslem succession are expounded by the Amir Abdurrahman in his autobiography, and will be discussed later.

CHAPTER VI

THE FIRST CLASH OF BRITISH AND AFGHAN

Affairs at Delhi from Panipat to the Coming of the British · The Great Fear of India · The Coming of Shah Zaman · Early British Missions to Persia · The British Mission to Afghanistan and the Sikhs

Affairs at Delhi from Panipat to the Coming of the British

Before the sequence of events which brought the British to Delhi in 1803, the Mogul throne was destined to pass through another generation of tragedy and contumely. At the time of the murder of Alamgir II by his Vizier Shahab-ud-din, Ali Jauhar, the Prince Imperial, was absent with the Nawab of Oudh endeavouring to attack the British and the Nawab in Bengal. After suffering defeat at the hands of Major Calliaud in January 1761, the Emperor joined the British at Patna and conferred on them the Diwani[1] of Bengal, and then returned to Delhi to take up the throne, on which he had been confirmed through the victory of Ahmad Shah, as already related. In 1764 we see him once again something of a fugitive from Delhi, but with the forces of Oudh and the Rohillas, who were then fighting the British. Beaten at Buxar by Major Monro in a fight in which the Imperial forces lost 130 guns, the Emperor came into the British camp once more. At Delhi his heir-apparent, Jawan Bakht, was now in the hands of the Rohillas, and he himself was only too glad to accept from the British the provinces of Allahabad and Kora, with a grant of twenty-five lakhs a year as his kingdom. Eventually the Marathas, recovering from the disaster of Panipat, reoccupied Delhi and invited the Emperor to

[1] Viz. the right to administer the revenue.

return; which he did, and was enthroned with great pomp, but was induced to offer Kora and Allahabad to the Marathas. This, however, the British refused to allow, taking over those districts themselves, in pursuance of their policy to put a barrier between the Marathas and Bengal.

From this time onward the Emperor was but the puppet of contending influences of Maratha and Rohilla, being eventually blinded by Ghulam Qadir the Rohilla, the grandson of Najib-ud-daulah, in vengeance, it has been said, for having been made a eunuch at the Emperor's hands when a lad.

In 1785 Sindia came to Delhi at the invitation of the blinded Emperor, and was appointed commander-in-chief of the Imperial forces. Ghulam Qadir falling into the hands of the nobles, who resented his treatment of the Emperor's still sacred person, was cruelly maimed in his turn and carried about crouched in a cage for many months, in a vengeance that he had certainly deserved. In this cruelty and outrage the last vestige of the Delhi throne went down, while the rising power of the Afghan Rohillas—a power which they were quite unworthy to exercise—was suppressed by the Vizier of Oudh, assisted by the British.

The struggle for the mastery of India was now one between the British and Marathas. The latter would not let the British alone, and at last the Governor-General was compelled in self-defence to break their power once and for all. At Patparganj, outside Delhi, in 1803, the Maratha troops, led by French officers, were defeated by Lord Lake, and the blind Shah Alam, rescued from what was now practically durance in the Maratha hands, was pensioned and restored to comfort and some shadow of dignity. And then Lord Lake must needs drive the Sikhs from British territory and pursue the Marathas up to the Punjab, before it was possible to settle down to the reconstruction of the narrow area round Delhi which alone comprised the remnant of Mogul belongings.

And this in outline is the sequence of events which brought the British to the Sutlej and to march with the nominal boundary of the Afghan kingdom, after watching for ten years the threat of Shah Zaman to overrun Southern India once again, as must now be told in more detail.

The Great Fear of India

In this strange story of the crumbling of the Mogul Empire of Delhi, and the struggle between Maratha and Afghan for the domination of the Delhi throne which has just been described, it can well be believed that the very name of Afghan was a horror to the inhabitants of the Punjab, whether peaceable peasant and yeoman, or factious knight and squire. Between the death of Ahmad Shah and the accession of Shah Zaman the continuous inroads of Afghan and Turki horse had stopped, though many had remained the holders of land in fief. Timur Shah had been nominally head of the Punjab, both by treaty and conquest of his father and by his own marriage with a princess of Delhi; but he had done little to emphasise that position or to press for his revenues. His son, Shah Zaman, who succeeded in 1793, was not disposed to so nominal a sovereignty. The empire of Ahmad Shah to him was bounded by the Indus and the Sutlej, and he was anxious that it should be so again. That must mean that once again would huge armies of Afghan and Central Asian horse march by the great ways through the mountains, by Kabul and Ghuzni on Peshawar, or by Kandahar on Multan, where the Afghan settlers always formed a bridge-head for their compatriots to use. So the fear, the sleepless horror of the Afghans, of their atrocities and their pillaging, were once more aroused when Shah Zaman's armies appeared on the banks of the Indus. This dread was a household word in the villages far down into even the Gangetic plain, and in the Punjab, women would quiet their children with the threat of the coming of the Afghans. During the generation that had just passed two conflicting currents had been at play: first, the desire of the Moslems of India, especially the later Afghan colonies, to maintain an Islamic throne at Delhi; second, their gradual and occasional identification of themselves with the land in which they lived. It was chiefly the Afghan settlers and descendants of converted Indians who had invited and sided with Ahmad Shah when he invaded Delhi and destroyed the flower of the Maratha chivalry, and it was the Moguls who co-opted the Maratha. The rise of the Sikhs and the internecine struggles in which they were engaged with Mogul and Afghan had further turned the thoughts of the Moslems in Northern India to the idea of the Durani dynasty coming to the throne of Delhi, mindful of the fact that the great Babur had himself been King of Kabul when he conquered India. To many in the face of Maratha and Sikh oppression or British encroachment the Shah of Afghanistan seemed the only hope of Islam. As far south as Mysore, Tippu, finding he could not drive the British into the sea, had appealed to Shah Zaman to save him. The Shah actually entered India in response to this call; but, fortunately, troubles in Afghanistan had recalled him, and Tippu went to his fate unaided and unmourned, save that Islam shuddered to see that another Moslem power, however so recently usurped from a Hindu kingdom, should fall.

India was now entering into the sphere of world politics. Napoleon was in Egypt, openly boasting of his road to the East. He had been in communication with Tippu, and the French officers, either the remnant of the original French in the south, or refugees from the Revolution who, with others now sent with Napoleon's blessing, were active at Tippu's Court and with all the armies of the Maratha states. Napoleon and the Emperor Paul of Russia were actually planning an invasion of India as early as 1800.

Seven years later the peace of Tilsit enabled Napoleon and the Tsar to concoct fresh schemes, which were by no means impossible, for invading India via Persia or Afghanistan. This policy, however, was not yet apparent, and because of the great fear which Northern India had of the Afghans, and the desire for some freedom from the come-and-go of marauding armies, the British Government of India despatched a mission to Persia with the idea of inciting the Persians to attack Afghanistan and recover some of their ancient provinces. It was this fear of Persian attack on Herat that was afterwards to make Afghan affairs so important a feature in Anglo-Indian frontier politics; thus the reflection is not without a suggestion of humour that we find ourselves at the very beginning of the nineteenth century inflating the bogy that so disturbed us later.

The diaries and despatches of the period when the Marquis Wellesley was Governor-General are full of reference to this fear of France and Russia, and these fears had definite result in the sending of missions to Persia, to Afghanistan, and to Lahore, with the view of forming alliances or engagements that should impede the advance of the forces of the Bear which Napoleon was inciting to the conquest of India. It has in later years been the fashion to pooh-pooh these apprehensions as the fear of the merest bogy, but a more careful consideration will show that there was something very tangible in the apprehensions of India. Russia was already on the borders of Persia, and had concluded overriding treaties with that country. What Nadir Shah had done in 1738 was perfectly possible for Russia, France, and Persia to do in the early nineteenth century, especially if Afghanistan could be incited to join. It is also to be remembered once again how involved from earliest times was the Persian overlordship of Afghan provinces, how Nadir Shah in recent times had installed Persian governors throughout the country, and how Herat and Kandahar had often been Persian provinces for long periods on end.

The Coming of Shah Zaman

Shah Zaman succeeded to the throne of Kabul in 1793, and commenced his attempts to reassert control over Ahmad Shah's Indian Empire by crossing the Indus in 1795 and advancing to Hassan Abdal on the road to Rawalpindi. From thence he sent forward to capture from the Sikhs Sher Shah's fort at Rohtas that guarded the approaches from the plains to the Pindi uplands, and which had so often before been a point of importance in the struggles between India and Afghanistan, but he was recalled by troubles in his western provinces. In the cold weather of 1795–96, Ghulam Muhammad of Rohilkhand, and after him agents of Asaf-ud-daulah of Qudh, proceeded to Shah Zaman's Court to invite the Shah to deliver Islam in India from Maratha domination. So in 1797 Shah Zaman, whose book it obviously suited to appear in his grandfather's rôle, crossed the Indus, but was compelled a second time to return, by trouble elsewhere at the hands of his brother Mahmud. In 1798, however, he came a third time and actually reached Lahore, where Nizam-ud-din of Kasur joined him. This for the moment appeared to make effective once more the Afghan dominion of the Punjab to the boundary of the Sutlej, the rising Sikh chief Ranjit Singh acknowledging his overlordship. Anxious to return, Shah Zaman then appointed Ranjit Singh Governor of Lahore in reward for the assistance given in getting the Afghan guns across the Chenab; and incidentally from this period dates the occupation of the ancient Mogul stronghold of Lahore by the Sikhs, nominally as the retainer of the Shah of Afghanistan.

With Shah Zaman at Lahore, and Tippu, whose final trial of strength with the British was approaching, calling for his aid, the British inaugurated their first cantonment in the north at Anupshahr, and assembled an army of observation, lest the Afghans should once again sweep into Hindustan.

Early British Missions to Persia

The British stimulants to Persia already mentioned are worthy of reference in more detail. The Governor-General, among the many possible measures to counter the plans of the French and also to minimise the danger of Shah Zaman's invasion, determined to send a mission to Persia which might induce the Shah to renew the threats to Kandahar and Herat. His selection fell on the rising young soldier-political Captain John Malcolm of the Coast Army.[1] At the end of 1799 Malcolm sailed for the Persian Gulf, a mission which he thus describes: "To relieve India from the annual alarm of Shah Zaman's invasion, which is always attended with serious expense to the Company, by occasioning a diversion upon his Persian provinces; to counteract the possible attempts of those villainous but active democrats the French; to restore to some part of its former prosperity a trade which has been in a great degree lost . . . are the leading objects of my journey."

Malcolm was at Tehran in November, where he had a splendid reception and presented handsome gifts from the Governor-General. But troubles of his own had already compelled Shah Zaman to abandon his designs on India. The French menace, however, remained, and a treaty was signed in which Persia and Britain together were to attack any attempt of the French to invade or occupy any part of the Persian dominions, while the King of Persia would never allow the French or any European force in alliance with them to build a fort or settle in any part of the Persian dominions. Whatever the value of this treaty, the mission and its presents made for good relations, and left a pleasant memory. With the difficulties in which Shah Zaman found himself, by the destruction of Tippu Sultan, and, above all, from the surrender of the French in Egypt and Buonaparte's return to France, the dangers anticipated disappeared for some years. They revived, however, with more force after the peace of Tilsit in 1807, when Napoleon and the Tsar met and planned Asiatic enterprises. An unfortunate incident occurred in 1802 when the Persian Ambassador, who had come to ratify the treaties, was shot in Bombay, and Malcolm went to explain and express regret. The grants made to all who suffered by the mischance were so liberal, that it was said afterwards in Persia that the English might shoot a dozen ambassadors if they liked.

In 1807 the conferences at Tilsit and the plans for the conjoint campaign, "*Contre les possessions de la compagnie*

[1] The old name for the Madras Army.

6

des Indes," were in progress. The King's ministers had long contemplated another mission to Persia. They refused to have Malcolm, as was suggested by the Marquis Wellesley, and sent "Bagdad" Jones, making him a baronet. He was to have proceeded through Russia, but the sudden change in Europe due to the peace of Tilsit and the Russo-French *rapprochement* not only emphasised the importance of the mission, but compelled it to come via India. The Government of India, however, was even more impressed with the urgency of the occasion. Already had Russia been at war with Persia, and already had she encroached on Persian dominion, and been coquetting with parties in Persia. In the expectation that Sir Harford Jones would be delayed in coming, Lord Minto, the then Governor-General, decided to send Malcolm to the Persian Gulf once again.

It has long been forgotten how this joining of Russia with France, after we had expected that she would help us stem the adventures of Napoleon, had dismayed the statesmen of Great Britain. Shah Zaman was now a blind nonentity, but Afghanistan and the shade of Ahmad Shah still stood in the near distance. With Russia definitely allied to our ambitious foes, and already pressing forward to the Oxus, there was much to cause genuine apprehension. Malcolm unwittingly sailed just as a king's ship with Harford Jones on board was approaching the port. Lord Minto had written that the whereabouts of Sir Harford Jones were not known, but that his instructions were framed in such a manner as not to clash with the rôle of the minister. Malcolm reached Bushire and was well received, but had to report that the French were already in possession, having the dominant influence in Persia and busy drilling the Persian troops. General Malcolm [1] was not permitted by the Shah to go to the capital, nor was a messenger of his even allowed to go beyond Shiraz. Malcolm decided to return at once rather than lose face by waiting at the coast, and reported himself to the Governor-General at Calcutta. The latter ordered Sir Harford Jones not to proceed, and decided to

[1] He had the temporary rank of brigadier-general.

send Malcolm with three thousand men to occupy the Island of Kharg at the head of the Gulf and threaten the Persian coast.

Sir Harford Jones, however, had just sailed from Bombay for Persia when the Governor-General's instructions to him arrived, and somewhat better news from Europe decided Lord Minto to cancel his plans. But the story, while also illustrating the difficulties of managing a world-wide empire before the days of the telegraph and deep-sea cables, also indicated an overlap between Whitehall and India which even now at times is not unknown. Chiefly is it of interest in the study of Afghanistan and the protection of India, as showing how deep was the anxiety in such matters that prevailed amongst those whose business it was to peer ahead into the loom of the future.

The British Mission to Afghanistan and the Sikhs

As part of the measures to be taken to minimise the threat of the Treaty of Tilsit, Lord Minto decided to send a mission to the Courts of Lahore and Afghanistan, to explore the situation as regards combination in the event of a Russo-French move on India, and incidentally to develop the British aim of trade facilities and markets. There were two brilliant young civil servants available, afterwards destined to make a great mark, in the shape of Mr Mountstuart Elphinstone and Mr Charles Metcalfe.

Elphinstone proceeded by Bikanir and the Moslem State of Bahawalpur in the Southern Punjab, and thence via Multan and the Derajat, reaching Peshawar, where the Afghan Court was in session owing to troubles northward, on the 25th February 1809. Elphinstone found Shah Shujah a courteous, well-mannered gentleman, and, like everyone else, was much attracted by the Afghan bearing and demeanour. It was almost the first time that any responsible British official had met what may be called the Afghan in a free state, rather than those Afghans who had been some generations in India, and had lost something of the charm of the wilder races who spend their winters in snow. But the Shah was in the throes of a dangerous rebellion, and had not much to say unless the British were prepared then and there to give him assistance. The Afghan ministers were astute bargainers, and not unnaturally failed to see how the British could expect help from Afghanistan if they were not prepared to give it themselves. They also said that the Shah's half-brother, Shah Mahmud, now in rebellion, could not maintain himself without Persian support, and that it would pay the British in their fear of Persia and her friends to back up Shah Shujah.

They rather minimised the Russian, French, and Persian danger to themselves, saying what was true enough, that Afghanistan was a hard country for invaders; and they were not much impressed when warned by the envoy of their own danger.

But they were really anxious for help against Shah Mahmud, and disappointed that Mr Elphinstone had little definite to offer. All that the missioner could do was to promise to put the Shah's views and requirements before Lord Minto, which was but cold comfort to the harassed monarch.

The Afghans were still full of the proud memories of Ahmad Shah; and Elphinstone records that Mulla Jafar said to him that if 10,000 French were in each of the cities of Kabul, Herat, Kandahar, and Peshawar, nevertheless the word of one Mullah would be sufficient to destroy them without the assistance of a single soldier! If the Afghan king gave them passage he would join them also, and the British would find the Duranis very different customers from the French. He further said "that our (*i.e.* the British) reputation was very high for good faith and for magnanimous conduct to conquered princes, but he frankly owned that we had the character of being very designing, and that most people thought it necessary to be very vigilant in all transactions with us."

The poor Shah was very soon after heavily defeated by his brother, and the envoy came away. Among other points that he had put forward was a suggestion that we might obtain the Shah's rights over Sind in return for some form of assistance and treaty; but this was severely negatived by the Governor-General, as showing a failure to realise the true situation in Sind.

Before he left by way of the Punjab he had, however, negotiated a treaty of friendship with the Afghan Shah. The latter undertook to prevent the passage of the French and Russians through his kingdom, and the British undertook to finance such opposition. Shortly afterwards came the news that the "King of Kings"[1] had also undertaken, as in the case of Malcolm's first mission, to permit no European force to approach India through Persia. There was not very much in either of these treaties, but they gave us a very definite *locus standi* as being much concerned in the integrity of both Afghanistan and Persia. Elphinstone, though he had not been farther into the country than Peshawar, did manage to collect a very great deal of information about Afghanistan generally.

While the latter had come up to Kabul via Afghan land on the trans-Indus side of the river, young Charles Metcalfe was despatched shortly after to Lahore on a similar mission. At Lahore the envoy had to deal with brains quite as astute as those of the Afghans, and the danger of the Persian and French aggression did not strike Ranjit Singh and his advisers as very serious. He was somewhat suspicious of Metcalfe's presence, and was anxious to get the British to recognise his right to control the cis-Sutlej Sikh States. This, however, was not to be thought of, though eventually the envoy was able to conclude a straightforward treaty of mutual friendship and alliance which served its purpose for many a long day. It was said that Ranjit Singh was persuaded to this by seeing an attack of fierce fanatical Sikh Akalis repelled steadily by the small sepoy detachment which had accompanied Metcalfe, and he felt that a race that could so train men to serve them was worth being on friendly terms with. And thus ended for the time being the attempts of the British to put matters

[1] Shah-in-Shah, the Persian Shah's full designation.

on the north-west frontier of India on to some sort of recognised footing. The history of the next thirty years is that of constant and unprofitable war and raid between Afghan and Sikh, to the despair of the trade-developing and peace-needing British, which eventually called for the adoption of some definite policy.

CHAPTER VII

THE FALL OF THE DURANI EMPIRE AND THE RISE OF THE BARAKZAIS

The Collapse of the Durani Empire · The Struggles of Shah Shujah · The Blinding of Fath Khan and the Flight of Mahmud · Shah Shujah attempts to Regain the Throne · Ranjit Singh's Encroachments on the Afghans · The British and the Indus · The Hindustani Fanatics · Shah Shujah's Second Attempt · Appeals to the Paramount Power

THE COLLAPSE OF THE DURANI EMPIRE

IN his autobiography the Amir Abdurrahman states very properly that his dynasty and kingdom is Durani, and that his folk the Barakzais are as much Durani as any other of the Abdali. This is perfectly true, but it has been the custom to speak of the "Durani" dynasty as that of the "Saduzais," the original royal clan to which Ahmad Shah belonged; and if we take the termination of that dynasty to be 1827, when the Dost asserted his ascendancy, or 1842, when the restored Shah Shujah was shot in a ditch, the fact remains—the Saduzai dynasty lasted less than the century.

It has been recorded how Ahmad Shah was largely maintained in his chiefship by the support of Jamal, the head of the larger Barakzai group of clans and families. His eldest son, Payindah Khan, had even more influence behind the Durani throne and was minister to Timur. When Timur Shah died in 1793, leaving a very large family, five of his sons were governors of provinces. Humayun, the eldest, had Kandahar, Shah Zaman Kabul, Shah Mahmud Herat (with whom was his full brother Firuz-ud-din), Kuhn Dil had Kashmir, and Abbas Peshawar.

By the influence of the able Barakzai minister Payindah Khan, Shah Zaman, Governor of Kabul and second son of Timur, was able to seize the throne. Humayun resisted, but was defeated and blinded. Mahmud at Herat and his brother acquiesced in Shah Zaman's accession.

At this time Shah Zaman was a popular enough ruler, but his three invasions of India distracted his attention, which was needed nearer home, and his influence faded. Further, Payindah Khan, not being satisfied with Zaman, was planning to place the Shah's brother Shujah-ul-mulk on the throne. Shah Zaman hearing of this took the law into his own hands, and put Payindah Khan and several other nobles to death. This stirred the general resentment against the Shah. Fath Khan, eldest son of Payindah, summoned Shah Mahmud from Herat, who, supported by numerous adherents, occupied the throne while Shah Zaman and his minister, one Wafadar Khan, took to flight, only to be handed over to Mahmud by a treacherous noble. The minister was murdered, and the unfortunate Shah Zaman was promptly deprived of his sight, and for a short while Mahmud reigned in his stead.

With the blinding of Shah Zaman, the "Ruler of the Age," the Durani Empire practically came to an end, though Saduzai princes ruled in some sort at Kabul for some time longer, as already related.

Mahmud himself was little fitted to sit in the saddle of Ahmad Shah, and he was almost immediately ousted by Shah Shujah, the whole brother and inseparable companion of Shah Zaman. But Shah Shujah had too forgiving a nature to handle the fickle Afghan, and spared his half-brother's life and eyesight, only to be ousted by him later on. He ruled, however, in the face of rebellions of this and other brothers, till 1810, during which period he had received, as has been described, the British Mission of Commerce and Friendship, headed by Mr Mountstuart Elphinstone.

In 1810 Fath Khan, who was not satisfied with his position and influence at the Court of Shah Shujah, supported Shah Mahmud in once again seizing the disputed throne.

The Struggles of Shah Shujah

With the expulsion of Shah Shujah from Kabul in 1810 began that era of disturbance and incident on the Indus from which eventually evolved the British policy of 1838.

The expelled Shah was now coming eastwards to look for help, and Ranjit Singh, mindful of how he himself had received the grant of Lahore from Shah Zaman in return for some help, was a little apprehensive lest the loan of a few British battalions might not precede a similar grant to the British, since in theory the kingdom of Ahmad Shah still stretched to the Sutlej.

He made some offers of helping the ex-Shah to recover Multan and Kashmir, and went to meet him at Shadiwal, with no great result; but the crafty Sikh, before they closed their discussion, saw fit to demand that ancient bone of contention, Multan, from the Afghans "on behalf of Shah Shujah." He even brought Zim Zammah (or Zem-Zem, the Bungi Top, the gun of "Kim") from Lahore to batter its walls. But the Governor of Multan, Muzaffar Khan, was already offering his allegiance to the British, so apprehensive were all Afghan chiefs of each other and of the Sikhs. This first instance of the Afghans acknowledging the British as rulers of the Mogul Empire, to which the Afghans really belonged, is of great interest, since for the next twenty years it was to be followed by several more, even from the throne of Afghanistan itself. Ranjit Singh also tried to borrow a British siege train, and proposed a division of the spoil.

Shah Shujah, disappointed of Sikh support, proceeded to attack where another Barakzai brother was prepared to help him, and he remained in possession of Peshawar for six months. Then another brother of Fath Khan, Muhammad Azim Khan, drove him forth; but after an attempt to get help from Multan the ex-Shah again secured Peshawar, after first suffering a reverse and then gaining a victory. But the inherent faithlessness of the Afghans was against him. Intrigues on all sides resulted in Jahandad Khan, the Governor of Attock, seizing him in 1812 and sending him off a prisoner to Kashmir, where he remained in easy durance a twelvemonth.

While Shah Shujah was endeavouring in 1811 to get help from Multan, Shah Mahmud himself came down to Peshawar and crossed the Indus with the object of deterring the Governor of Kashmir from helping him. There Mahmud and Ranjit Singh had a meeting of ceremony and mutual appreciation, and the Shah went home. That year (1811) blind Shah Zaman came to Lahore and took shelter, and with him his own family and that of Shah Shujah. Yunus his son came for a while to Ludhiana, but was not welcomed with much enthusiasm and wandered off to Central Asia. Ranjit Singh then prattled to Shah Shujah's wife of his hopes of helping the ex-Shah and placing him on the throne of Kashmir. But in 1812 Fath Khan, the Kabul Vizier, crossed the Indus with the intention of preventing Kashmir and Multan taking Shah Shujah's part. Ranjit Singh went to meet him also, each hoping to fool the other. Together they advanced to Kashmir by different routes, but Fath Khan succeeded in maintaining his claim to the province, allowing Shah Shujah to take refuge in Lahore, where he became practically a prisoner.

Ranjit Singh, however, generally got something out of every bargain, and, to the anger of Fath Khan, he persuaded the rebel Governor of Attock Fort to render it to him. This led to hostilities, and in 1813 the Sikhs, under Ranjit Singh's minister Mokhum Chand, defeated the Afghans near Attock.

The Sikh Maharajah, who was acquisitiveness personified, wished to retain Shah Shujah at Lahore, knowing well that "prisoned princes are priceless" and valuable Eastern counters in the game of grab. Further, the Shah still held the great Mogul jewel, the Koh-i-nur diamond, and that above all things Ranjit Singh coveted, as had various Barakzai chiefs. Long was Shah Shujah obdurate, but at last he and the Sikh exchanged turbans, and with the turban went the jewel in return for vague promises of help and a *jaghir* in the Punjab.

Treated with contumely by Ranjit Singh, the beggared Shah soon escaped to the hills towards Kashmir, hoping that he might yet be acceptable to the Afghans there. He was supported in this enterprise by the Rajah of Kishtwar, a state in the Himalayas adjoining Kashmir. Finding, however, no prospects of success in that direction, he threw himself on the protection of the British at Ludhiana, where his family had already preceded him. Almost immediately after the Shah's effort to secure Kashmir, Ranjit Singh himself had led a powerful expedition into that country with a similar purpose, but Muhammad Azim Khan, the Barakzai Governor, defeated him with heavy loss, and the Sikhs retired to the capital to lick their wounds.

The Blinding of Fath Khan and the Flight of Mahmud

For a few years Shah Mahmud, with the support of Fath Khan, ruled ineffectively at Kabul, still further increasing the Barakzai contempt for the dynasty of Shah Ahmad. His full brother, Prince Firuz, known to history as *Haji* Firuz, ruled in Herat, and the Shah had given his daughter in marriage to the Haji's son.

Ere long Fath Khan and Mahmud thought it desirable to evict Haji Firuz, and the royal troops were set in motion under the leadership of Fath Khan. Now occurred one of those typical Afghan tragedies which have blackened the character of Afghan chiefs throughout Central Asia. Fath Khan gained possession of the citadel of Herat after defeating a Persian army threatening the city. The young Dost Muhammad, a brother of Fath Khan, thought it fitting to violate the zanana of Haji Firuz and insult, if not dishonour, the daughter-in-law of Prince Firuz, no less a person than the daughter of Shah Mahmud. A chorus of indignation followed from all of any standing, and the Dost fled. The vindictive Saduzais, however, must needs have revenge, and Prince Kamran, son of the Shah, seized Fath Khan on the pretext that he was responsible, and with his own hands put out the Vizier's eyes with a dagger.

It has been said of this cruel act that "the shout of Vizier Fath Khan as the knife of the executioner was thrust into his visual organs was that of the expiring Afghan monarchy." It certainly turned the whole of the Barakzai family and influence against the Shah, and civil war at once broke out. Mahmud and his son, Prince Kamran, before they fled from Kabul seized the unfortunate Fath Khan and hacked him to pieces with every refinement of cruelty. This last dastardly act put an end to the miserable travesty of a once famous throne.

Shah Shujah attempts to Regain the Throne

Fath Khan's brother, Muhammad Azim Khan, from Kashmir now came to Kabul, and made an offer to Shah Shujah to place him in power once more.

From this period when the Shah alternated between attempts to regain his kingdom and pensiondom at Ludhiana, dates the sequence of events and the long periods of unrest along the Indus and in Afghanistan that so thwarted the British attempts at developing a prosperous trade on the Indus and with Central Asia. The British are a trading people, the East India Company was a trading company first and last, and the development of trade was always at the back of our policy.

Through periods of anarchy in Afghanistan and of an internecine war on the Indus, the policy that matured under Lord Auckland was slowly becoming possible and even desirable, and for this reason this involved period is of itself worthy of study in some detail.

In 1818 Shah Shujah made his first attempt from a British asylum to recover his kingdom and accept the offer of Muhammad Azim Khan. Leaving Ludhiana, with the help of the Nawab of Bahawalpur, the Moslem principality on the Sutlej, he occupied Dera Ghazi Khan, and thence sent his son, Prince Timur, to seize Shikarpur, moving himself to Peshawar. But Muhammad Azim Khan had changed his mind, preferring to instal another puppet Saduzai brother, Shah Ayub, who died shortly after, on the throne of Kabul in the hope of becoming minister himself. Pressed by Muhammad Azim, Shah Shujah fled to the Khyberrees, who had always favoured his cause, and thence made his way through the Derajat to Shikarpur, where with the help of the Amirs of Sind he maintained himself for a year, not, however, without abandoning his claim for dominion over Sind in return for the said assistance.

A little later, however, the Barakzai minister put in his appearance and bribed the Amirs of Sind to expel the Shah, who now returned crestfallen to Ludhiana, to find that his faithful Begum Wafa had drawn his allowances (24,000 Rs. per annum), and that the British would allow him asylum once again. And so ended in failure the Shah's first attempt to recover "the throne of his ancestors" from within British India.

Ranjit Singh's Encroachments on the Afghans

Ranjit Singh had not the least intention of abandoning his designs on the Afghan territories about the Indus, whoever might be ruler at Kabul, and in 1818 succeeded in carrying the city and fortress of Multan by storm, killing the Afghan Governor, Muzaffar Khan, and two of his sons. It was during this summer-time that Fath Khan had been blinded and murdered, and Ranjit Singh now turned his attention to Peshawar under cover of the confusion that was in progress at Kabul. The Afghans evacuated the former city, and Ranjit Singh made his old ally of Attock, Jahandad Khan, Governor in his interests; but on this occasion with little success, as the returning Barakzai Governor, Yar Muhammad, another brother of Fath Khan, soon ejected him. Ranjit Singh for the moment was preoccupied with his designs on Kashmir, now governed by Jabbar Khan, still another of the innumerable Barakzai brothers. Preparing a well-equipped mountain force, he crossed the Pir Panjal mountains, and on this occasion attained an easy conquest of the beautiful upland valley.

Thence the Sikh turned his arms to the trans-Indus and acquired Dera Ghazi Khan and the Lower Derajat, which he gave to the Nawab of Bahawalpur in fief. In 1821 he further deprived the Afghans of Dera Ismail Khan and the Upper Derajat, making the Nawab there his feudatory in return for the rendition of the great fort of Mankera on the hitherside of the Indus. That meant a considerable nibble into the Afghan riverine territories; but in 1822, however, Muhammad Azim Khan, the new minister, came down from Kabul himself to see if he could get rid of the Sikhs from their stronghold of Khairabad on the Afghan side of the Indus, bringing with him the Sikh chief, Jai Singh Atariwala, a refugee from the Punjab who had long been serving with him. This brought Ranjit Singh up to the Upper Indus again, to put forward his demand for tribute from Peshawar. Yar Muhammad, however, bribed him with a tribute of horses. This rendering of tribute in any form angered the Vizier, and Yar Muhammad fled to the Khaibar from his brother, and the latter entered Peshawar once again in 1823. The Sikh, who had but accepted the horses so as to be free to negotiate with the British, having settled that matter, returned to assert his claim over Peshawar, crossed his guns over the Indus and forgave Jai Singh, who returned to him.

We may pause a minute here to consider the importance of the great Mogul fortress of Attock on the hitherside of the Indus, which the British still hold with modern guns, and the position of Khairabad on the heights on the other bank, under which the great fortified railway bridge now spans the mighty Indus. We shall see them later playing a considerable part in the fortification of the frontier after the Russian War scare of 1885.

The Afghans now proclaimed a holy war against the enemies of Islam, and 20,000 tribesmen of Khattak and Yusufzai flocked to the defence of the valley, taking post on the heights about Nowshera, on the left bank of the Kabul River. Muhammad Azim Khan and the Afghan troops remained on the right bank. A fierce and pitched battle ensued, Ranjit Singh loosing the Sikh Akalis against

Akbar Khan

The son of Dost Muhammad, our principal opponent in 1841–42

the Moslem ghazis. The Sikh leader was killed and the ghazis rushed on the Sikh[1] regulars, who with the Sikh cavalry eventually turned the day. The tribesmen under their Pirzada were ready to continue next day, but when morning dawned the Afghans had gone. Peshawar was captured and sacked by the Sikhs, but in view of the hostility of the people, the prudent Ranjit preferred to place Yar Muhammad again as governor in the Sikh interest.

Shortly after this Muhammad Azim died, and with him also went the unanimity among the horde of Barakzai brothers, who were in possession of Kabul, Kandahar, and Peshawar. Shah Mahmud and his son Kamran still remained rulers of distant Herat, while Shah Ayub remained a powerless Saduzai puppet in Kabul.

With the death of Muhammad Azim, Dost Muhammad, the "Cinderella" brother, but by far the ablest of them, gradually became the most prominent, and was at last recognised as Amir, or leader, by the chiefs of the eastern provinces—viz. Kabul, Ghuzni, Jalalabad, but not at this stage of Kandahar, Herat, or Turkistan. But it is to be noted that because he was Amir of those parts that were in touch with India, therefore he appeared to be the only Amir in Afghanistan who mattered, as indeed he was.

It is also worthy of note that Ranjit Singh was now (in 1823) in possession of all the Afghan riverine provinces from the Indus to the foothills—exactly as when the British took over the Sikh kingdom and the Sikh frontier, and also exactly where for the most part the administrative British border stands to this day.

Another fact of interest is that the presence of a "prisoned prince" at Ludhiana set half India busy plotting new combinations. As early as 1816, before Shah Shujah set forth on his venture as just described, one Bir Singh of Nurpur had suggested to the Afghan a combination against the rising power of Ranjit Singh, whilst some three years later Appa Sahib, ex-ruler of Nagpur, was

[1] It is of interest to read that Ranjit Singh's Gurkha troops alone withstood the ghazi rushes.

planning with Prince Haidar, son of Shah Shujah, and Sunsar Chand, the Katoche chief, an Afghan rule at Delhi. Such happenings are further proofs of the intimate connection of anything Afghan with other pieces of the broken Mogul Empire which so long remained a potent tradition in the enduring memories of the East.

The British and the Indus

During the next ten years the situation in the Punjab was growing more modern, and the trading policy of the Company was much to the fore. What the Ganges had done for Hindustan, the Indus and the Sutlej, as well as the other rivers, could do for the Punjab and Afghanistan. The position of Great Britain was very different from that when she had sent to Ranjit Singh and Shah Shujah in 1809 to enlist their assistance in the defence of India from France and Russia. France had long been crushed into decency. The princes of India, whether feudatories of the Mogul or upstarts of the lawless period of decline, had fitted into their places as the peaceful, non-aggressive holder of their legitimate realms, and the *Pax Britannica* was spreading over the whole of Hindustan. The British now began to talk of opening the Indus to the commerce of the world, and were anxious to obtain from the Amirs of Sind and from the Sikhs an agreement for the navigation of the Indus by a steamship flotilla.

The position of Sind needs to be fully understood. Until the coming of Nadir Shah, if not indeed till conquered by Ahmad Shah, Sind had been a province of Delhi, and later of the Durani Empire. It now either belonged to Delhi or Kabul, since no one of due authority had ever recognised any other status. Ranjit Singh was casting envious eyes on it, especially on that Afghan district of Shikarpur and centre of trade below the Derajat which Shah Shujah had recovered for a while in 1817, and from which Muhammad Azim Khan had expelled him, but which the Mirs of Sind had occupied when the Afghans had withdrawn. The Governor-General sent Colonel Pottinger to Hyderabad to press for the opening of the Indus, and in 1831 Lieutenant Alexander Burnes had been sent to Lahore to bring by water a present from the King of England to the Maharajah, and incidentally to observe the navigation facilities while *en route*.

While these events were in progress, Ranjit Singh was finding occupation of the Peshawar valley no easy matter. In 1824 the Black Mountain tribes on both sides of the Indus above Attock rose against the Sikhs, and administered a severe check to Hari Singh, the favourite general of Ranjit, so that the Maharajah had himself to hurry to the rescue.

The Hindustani Fanatics

In 1827 a new menace arose, with the shadow of which the British have been very familiar during the last fifty years, and which still at times looms across the frontier situation. Among the followers of the Pindari leader, Amir Khan, himself of Afghan origin, was one Ahmad Shah, a young Hindustani of fanatical and zealous Moslem tendencies, belonging to a family of Sayyids at Bareilly. At the termination of the Pindari War (1819), when Amir Khan was made Chief of Tank, Ahmad Shah went to Delhi, where he achieved some notoriety for his religious zeal and upholding of the simple laws and faith of the Qoran. In 1822 he led a band of followers from Calcutta to Mecca and Medina, and after four years returned to Delhi and proclaimed a religious war against infidels, implying, however, that he referred to the Sikhs and not to the British. In 1826 he went to Tank, and thence, after obtaining considerable support from the young Nawab, son of Amir Khan, went through the desert to Sind, whence he led a band of devotees to Kandahar. The Barakzai brothers in possession gave him no encouragement, and wandering through the Ghilzai country, he eventually arrived with his following at Panjtar in the Yusufzai hills, where, admired for his doctrines and his teaching, he founded a colony to which from time to time came Moslem puritans, especially from the Wahabi fraternity at Patna, and which was swelled in 1857 by Moslem mutineers.

Thus was founded that fanatical colony of Moslem zealots who for so many of the later years have seized every opportunity, in-season and out-of-season, of flinging themselves on British bayonets.[1] Soon after his arrival in Yusufzai, Ahmad Shah *Ghazi* hurled himself on the Sikhs at Akora in the Peshawar valley. The Sikh commander beat off the fanatics, but as he could not pursue them, their prestige was but increased. In 1829 Ahmad Shah accused Yar Muhammad, who was still Governor of Peshawar in the Sikh interest, of an attempt to poison him, and attacked Peshawar. The Governor was killed, and but for a Sikh force under Sher Singh and General Ventura, another brother, Sultan Muhammad, would not have succeeded to the governorship. The Sikh troops then withdrew east of the Indus. Ahmad Shah now crossed that river into the hills, raising the mountaineers and attacking a Sikh force under Generals Hari Singh and Allard, who defeated him. Nothing daunted, with his hand against every man, he attacked Sultan Muhammad, and actually defeated him and occupied Peshawar with his *ghazis*. But he was now unpopular with his Yusufzai hosts, and was driven from Peshawar by Sultan Muhammad. He then turned to attack the Sikhs, but after desultory mountain warfare was surprised by the latter early in 1831 at Balakot and was slain. His followers were then dispersed by the tribesmen for the nonce. Such doings, however, but contributed to the general unrest along the Indus, and to the hindrance of trade.

Shah Shujah's Second Attempt

Ranjit Singh was now at the zenith of his prestige and in fairly complete possession of the Afghan territories of Kashmir, Peshawar, the Derajat, and Multan. Shah Mahmud at Herat had entered into friendly correspondence with him, and Ranjit Singh himself was inclined to stimulate the Amirs of Sind as a possible antidote to the now dreaded prestige of the British.

The doings of Ahmad Shah *Ghazi* in the Peshawar valley

[1] See p. 233.

had inspired Shah Shujah in his Ludhiana asylum, and he was informed by the British that there was no objection on their part to his attempting his fortunes once again, though they would not guarantee a pension a second time should he fail. The Shah therefore entered into correspondence with Ranjit Singh, who now was prepared to discuss action with him, taking, however, a somewhat lofty line, as, according to Captain Cunningham in his *History of the Sikhs*, the Shah was to agree to prohibit the killing of kine in Afghanistan, and also was to agree to the restoration of the gates of the Temple of Somnath, carried off to Ghuzni by Mahmud in the eleventh century, and there erected at the shrine of the great conqueror.

The Shah countered the first suggestion by pointing out that Ranjit's friends the English did not prohibit cow-killing. The second item is of great interest to those who remember with what derision and contumely the public regarded Lord Ellenborough's bringing away of the gates after the victorious march of General Nott via Ghuzni to Kabul, as an act of truly Ellenburian bombast and false sentiment, whereas in truth it was originally proposed by no less a person than the Lion of the Punjab himself, as a point of value to Hindu sentiment.

Cunningham also records that Moslem opinion was much concerned at their removal later, and would have welcomed the subsequent return of the gates to Ghuzni.

Ranjit Singh had at that time no real intention of assisting the Shah, but the Amirs of Sind, afraid of the British, now commenced treating with him as their titular king, and talked of assisting him.

In 1832 came a rumour of a Persian attack on Herat, and this still further stimulated Shah Shujah. The Amirs of Sind now offered him assistance if he would forgo his claim to the supremacy of Sind, while Shah Shujah offered to Ranjit Singh to forgo any claim to Peshawar, and also to give a quittance for the hitherto compulsorily retained Koh-i-nur, in return for assistance in men and money.

Ranjit Singh was willing enough to secure agreement concerning Peshawar, but wanted the British to be a partner to any such pact, as he would trust no Afghan alone. Incidentally he is believed to have welcomed an arrangement whereby he might check British influence in Sind, while the Amirs of Sind, on the other hand, were anxious to defeat the Sikh claims to Shikarpur. These intrigues and plottings, trivial enough as they may seem at this distance of time, are in reality of considerable interest in showing very clearly how the British policy of 1838 had its origin.

The Shah finally entered into a treaty agreeing to forgo his claim to any of the trans-Indus districts which the Sikhs had for the moment wrested from the Afghans. The British now grew more interested, and did not insist on their warning as to a forfeiture of pension should Shah Shujah leave their protection, and actually advanced to him a third of his yearly allowance. But they disclaimed to him and also to the Dost any desire to be his partisan.

Dost Muhammad from Kabul was now engaged in warning the Amirs of Sind against coquetting with the British, saying that if the Company was allowed to establish a factory at Shikarpur, Shah Shujah with an army would soon follow. But he also entered into correspondence with the British, as has been already described.

The Shah left Ludhiana on his second attempt to recover his throne in February 1833, having raised a contingent in the Punjab and at Ludhiana of some 3000 men, and he had with him some two lakhs of rupees (200,000). Obtaining camels and guns from the Nawab of Bahawalpur, he entered Shikarpur in the middle of May. The Amirs of Sind, after some hesitation, broke with him and actually attacked him, but were defeated in January 1834, after which they willingly paid five lakhs of rupees to get rid of him. The Shah then proceeded to Kandahar, where he was strong enough to remain for some months.[1] Here, however, he was eventually defeated by Dost Muhammad and his brothers, and fled. After appealing for help to Shah Kamran, who had now succeeded his father at Herat, and after attempting to recover Shikarpur, he

[1] See p. 115.

Shah Shujah-ul-mulk

returned to his old asylum at Ludhiana in March 1835, having still with him some two and a half lakhs of his treasure.

While this was in progress, Ranjit Singh determined to make effective once more his occupation of Peshawar in view of the Shah's agreement. A large Sikh force, under the Maharajah's grandson Niao Nihal Singh and General Hari Singh, moved up the valley. The Governor, Sultan Muhammad, nominally in the Sikh interests, failing to give up the citadel, the Sikhs carried it by assault on 6th May 1834. They had also been making good the Tank and Bannu territory under cover of Shah Shujah's diversion.

After the failure of Shah Shujah's attempt much discussion and intrigue occurred between Sikhs, British, and Sindians over the country of the Lower Derajat, with the result that eventually the Sikhs were recognised as the overlords of the long strip of riverine territory between the Indus and the Sulaiman mountains in the Lower Derajat, through which the famous routes from Kandahar head for Multan. To protect their plains from mountain raiders the Sikhs repaired the ancient border fortresses—fortresses at the mouth of passes where the Græco-Bactrians, whose remains stand to this day, had also built forts for the same purpose.

Appeals to the Paramount Power

During these last few years of strife, strife all along the Indus between Sikh and Afghan, between Ranjit Singh's armies and frontier fanatics, as well as among the rulers of Afghan provinces and their struggles for the Afghan kingship, the habit of appealing for British help had arisen. Shah Mahmud of Herat had appealed for support against the Barakzais. One of the latter, Jabbar Khan, Governor of Kabul, had also appealed to them to recognise him as an independent ruler. Even the Dost himself had called on them in 1832 to protect him, and also against the Sikh encroachments. Ranjit Singh, too conscious of the continual interest aroused in India by the presence of the grandson of Ahmad Shah in British territory, had occasionally asked the British to guarantee him against any hostile attitude or action by the Shah, in whose breast not unnaturally the trick by which he had lost the Koh-i-nur still rankled. Ranjit Singh continually regretted that his unseemly treatment of his guest had caused the latter to depart from his coasts.

In fact there was an instinctive tendency, never perhaps recognised as such, to look on the holder of the power that had once been the Moguls as being in the same relation to all and sundry as that power was in its heyday, from which one by one they had slipped their moorings.

In 1829 Sultan Muhammad Khan of Peshawar wished to negotiate with the British as an independent chief. Finally, when Shah Shujah advanced on Kandahar in 1834, and the Sikhs were again pressing on the Indus, Dost Muhammad actually tendered his submission as a dependant of Great Britain, appealing also to them to help him to recover Peshawar. His nephew, son of Jabbar Khan, was sent to Ludhiana to learn the ways of the English. These points, which have been so neglected in the study of the politics of the period, are not to be forgotten when trying to follow the conditions preceding Lord Auckland's great adventure.

CHAPTER VIII

DOST MUHAMMAD AND THE FIRST AFGHAN WAR

The Battle of Jamrud · Captain Burnes' Mission · Lord Auckland's Central Asian Policy · The Persians at Herat · The Tripartite Treaty · The Army of the Indus The Order of Battle · The Shah's Contingent · The Question of Sind and Baluchistan

THE BATTLE OF JAMRUD

THE situation on the Indus was to get much more complicated in the next few years. The commercial policy of the British people required that peace and industry should be at once introduced among the half-barbarous tribes of Sind, Khurasan, and the Punjab. It was greatly desired to give fixed limits to newly founded feudal governments and to impress moderation of desire upon grasping military sovereigns, and that Ranjit Singh should be content with past achievements. It was equally to be desired that the Amirs of Sind and the chiefs of the mutually independent chiefs of the principalities of Kabul, Herat, and Kandahar, into which the remnant of the Durani Empire had broken up, should feel secure within themselves, but incapable of obtaining more—a frame of mind into which the British in India had been successful in bringing the warring Maratha kingdoms. It was also fervently to be desired that the restless Shah Shujah should abandon his day-dreams of a recovered empire.

The British Government offered mediation between Dost Muhammad at Kabul and the Sikhs in the constant struggle for Peshawar and the Derajat.

The victory gained by Dost Muhammad over Shah Shujah in 1834 somewhat modified his desires to become a protected British state, and he assumed the proud epithet of "Ghazi," or "Champion of the Faith," and also styled himself Amir, or "leader." He dare not style himself "Shah," for his brothers, some of whom governed in his name and others as independents, were all jealous of him, and all prepared to fight for their own ambitious hands. In gazing on these bellyings of the Afghan curtain, it is to be remembered that Dost Muhammad was for long the Cinderella of the fraternity, the son of a despised Persian mother, and only entitled to such respect from the others as his courage, address, ability, and ferocity could gain for him.

And all the while Peshawar rankled in his mind as Calais on that of Mary the Queen. Ranjit had succeeded, as has been related, in detaching Sultan Muhammad to his interests, and in 1835 the Dost came down the passes to the eastern end of the Khaibar. Sultan Muhammad had no confidence that the Dost, if he were victorious, would not remove him from Peshawar, and he sat tight. On 11th May, however, the Amir, while engaged in pour-parlers with Ranjit, was nearly surrounded, and escaped only by abandoning some guns and baggage. So again he appealed to the English, as did also the brothers at Kandahar, who were pressed by Shah Kamran. The Dost, moreover, had lost much prestige by retreating before the Sikhs, and a battle must be fought to restore it. So once again the Afghans marched through the Khaibar under Akbar Khan, the most determined of the Dost's own sons. The Sikhs under General Hari Singh were entrenched about Jamrud and on the foothills. On the 30th April the Afghans attacked Jamrud, and the Sikhs, to draw them into the plain, fell back. In the battle that ensued the Sikh general was killed and his army routed. But only two of the Sikh guns were captured, and the Afghans could take neither Jamrud nor Peshawar, and eventually retired into the pass again rather than face a reinforced Sikh army. Interesting details are on record of the forced marches made by the Sikhs to recover themselves and the mass of guns that Ranjit Singh pushed up. The Maharajah himself came up to Rohtas, and Diyan Singh, one of the

Sir Alexander Burnes

Murdered at Kabul in 1841

notorious chiefs of Jammu, laid the foundations of a vast fort at Jamrud, which stands to this day, and hard by is a tower that marks the place where the Sikh general fell, known also to this day as the Tower of Hari Singh. And it is from this period that the Dost's fears that the British would not take control and forbid the Sikh aggression, as they had forbidden it against Sind, seems to have turned his thoughts towards Russia, thoughts which the result of the Burnes Mission further developed.

Captain Burnes' Mission

Captain Alexander Burnes had for some time been looked upon as a young man specially devoted to, and unusually well informed and experienced in, Central Asian matters. He it was who, when an assistant with the political mission to Sind, had brought up to Lahore the present of horses from His Majesty to Ranjit Singh, and from thence had proceeded to Simla, where the Governor-General, Lord William Bentinck, was spending the summer. Lord William's thoughts had been turned from his measures for the betterment of India to the advantages to the human race of a peaceful and tradeful Central Asia. Hearing that an officer was wanted to tour through Afghanistan, Burnes volunteered for the duty, and was accepted. At this time, too, the loom of Russia in her start to absorb the khanates, which had been so strongly felt in the days of Napoleon and the Tsar Alexander, was again attracting attention, and it was felt that it was a question that must ere long be faced with some show of statesmanship and knowledge. On January 1832 the young traveller went forth over the British frontier at Ludhiana and passed through Lahore and the Punjab, crossing the Indus at Attock in March and reaching Kabul on 10th May. At this time the fierce fanatical wars of the next few years between the Sikhs and Afghans had not yet produced that frontier fanaticism which the British were later to inherit with the Sikh border. Burnes' travels were pleasant enough, and he met with friendliness and hospitality. He stayed some time at Kabul with the Nawab Jabbar Khan, one of the Barakzai brothers, who was hospitality itself, and he then travelled on in Afghan guise through Afghan Turkistan to Bukhara, where he had an equally kindly reception from the King and his vizier, and thence to the Gulf through Meshed and Persia and back by sea to Calcutta. He was shortly afterwards sent home to England to explain the Governor-General's views on the Central Asian question, and received an ovation on all sides. Specially did he emphasise his view of the disastrously dominant position of Russia as regards Persia, and the relentlessness of her march to the Oxus, as well as the necessity for our maintaining Afghanistan or Khurasan—to use its still popular name—intact from Russian influence.

In 1835 Burnes found himself back in Sind. Lord Auckland, who had met him in England, had now taken the place of Lord William Bentinck as Governor-General, and ere long Burnes was directed to undertake a mission to Kabul, accompanied by Lieut. Robert Leech of the Bombay Engineers, Lieut. John Wood of the Indian Navy, and Percival Lord, Esq., of the Medical Service. This party was to proceed via the Indus to still further develop the navigation and trade policy. The mission was called the "Mission of Commerce," and in due course, delayed only by the war between Sikh and Afghan at the mouth of Khaibar, arrived at Kabul in May 1837, where it was received with pomp and ceremony by Akbar Khan on behalf of the Dost.

At Kabul the Dost unburdened himself to Alexander Burnes, known to all as "Sikunder," "the Fortunate," that Eastern rendering of Alexander. He was torn many ways and needed help. The Sikhs were pressing at his gates on the one hand; the Persians were not only at the doors of Herat, but Russian officers were supporting them. Nor was he the master yet of even the Afghan part of Ahmad Shah's empire. What he wanted was definite support—arms, perhaps money, something to help him to make himself king in reality—and then he would talk about alliances. Oh, yes! the Afghans many of them were enterprising merchants true enough, but that came when a strong rule had been perfected. What could "Sikunder" Burnes offer in the way of practical friendship? And Sikunder had only hot air to offer, he had no authority. That puzzled the Dost—an envoy who had no authority to bargain and who could but refer!

In vain Burnes wrote to the Governor-General that in his opinion the Dost could "deliver the goods" if we gave him support. The Dost wanted immediate help, and Russian officers had been sending many promises to many quarters in Afghanistan, and the harassed Dost, finding "nothing doing," or rather that nothing immediate was to be had from Burnes, turned perhaps reluctantly to Russia. For weeks and months no definite proposal came from the British, and a Russian agent had arrived at Kabul, his tongue full of promises and his hands full of goods. Burnes, whose business was to secure the goodwill of the Amir, had failed because he was not supplied with the wherewithal. With the Russian agent flaunting himself before his eyes, he left. And it was a tragedy that it should have been so. It is a point where those who want to attach blame can freely do so. To send an envoy so far, before the days of telegraph, when conditions were critical, with no powers to offer anything needful, was a serious blunder, though those competent to criticise personalities have always doubted the fitness of Burnes, or Dr Lord, who later became a political officer, for so delicate a mission, pointing out that energy and courage as travellers do not necessarily connote diplomatic abilities.

Lord Auckland's Central Asian Policy

It is not to be wondered at that the march of the troubled years of the twenties and thirties should culminate in a point where the British found it necessary to take a strong hand in endeavouring to put an end to the years of quarrel and even anarchy that were so militating against peace and prosperity in Northern India. But it was a policy that, while it did eventually result in what was aimed at, did so by long and weary ways, and was conspicuous by the immediate failures, both political and military, which resulted therefrom. For this reason it has been the custom of many European writers of the Victorian era, notably Sir John Kaye, the principal historian and biographist of the period, to criticise severely all and sundry connected therewith, accusing the British of unworthy and unchristian conduct in interfering at all. Many who have written subsidiary accounts of the period have taken their views of this nature from Kaye without looking further, as Macaulay took his from James Mill, and together with Burke's Speeches produced such entirely unjust accounts of Warren Hastings' transaction of the Rohilla War, referred to in Chapter III. But a close study of the period and the preceding years tends to show that the British had every right to do as they did, and much warranty therefor, though singularly unfortunate in the officials they selected to give effect to their policy. Further, miserably were they served by a small portion of their soldiery, and still worse served by themselves, by withdrawing their hand from the half-ploughed furrow when they found that the cost which they had not previously counted bid fair to be excessive.

We have seen in our study of the period that Afghanistan was the victim of centrifugal forces, torn with bitter civil war for years after the death of Timur Shah. We have seen that Dost Muhammad, though apparently the most enduring and capable of the Barakzai brothers, ruled but Kabul, Ghuzni, and Jalalabad, had no jurisdiction over Herat, where a dynasty of the Royal House still reigned, had practically no control over his brothers at Kandahar, had lost Kashmir, Peshawar, the Derajat, and Multan, and that the Amirs of Sind and the Khan of Kalat snapped their fingers at any claim of his to the dominion over them that was Ahmad Shah's.

We have seen almost every governor of an Afghan province, whether independent or part of the Dost's territories, appealing to Great Britain, as the paramount power, for some guarantee of his own independence, and we have seen even Ranjit Singh at times render involuntary homage to the power that ruled where the great Moguls had sat.

Then in 1837 the bitter war between Sikh and Afghan had broken out again in even more serious form, as the Sikhs enhanced their grip of the Peshawar valley and Avitabile, an Italian General in the Sikh service, set up his gallows at the four corners of his house in Peshawar city. Added to it all there came the news that Persia, with Russian officers abetting, was endeavouring to capture Herat, and thus destroy that block of Afghan provinces, whether a kingdom or a confederacy, that the British deemed a solid necessity between the trans-Oxus Khanates and India. It was to Lord Auckland that fell the task of designing a Central Asian policy, but Lord William Bentinck was the statesman who saw that the time had come to take a hand in some form in trans-Indus and Central Asian affairs, just as the Marquis Wellesley had seen far ahead of the Court of Directors and the Cabinet in the British destiny in India. Lord Auckland but tried to shape the policy, and spent the summer of 1838 in Simla, so cheaply described by Kaye as "the great hotbed of intrigue on the Himalayan hills, where the Governor-General and his secretaries were refreshing and invigorating themselves, and rising to heights of audacity which they might never have reached in the languid atmosphere of Calcutta."

While Burnes was at Kabul, the clever secretaries of the Foreign Department, Messrs Macnaghten, Torrens, and Colvin, all men of great ability, had been planning how to give effect to the policy which Lord William Bentinck had been studying—the extension of British influence to Central Asia in the name of humanity as well as of trade.

The line they took was not an unnatural one. The rightful holder of the Afghan throne, an agreeable, kingly personality, was a refugee, a political guest, in their hands. He was obsessed with the idea of recovering his kingdom. He and Ranjit Singh were known to each other. Could he be restored to his throne? He had a nephew already installed at Herat who had not submitted to the Barakzai dominion. He had maintained himself for the best part of two years in Southern Afghanistan but a couple of years before. Dost Muhammad was, so far as they knew, little more stable than any other of the warring Barakzais, and Shah Shujah had obviously partisans among his countrymen.

Given these premises, it was not hard for clever men to persuade themselves that the solution of the problem was to restore the Shah, after signing a treaty defining his position and attitude towards the British which would put our mutual policy on a sound basis, and that the Shah and Ranjit Singh should be so bound together and interwoven into the agreement that their frontier differences should terminate. It was from many aspects a highly statesmanlike proposal if an active forward policy was to be tried, but it involved two suppositions, and also a deep-seated economic problem. Those points were the certitude that Shah Shujah was sufficiently acceptable to the Afghan people for his restoration to produce the effect desired, and consequently that the Dost in his present position was not likely to be the better of the two.

The economic problem was this: Were the resources of the army in India in stores and transport sufficient? Could the army be maintained so far from its bases in a country where the old Mogul system of contract supply was the only one known? Was it adequate for the entirely novel and distant undertaking? For it must always be remembered that in 1838 there was not a mile of railway in India, while the Punjab that lay between the north and Afghanistan was a Sikh country, and in the south the territories of the Amirs of Sind intervened. Further, was it not necessary to probe the possible mishaps and their cost to India before launching the venture?

When Burnes returned to Simla in chagrin he found that matters had gone far in a policy which aimed at ousting the Dost and restoring the Shah. He was convinced that we were backing the lesser horse of the two, with some injustice to the Dost; but in common with most others he felt that the time had come to assert our influence, and that the Russians and Russian influence must go, and he was quite prepared to work for the restoration of the Shah if that policy was accepted.

Whatever our later experience of the Dost and his position *vis-à-vis* the Afghan peoples, it was fairly obvious that he had only recently achieved for himself any real position of eminence during the years of turmoil that had followed the ejection of the Saduzais. And it was a fact that Shah Shujah himself was an object of some devotion to the Khyberrees, or, as we should now say, to the Afridis; which alone was an important factor, at any rate in his position as regards the Punjab and the Sikh imbroglio. The critics of the time are pleased to say that very undue attention was paid to the reports of British newsagents elsewhere as to the Shah's position in the regard of the Afghans of Kandahar and its neighbourhood. But unless we are prepared to attribute very culpable false representation to the secretaries of the Foreign Department, we must assume that the balance of evidence in that movement was based on reasonable judgment; though gossip, it is true, does say that when Burnes came to Simla he was implored by the secretaries not to upset the Governor-General's mind by throwing doubt on the policy which all plans were now ready to put into force.

Before going further into the doings that furthered it, we may turn aside to see the conditions as to one of the chief ingredients of that policy—the siege of Herat by the Persians, and the achievements of young Eldred Pottinger.

The Persians at Herat

While Lord Auckland was planning the mission of Burnes to the Kabul Court, the age-old quarrel between Persia and Khurasan had developed another phase. It will be remembered how, a generation earlier, the British Government, bewildered by the threat of Shah Zaman to invade India with his Afghans once again, had endeavoured to stir up the Persians to threaten Herat and Kandahar.

Perhaps our own policy was now coming back to us as a boomerang. In September 1837 news came to Herat, which was still ruled over by Shah Kamran with a strong, ruthless, slave-dealing Afghan, Yar Muhammad, as his vizier, that Muhammad Shah, King of Persia, with whom Herat had many border bickerings, was advancing to its capture.

Just as this occurred there arrived travelling in Eastern dress one Eldred Pottinger, a young artillery officer, and assistant to his relative at the court of the Amirs of Sind, who had also been encouraged to follow in the steps of Burnes and travel in Khurasan.

Pottinger offered to help in the defence of Herat, and Yar Muhammad realised what a trump card the presence of an Englishman might be. With the Persian army were Russian engineers, and curiously, with the force was a British officer, Lieutenant-Colonel Stoddart, who belonged to a British mission in Persia.

For some months Pottinger was the active spirit of the defence at a singularly ineffective Afghan headquarters, and at last, in January, he agreed to proceed on a mission to the Persian Shah.[1] To the great surprise of Colonel Stoddart, to whose tent in the Persian camp Eldred Pottinger had demanded to be taken, the Afghan envoy proved to be no other than a British lieutenant of artillery. Pottinger eventually was taken to see the Shah, and conducted his business. The Shah was apparently not to be moved from his intention to take Herat as a fitting ending to a long string of grievances against Shah Kamran. Further parleys occurred, while the siege dragged on its interminable and ineffective course.

But the British minister to the Persian Court had now arrived, and with him another officer of the Company's artillery, Major D'Arcy Todd, also attached to the military mission that was in Persia. Shortly after Todd was sent into Herat with a message. Major Todd, in full British regimentals and cocked hat, had come to state that

[1] Neither siege nor defence was remarkable for persistence or energy.

Muhammad Shah had requested the British to mediate. Very shortly after Sir John McNeil, the British Minister to Tehran, himself arrived. His mission too, however, was of no avail, and the siege dragged on into May and June. On the 25th of the latter month the Persians made an attempt to storm Herat, and in their repulse Pottinger took a leading part.

As the Persians would not accept the British advice and remonstrances against their policy in attacking Herat, the latter now sent a force to occupy the Persian island of Kharg, near the head of the Persian Gulf, and this mark of their earnestness eventually decided the Persians to raise the siege. Our attitude to Persia, however, has been the subject of not unreasonable criticism. We had a treaty with Persia that bound us not to interfere in disputes between her and Afghanistan, and it was only by offering ourselves as mediator that we were able to get over this. But times had much changed since we sought the alliance of Persia in 1800 and 1809. Stability beyond the Indus was the prime motive of our policy, with régimes that would eliminate the intrigues of rival groups of clans and chiefs; and this was but in the natural course of the spread of the civilisation of trade and markets.

Colonel Stoddart and Pottinger remained some time longer endeavouring to help the starving Heratis, whom the minister was inclined to sell as slaves to restore his master's coffers. The two British officers were able to improve their abject conditions by drawing to some extent on British Government credit, but were at last compelled to leave by the hostility of Yar Muhammad. Stoddart then went on his fatal journey to Bukhara,[1] and Pottinger after a while got back to Herat, before finally coming away, and however much Shah Kamran and his vizier might dislike the young Englishman, the whole countryside itself rang with the knowledge that it was Pottinger who had made the defence of the town possible.

[1] He was beheaded by the Khan at Bukhara.

THE TRIPARTITE TREATY

The results of the Battle of Jamrud and the abomination of years of disturbance, as has been described, decided the Governor-General to put an end to the supremacy of any of the Barakzai brothers. Peace and goodwill must be engendered, and the only way was the establishment of Shah Shujah-ul-mulk, to give him his full title, on the throne of his ancestors. Much has been written of the ineffective character of the Shah, but there was a good deal on the other side. As far back as 1809 he had favourably impressed Mountstuart Elphinstone; and Captain Wade, the political agent at Ludhiana, had long felt that the Shah was the man for our money. Writers, notably Sir Marion Durand, have held up Wade to scorn, and have indeed written in no sparing terms of the fatuousness or folly of most of the young "political" officers of the day. However just that may be, Wade was strongly in favour of the Shah and of putting him back on his throne.

So the Governor-General adopted, or if the phrase be preferred, was persuaded to adopt, an extremely forward policy, and Mr Macnaghten was sent to Lahore to negotiate the business with Ranjit Singh, who was nearly at the end of the debauched life into which his strenuous career had finally slipped. But debauched or not he was an extremely astute politician, and saw well that whatever came of it he was likely to be the gainer. The British would either be successful, and by such success he would hold his debatable territory and acquire more, or if they failed, the British would lose heavily in men, prestige, and money, and would therefore be less to be feared as a neighbour. In his searching for the best plan for putting a barrier between Russia and India, Lord Auckland had at one time thought of a Sikh rule at Kabul; an idea not so absurd as it would seem, if we remember the success of Sikh control over the Moslems of the Punjab. In this connection it may be remembered that even in the twentieth century there are but three million Sikhs out of forty million Punjabis who are chiefly Moslem.

Lord Auckland had originally proposed to put the Shah on his throne by means of his own contingent, led by British officers; a scheme also less wild-cat than we should now think it, when we realise that at the Battle of Kandahar, which the Shah fought with Dost Muhammad in 1834, two mercenary Hindustani battalions in his service raised at Ludhiana and commanded by an Eurasian named Campbell bore the brunt of the battle with some success. Burnes, however, was emphatic in his advice that British troops must accompany the force, or at any rate back it.

The method of entering Afghanistan needed some thought, for since the British frontier lay on the Sutlej, with a cantonment at Ludhiana only, the Punjab and most of the five rivers, as well as the Indus, lay between the British and the Khaibar Pass, while the Sikh Army was a formidable force to have as an uncertain factor on a line of communications. Nor was Ranjit Singh anxious to see the northerly road the main line of communication.

From the British point of view, as a strategical operation, the forcing of the succession of passes and threading the tumbled mass of mountains between Peshawar and Kabul had no particular attraction, while an advance on Kandahar would bring the army into a far easier country, producing more supplies and having easier routes than the much shorter one by the Khaibar. It was, it is true, a long way off—from Ferozepore to the point of crossing at Sukkur was 446 miles, and thence on to Kandahar alone 404 more —850 miles in all. From Kandahar to Kabul was another 325 miles. On the other hand, the move to Sukkur meant the presence of a river alongside for the whole route, so that water for transport and for drinking would produce no difficulty, while as the force proceeded it would be able to pick up more and more camels.

The original plans aimed at taking two [1] Bengal divisions by this route, and sending the Shah's eldest son and the Shah's family, together with a British escort and a force of Sikhs, to Kabul by the Khaibar.

In June 1838 the Tripartite Treaty was signed at Simla,

[1] Since it might be necessary to attack the Persians at Herat.

at the still extant house of Chapslee,[1] and orders went forth to assemble the Bengal troops. They had to come from far and wide, and it meant many months of marching for the more distant units before the huge camp at Ferozepore, on the banks of the Sutlej, was reached, to which came Lord Auckland himself, Shah Shujah with his contingent, and Sir Harry Fane, the Commander-in-Chief, who was himself to command the army. To this gathering, too, came the third great partner of the treaty, Ranjit Singh, and with him also a large organised army. And, indeed, it was one of those great gatherings and *tamashas* for which India has been so long famous.

The treaty provided for the co-operation between the Governor-General, the Maharajah of Lahore, and Shah Shujah, for the restoration of the latter, for an amicable alliance for the future, and for the settlement of debatable points of Afghan and Sikh, and Afghan and Sindian territories.

The Army of the Indus

As this was the first campaign of the British Army of Queen Victoria's reign, and the first of a series which finally completed the British dominion from Cape Comorin to the Indus and ushered in the India of to-day, as well as laid the seeds of the Indian Mutiny, the army that assembled and its system are worthy of some notice. It was known by the stirring and suitable title of "The Army of the Indus."

It is first of all to be remembered as an interesting, futile, but romantic fact, that the army in India was clothed, at any rate in winter, as was the army in Europe, and the regular part of the Indian Army, both native cavalry and infantry, were dressed in the dress of the British line—in chakos, coatees, and white cross-belts. This was origin-

[1] So long known as the residence in modern times of Sir Arthur and Lady Ker on the spur below the Lakri Bazaar, but in 1837 the residence of Lord Auckland and the Hon. Miss Eden.

Sir William Hay Macnaghten

The British Envoy to Afghanistan. Murdered at Kabul in 1841

ally done that the appearance of the long red lines and red masses should impress their Indian foes, which no doubt it did. In this campaign as in all others, for instance, the Bengal Horse Artillery were in brass dragoon helmets with leopard-skin rolls, white buckskin breeches, and high jack boots; and in this kit, too, was made that dramatic charge of the guns at the last barricade in the retreat from Kabul, when the last Horse Artillery gun was the last rallying-point. Only the Irregular Horse were clothed in the style that is now universal in the Indian Army to-day.

But the army, magnificent to behold and splendid in fair fight, was by no means equipped and organised for the type of operation for which it was now designed—a campaign far away from all its bases of supply. The belief that the Almighty fed armies by means of ravens and cruses of oil was as prevalent in high circles then as it often is now, and the secret of maintenance was understood by very few.

The army in India was organised on the old Mogul principle which had obtained from time immemorial, and which worked when the Moguls moved up and down the length and breadth of Hindustan with huge escorts and retinues in peace, as well as when they marched armies in war. The Indian Army supplied itself from a huge moving city of shops which followed it a-pack-a-back. In Lord Lake's day only the outposts drew rations. The regimental merchants and agents fed the men in staples, shoes and equipments were mended in the bazaars, and every requirement, legitimate or otherwise, except fighting stores and equipments, could be bought from the hucksters and sutlers who followed the army.[1]

With the army or with the Moguls' encampments marched a huge and efficient staff of tent-pitchers—a race which endures to this day, and under whose guidance canvas cities rise in incredibly short time.

Everything other than the fighting troops and organised units was controlled by a bazaar-master. As soon as the Quartermaster-General's staff had indicated the encampments of the troops and of the bazaar, up went the bazaar-

[1] The system remained practically unchanged till 1917.

master's flag, and when that went up, the stream of followers and merchants knew exactly where their quarters lay. Within an hour up went the long streets and cross streets of the shops, each in the same relative position day in and day out. The last time this was perhaps seen in India in even a small way was at the great camp at Shinwari, below Dargai, in the Tirah campaign of 1897.

The huge numbers of followers who maintained these shops, pitched tents, and the like, made sanitation beyond the power of man to establish, and when cholera came it swept the camps.

The merchants and *bunniahs* with the corps and in the bazaars had relatives in business, or business connection in every town in India, and these were anxious enough to supply the armies. Large fraternities of hereditary carriers who managed the grain trade of India were eager enough to carry the stuffs to the camps, and it was for their protection that so large a number of irregular cavalry regiments grew up in India in the first half of the nineteenth century. The Brinjaras, with their pack-bullocks, were the most notable of these carrying races, and their goodwill was the special care of Sir Arthur Wellesley in his campaigns in the Deccan, and indeed of any good commissariat officer and commander. Army transport as we know it now did not exist.

The mobile artillery of the army in India consisted chiefly of horse artillery. Horsed field batteries hardly existed at all, and the light field batteries drawn by bullocks were not especially prominent. Horse artillery guns which, when outclassed, as they often were, galloped in to closest range to get effective, or the heavier, slow-moving field guns, with elephant or bullock draft, were the artillery features. Pack artillery was hardly known, though now and again it had been extemporised for campaigns in very wild terrain.[1]

[1] The Bombay Artillery furnished a mountain train for service in Khandesh.

The Order of Battle

The army was originally to have been commanded by General Sir Harry Fane, the Commander-in-Chief in Bengal and of the Queen's troops in India, a distinguished soldier to whom all the army looked with confidence, and with him were two Bengal Divisions under Generals Cotton and Duncan respectively. But while the British force was sharing in the parades with the Sikh forces at Ferozepore, came the news that the Persians had abandoned the siege of Herat, and thereby one of the important reasons for moving an army into Afghanistan disappeared. It was decided, therefore, to reduce the army by one division, and that then Sir Harry Fane should not go in command. General Cotton was to go with the Bengal Division, while General Sir John Keane,[1] who was bringing up a Bombay Division, would command the army.

But it must be remembered that we were not going to make war on Afghanistan. We were accompanying a sovereign who, with an army of his own and many supporters, was returning to claim the throne of his fathers. We did not enter the country as an enemy but as a friend. Therefore the principal personage was the representative of the Governor-General at the Court of Shah Shujah, no less a person than Mr Macnaghten himself, who, unless actual hostilities were in progress, was not unnaturally supreme.

The infantry brigades, as was then the custom, consisted of three battalions, usually one European to two native, and the cavalry in the same combination.

The reduced force, under Sir Willoughby Cotton, consisted of three infantry and one cavalry brigade, and that under Sir John Keane, coming up from Bombay via Karachi, two of infantry and one of cavalry. The 2nd Bengal Division was left behind at Ferozepore, where a cantonment was to be established.[2]

[1] Commander-in-Chief in Bombay.

[2] The detail of the corps is given at the end of this chapter.

The Shah's Contingent

Among the most interesting side-stories to the history of this period is that of the Shah's contingent, of which the whole story has yet to be written. It has been related how Shah Shujah, in his attempt to recover his throne in 1854, had been permitted to raise a force at his own expense in Ludhiana. This contingent contained, among other adventurers, some two battalions of Hindustanis, that is to say, men of Oudh, the hereditary foot-soldiers of Hindustan from time immemorial. No doubt many of them had served in the Company's army. It has also been related how these battalions, under a Eurasian officer,[1] had been the *pièce de résistance* in the battles at Shikarpur and Kabul. It was therefore to be expected that a properly organised force of six thousand men, with British officers and N.O.'s, and N.C.O.'s specially selected and promoted from the regular army, would become a valuable force.

It consisted in the first instance of—

> 6 battalions, 2 cavalry regiments (irregular), 1 troop of horse artillery.

The force was clothed and equipped on the Company's model, and the commander was Brigadier Simpson from the 19th Bengal Infantry.

The contingent had to start long before its training was complete, and it was largely increased from local levies later. In its first composition were Hindustanis and Pathans and Moslems from the Punjab, as also a battalion of Gurkhas; for the men of Nepal were always to be found in Northern India seeking military service from the Sikh as well as from the British Government. Its doings will be recorded in the course of the narrative, but it is interesting to note that Brigadier Roberts,[2] the father of the Field-Marshal, commanded it later at Kabul.

It disappeared with the disasters that overwhelmed the Shah, with two exceptions; one the 3rd Shah's Infantry,

[1] See p. 115.

[2] Afterwards General Sir Abraham Roberts, G.C.B.

which so distinguished itself in defending Kelat-i-Ghilzie [1] and, accompanying General Nott to the end, was absorbed into the Indian Army as the Kelat-i-Ghilzie Regiment. It also survived the Mutiny and became the 12th Bengal Infantry, remaining to this day as the 2/2nd Bombay Pioneers (Kelat-i-Ghilzie). The other is the troop of Horse Artillery.[2]

The Question of Sind and Baluchistan

The position of Sind *vis-à-vis* the Durani Empire and the British has already been alluded to, and the fact that it was for centuries a part of the Mogul Empire, then of the dominion of Nadir Shah as wrested from the Moguls, and eventually fell to Ahmad Shah Durani when he established his empire. It had only been released therefrom when that empire crumpled of its own weight, and dominion over Sind was held by certain Amirs or Baluch chiefs who rode at their ease amid a peaceable population whom they oppressed terribly, maintaining their position by a large retinue of men-at-arms drawn from the Baluch of the hills or from the military and predatory class of Central Asia. If pressed, they must either yield to the ruler of Afghanistan or to the British, to whom the rule of India had fallen. They had not the slightest claim to any other position, and the cruelty and ruthlessness of their rule did, in fact, entitle them to little regard on any count. It has been related how Shah Shujah in 1818 and in 1834 had claimed their allegiance, and had actually discussed with them terms under which he would abrogate their obligations to him. The Tripartite Treaty freed them from any allegiance to the Shah.

As part and parcel of the trade policy of the British, but more especially of their Afghan policy, the status of Sind needed a definite solution. The British have been much criticised, however, by the Victorians, but without any good reason, for their treatment of Sind. In effect, the

[1] This is the spelling of the period and the Army List to-day.

[2] This troop is now T Battery, R.H.A. (Shah Shujah), the only memorial in the world bearing his name.

British demanded a passage for certain of their troops up the Indus and certain of their troops down the Indus. They also demanded the cession for the time being of the ancient fortress of Bukkur, on an island in the Indus, where the river cut its way through conglomerate beds. That fortress was one of the great places of the world, and the Amirs of Sind had but a fortuitous lien on it. The British made these demands on behalf of the claimant to the Durani throne, with whom they were in alliance, or failing that, as the rulers of the empire to which from time immemorial Sind belonged. If the Amirs accepted these demands in good part they would be the better for it pecuniarily, and if they would carry out their duties as rulers of the land with any sense of humanity and responsibility, they would have the support and protection of the British. Such in broad terms was the position, and it was eventually accepted in fairly good part. Consideration for princes in their position had always been a strong point in British policy, and the events which led up to the British annexation of Sind, though outside this story, really were due to the impossibility of the Amirs fitting into any scheme of semi-civilisation and progress.[1] To this may be added their failure to realise that their position on the lower waters of the Indus did not give them the right to ride rough-shod over all who would use its waterway.

When the Bombay column was on its way up, the Amirs of Hyderabad made to oppose it. The Bengal column was then at Bukkur. Sir Harry Fane was about to leave it and proceed to Karachi, but finding his progress down, and Sir John Keane's up, opposed, he led the Bengal column down to settle the matter. The Amirs gave way, the Bengal troops returned to Bukkur, Sir John Keane came up, and the campaign went forward.

Baluchistan, the wide mountain tract about the Bolan Pass which ran north along the Sulaiman mountains and south towards the coast, contained numerous Baluch clans controlled by chiefs whose authority they readily recognised. The supreme chief of the Baluch tribes, which formed a loose confederation, was the Khan of Kalat.[2] He,

[1] See p. 157. [2] The modern spelling is used here.

and his predecessors too, from time immemorial had recognised the Mogul and then the Durani overlordship, but during the decay of the Durani Shahs had achieved independence. It was the British purpose to obtain his assent to the progress of Shah Shujah and his allies, and also to see that he acknowledged once again the Durani supremacy—an ideal, however, peculiarly abhorrent to him.

APPENDIX

ORDER OF BATTLE OF THE ARMY OF THE INDUS

1st Bengal Division, Major-General Sir Willoughby Cotton :

1st Brigade, Brigadier Sale	13th Foot. 16th Bengal Native Infantry. 48th ,, ,, ,,
2nd Brigade, Brigadier Nott	31st Bengal Native Infantry. 42nd ,, ,, ,, 43rd ,, ,, ,,
3rd Brigade, Brigadier Dennie	3rd Buffs. 2nd Bengal Native Infantry. 27th ,, ,, ,,
Cavalry Brigade	16th Lancers. 2nd Bengal Light Cavalry. 3rd ,, ,, ,,

Bombay Division, Lieutenant-General Sir John Keane :[1]

1st Brigade, Brigadier Willshire	2nd Queens. 17th Foot. 19th Bombay Native Infantry.
2nd Brigade, Brigadier Gordon	1st Bombay Native Infantry. 2nd ,, ,, ,, 5th ,, ,, ,,
Cavalry Brigade, Brigadier Scott	14th Light Dragoons (two squadrons). 1st Bombay Light Cavalry. Poona Auxiliary Horse.

[1] Who took command from Sir Harry Fane and was succeeded by Brigadier Willshire.

CHAPTER IX

THE SUNSHINE AND CLOUD OF THE FIRST AFGHAN WAR

The March to Kandahar · Ghuzni and Kabul · The Accession of the Shah · Friendly Relations with the Afghans · The Occupation and the Break-up of the Army of the Indus · The Envoy and the Political Service · The Affairs of 1840 · The Crumbling of the Edifice

THE MARCH TO KANDAHAR

THE Bengal portion of the Army of the Indus, 9500 strong, and the Shah's contingent, 6000 strong, left Ferozepore early in November and marched down the left bank of the river Sutlej, through the territories of the Nawab of Bahawalpur, the Shah's contingent leading. Supplies were readily produced by the Nawab, and the march to Sukkur-Bukkur was uneventful, though in Sind supplies were not so readily forthcoming.

The Bengal Engineers constructed a magnificent bridge of boats over the Indus on both sides of the island, on which stood the fortress of Bukkur, now reluctantly handed over by the Amirs. The army crossed with enthusiasm, its trains taking several days in the process, which was not complete till 18th February. The Hindustani sepoys showed no sign of fear or reluctance to cross, despite certain expectations, mindful perhaps of the days when the Hindu kingdoms stretched to Kabul. The Bombay troops followed in rear, and the Shah himself crossed the Indus by way of Shikarpur.

Now it was that the troubles began to fall heavily on the army. The staff work dropped lamentably behind standard, for, in spite of the long wait at Sukkur, no plans for crossing the waterless plains of Kach Gandava had been made, and it was with great weakening and loss to the cattle and horses, and much irritation from the raids of the hill Baluchis, that the force was concentrated at Quetta early in April, much hampered by the failure of local supplies.

The Mogul system of transport and supply had failed. The army was beyond the reach of the Indian system of related merchants, eager to sell supplies, beyond the help of the carrier tribes and classes. The commissariat, ill-experienced in what was a very technical matter, tried with poor success to raise Government camel corps.

While waiting at Quetta, no attempts were made to reconnoitre the road over the Khwaja Amran range, and with the troops on half and followers on a quarter ration, the army struggled somewhat pitifully down into the lower and warmer plains of Kandahar, after one small skirmishing with bodies of Durani horse, still much irritated by the continued raids of the tribes, which they had not yet learned how to tackle.

However, by 24th April (1839) the Shah, ahead of his contingent, arrived at Kandahar unopposed and unwelcomed, and a couple of days behind him, the driving weight of the two British divisions.

Ghuzni and Kabul

The joint Amirs of Kandahar, Kuhn Dil Khan and his brother, with their troops, made off for Girishk on the road to Herat. The British Army, badly soldiered through the passes, was in need of considerable rest. Troops, followers, and animals needed a period on full rations, and this they now got, so that the force soon recovered its verve and spirits, though somewhat the worse for the lavish fruit harvest. It was some time before Brigadier Sale could march out to Girishk, where a battalion of the Shah's contingent was installed, the Amirs having fled towards Seistan. The envoy, said to be hugging himself with the delusion that the Shah's reception had been enthusiastic, prophesied that the march to Kabul would be unopposed.

The army had not organised its own intelligence staff, and was dependent on the political officers for information, of whose acumen a very low opinion was soon formed. In fact, the army was sadly defective for its purpose. It had an immense train baggage; and a young officer of the 16th Lancers, writing in his diary, records that a hurricane had swept the camp, but that luckily his tent was a small one, and his seventeen retainers had managed to hold it up. These would be *saises*, grass-cutters, tent-pitchers, and the like, as well as one or two personal servants. No wonder that the force stripped the country like a swarm of locusts! But that was India at its worst period of fighting efficiency.

By the 27th June, however, General Keane was ready to go on, and, resisting the urgings of the Envoy, decided to take most of his force with him. On 21st July the force reached Ghuzni without opposition *en route*, save for the ruthless slaughter of straggling followers. But it was now found that the ancient fortress was strongly held. Unfortunately, the weakness of the cattle had compelled the General to leave his heavy guns in Kandahar, and he had no metal that could hope to touch those massive walls. Ghuzni was held for the Dost nominally, with one of his sons, Haidar Khan, in command. In reality it was held by the pride of the Ghilzais, who did not easily brook strangers a-promenading in their lands. While the city was invested, the Ghilzais outside fell on that portion of the leaguer which held the Shah's contingent. The actual attack was to be made on the northern face, and the Kabul gate was carried after being blown in by Captain Peat and Lieutenant Durand of the Bengal Engineers. Fierce fighting with Afghan swordsmen occurred inside the gateway, and it was only after much severe hand-to-hand fighting that the place fell, the citadel itself, however, being found undefended. Of a garrison of from 4000 to 5000, 1600 were captured and some 500 killed, while a large quantity of supplies, many animals and much war material of sorts, were abandoned. The British loss was about 200. Leaving a garrison in Ghuzni with the sick and wounded, the British marched on for Kabul, having performed a very notable feat of arms, so far as the actual storming was concerned.

When news of the fall of Ghuzni reached the Dost he summoned his Sirdars, and then sent his brother, the Nawab Jabbar Khan, known to the British as the "good Nawab," to ask what terms they had to offer him. The answer was better than that which Harold the King sent to Harold Hardrada before Stamford Brig of six feet of English soil, but it was hardly less palatable: "An honourable asylum in India!"

When Jabbar Khan returned, Dost Muhammad concentrated his army, and found himself with 13,000 men and 30 guns, and with this he marched out to Argandeh on the Ghuzni road and set out his array, but knowing in his heart of hearts that no one was prepared to go into the last ditch on his behalf. There was, in fact, neither fight nor loyal following in those with him, and it is this fact that is the best argument in favour of Lord Auckland's policy, viz. that Afghanistan and the Afghans were not in any way wrapped up in the Dost, that his virtues merely lay in the fact that he had been able to carry on at Kabul, and that had Shah Shujah's affairs been properly managed, he and his line might have made good. How and why they failed we shall see. Apparently kings and amirs at best are things the Afghans detest, and they are no more set on one than on another, as indeed we may see in this year of our Lord 1929.

The Dost, it is related, rode among his troops, Quran in hand, and urged them in the name of God and his Prophet to fight for him and liberty. "Support the brother of Fath Khan in one last charge against the foreign dogs, and if that fails then go to Shah Shujah!" And not a soul responded. The American soldier of fortune, Harlan, who had been in the service of Ranjit Singh and who was in Kabul, related that his guards forsook the Dost and that the rabble plundered his pavilion, even took his bedding from under him, seized his prayer-carpet and hacked his tent to pieces. If that be true, well may the Persian proverb be repeated: *"Afghan! Afghan! Be iman! Be iman!"*

But the story rather upsets the idea of the king enshrined in his subjects' hearts, whom the British had replaced so unnecessarily.

So without an army and without a crown the Dost fled forth from Kabul, by way of Bamian, his son Akbar Khan covering his retreat with a few horsemen. It was Outram who, with a special party of officers, rode fruitlessly in pursuit, and with them the arch-turncoat of evil reputation, one Haji Khan Khakar, who had been the first to join the Shah and had not enhanced the latter's cause thereby.

The Accession of the Shah

On 6th August Sir John Keane camped close to Kabul, having found abandoned at Argandeh the somewhat pitiful array of all the Dost's guns.

On 7th August Shah Shujah-ul-mulk rode into Kabul at the head of a great cortège, looking, it must be said, with his flowing beard, kingly enough, and by his side the envoy and "Sikunder" Burnes. Bayonets gleamed and cannon roared, and the sight in the ancient city with its ring of hill was splendid and inspiring. It has been said that the Kabulis received him glumly; but the Eastern crowds do not shout, and you might have heard a pin drop when, in 1911, His Majesty drove through Delhi.[1] To him who would raise his voice on such an occasion the bastinado would be the customary reward. So the silent entry of Shah Shujah was not necessarily of evil portent.

It has been said that the Shah, who had been away from the Bala Hissar for thirty years, ran eagerly round its remembered courts, struck with the manner in which it had been neglected.

And thus the King came by his own again, and for the moment all seemed well. An Afghan Order was founded, that of the "Douranie[2] Empire," and His Majesty held an investment, Grand Crosses and Knight-Commanderships going to the great ones, and lesser stars to the lesser folk,

[1] A point that caused comment among the unthinking.

[2] The spelling of the day. The regalia of this order are in the R.U.S.P.

and everyone was mightily pleased, though those who were not recipients jeered heartily after the manner of the English. But indeed it was a fitting occasion, for the moment at least, to rejoice. Macnaghten was made a baronet, and Sir John Keane became Lord Keane of Ghuzni, while a medal[1] was to be issued by the Shah for the storming of that fortress.

But though the Shah was now on his throne, it was no part of Lord Auckland's programme merely to leave him there alone and to pass on before his position was secure. It was pretty obvious to all that he had not been restored by his own subjects and inherents, as the Simla Manifesto indicated, but by British weapons and bayonets. Even though Sir William Macnaghten might report that the Shah had been received "with feelings nearly amounting to adoration," it was not possible to suggest that he could remain supported by his own Contingent alone. Certain reductions of the force took place, but a strong British garrison remained. The chiefs of the countryside had not flocked to the Shah's Court, governors of prestige and devotion had not been forthcoming for the provinces, and therefore it seemed that the British must proceed to organise the government, which apparently the Shah himself was not in a position to do. And it is here that all the trouble began, and was bound to begin. Something was wrong in the whole make-up.

Friendly Relations with the Afghans

It is, however, to be remembered, and happily remembered, that the British came into Afghanistan in 1839 with no hostile intent and with no expectations of war. In fact, the description of the earlier phases of this period as the First Afghan "War" is sadly misleading—sadly, because it slipped into a war by ill-chance and ill-management.

When Dost Muhammad, abandoned by his supporters,

[1] It was not ready till after the Shah's murder, and was eventually issued by the E.I. Company.

left that pitiful row of guns, drawn up empty and unmanned, to oppose our advance on Kabul, no one was sufficiently enamoured of the Amir to die in the last ditch for him, and that city was occupied without hostility. Markets were opened, and the force encamped itself at ease as it would in friendly India. There were no outrages. Officers rode at will about the country with but an orderly. Young John Nicholson records how he and a friend rode in unescorted from Ghuzni to Kabul to attend the races. Afghans joined in the sports, and officers visited the gentry in their country houses for shooting and hawking.

Here is a description written at the time:

"Throughout the whole of the autumn (1839) the officers passed to and fro with a confidence which at this early stage of their acquaintance appeared to command a like degree of honesty among the people. . . . Parties rode hither and thither to visit and inspect such objects of curiosity as were described to them. . . . Horse-racing and cricket were both got up in the vicinity of Kabul, and in both the chiefs and people soon learned to take a lively interest. Shah Shujah gave a valuable sword to be run for. . . . Several of the native gentry entered their horses. . . . Being great gamblers in their way, they looked on with astonishment at the bowling, batting, and fagging of the English players. . . . Our countrymen attended them to their mains of cocks and quails and other fighting animals, betting freely, and lost or won their rupees in the best possible humour. In like manner our people indulged them from time to time in trials of strength and feats of agility, on which they much pride themselves, and, much to the astonishment of their new friends, threw the most noted of Kabul wrestlers.

"The result of this frankness was to create among the Afghans a good deal of personal liking for their conquerors (this is a wrong phrase). The chiefs, in consequence, invited them to their houses in town as well as to share in their field sports in their castles in the country."

The same writer records the amazement with which the Afghans saw the officers on skates which the regimental artificers fashioned, and cried, "Now we see that you really are men born in the North and used to vigour of body and mind."

The Afghan chiefs and sirdars freely dined not only

with the British heads, but also in the regimental messes, H.M. 13th Foot being especially forward in their hospitality.

Unfortunately, as we know, the attractive young Englishmen became too great favourites with the ladies of Kabul, and much jealousy and ill-will was finally engendered—a story of which a good deal might be written by itself. Afghan ladies enjoy greater freedom than those of India, yet were not used to the attentions and courtesy of the well-bred young Englishmen, and found them more than attractive compared with the rougher ways of their own people.

But the long and short of it was, that the Army of Occupation, in supporting the Afghan King against his enemies, was for a while received with goodwill and hospitality. The tragedy lies in the unfolding of the long series of events, events which should have been foreseen from the first, which made the situation impossible.

The Occupation and the Break-up of the Army of the Indus

The financial strain on the Government of India was, of course, considerable, and while the necessity of a military occupation at any rate till the next year was accepted, it was important to reduce the force by all unnecessary constituents. So in September the Bombay troops under General Willshire started back to their own provinces via Ghuzni, and thence to Kalat, where the Khan needed a lesson, while the next month the Commander-in-Chief returned to India via the Khaibar with most of the cavalry and horse artillery. General Sir Willoughby Cotton remained in command of the force at Kabul and its neighbourhood, while at Kandahar General Nott commanded a separate force. The distribution of the garrison was as follows, and it cannot be said that it was a large one for the purpose.

Between Kabul and Jalalabad:

1st Bengal Europeans.	48th Bengal N.I.
13th Foot.	2nd ,, ,,
35th Bengal N.I.	27th ,, ,,
37th Bengal N.I.	2nd Bengal Lt. Cavalry.

At Ghuzni:

16th Bengal N.I.

At Kandahar:

42nd Bengal N.I.	Skinner's Horse (with a squadròn at Ghuzni and Jalalabad).
43rd „ „	

Total.—Two British and eight native battalions with two regiments of native cavalry, in addition to the Shah's Contingent.

There were during the autumn some sharp hostilities on the far side of the hills at Bamian, where want of information got a force into some difficulties; but for the most part the country sat down to watch what manner of man the old King might be. And he, with the Envoy, spent the winter at Jalalabad, while the several battalions left at Kabul got through the winter in the Bala Hissar, the historical fortress on the hills near the city, with considerable success.

In any case the country is too snow-ridden for much to be done till the spring, and the hibernating Afghans had been able to think a bit harder as to their lot and their future; and in the meantime their relations with their visitors, as distinct from their visitors' policy, were excellent.

The Envoy and the Political Service

From this period there dates that pronounced hostility towards and dislike of the "Political" Service (which was so marked a feature at this time) which lasted over the Second Afghan War and the early frontier wars, and still rears its head whenever the "political officer" endeavours to exceed his rôle. The term "political" in India is used to denote what we should call the Diplomatic Service elsewhere. Nearly all our wars and campaigns in India have been against an internal foe whom we want to coerce without bloodshed, or against the recalcitrances of people on our border whom we are endeavouring to bring to lead a life of order.

The people who deal ordinarily with the native princes of India, and who carry on negotiations with semi-independent tribes and chiefs, are officers of the "Political" Service, a service recruited both from the Civil Service and from the Army.

Because, as has been explained, the avoidance of war, rather than the discomfiture of foes, is so often the prime object of our operations, political officers accompany the force, and it has usually been their duty to say when the ways of peace have failed, and to loose the dogs of war. They must therefore of necessity have a somewhat prominent position with the force they accompany. But as they are often drawn from the junior ranks of the army by chance, or by family influence rather than by ability, their position does not make them popular. The expedition to Afghanistan demanded that the Envoy should be the most important person therewith. He it was who represented the authority of Great Britain and all the ramifications of policy that the circumstances involved. For this he needed a considerable staff of assistants, which naturally grew. But the recognised Political Service of India could not spare many men, and the Envoy's staff was largely drawn from the young officers of the army, often selected for the inadequate reasons just described, whereon these young gentlemen left their corps to find themselves in places of authority, importance, and emolument. Their position up to a certain limit was essential. The army was not concerned with affairs. The Shah was our ally, his people our very good friends. The young politicals, who were soon sent out to the various districts, were representatives of the Envoy, helping the Shah's officials to get control of the country. So far so good. But very soon, by some extraordinary fatuity and incapacity, we see the army authorities abandoning all control of their own affairs. The Envoy decided what operations were necessary and detailed the troops, instead of being in close touch with the army commander and asking him, after due consultation, to undertake the necessary operations with the force and in the manner he thought necessary. The young politicals led out forces commanded by much senior officers and often took command, their ignorance and undue insistence at times being responsible for the military failures that occurred.[1]

As our position got more and more involved, so did this arrangement become more and more anomalous and dangerous, until, added to the want of personality and character of the senior soldiers when the crisis came, it was practically responsible for all the military failures, and probably the cause even of the civil collapse, since without military disaster civil prestige could have remained.

Happily, in modern times such a position is not allowed to arise.

The Affairs of 1840

In the spring of the second year things were quiet enough. The disturbing rumours of the autumn had died away. The Russian approach to Khiva, which had induced the Envoy to propose sending a force to Bukhara to dig out the refugee Dost and oppose the Russians, had been refused countenance by Sir John Keane, and the menace had wilted away as the Russians perished on the winter road to Khiva. So the Shah and the Envoy returned to Kabul as "the spring-time flushed the desert grass, and the kafilas wind down the Khaiber Pass."

The Ghilzais about Ghuzni were also in insurrection, and once again Nott had to put things right, occupying Kelat-i-Ghilzie in some hope of steadying the countryside.

On the long line of communications between Kandahar and the Indus, too, trouble had arisen. In November 1839 General Willshire had stormed Kalat with some brilliance

[1] We had much the same position in Mesopotamia, where the growing needs of administration of occupied territory demanded an increasing political service. Excellent young men were found in the army; they were admirably controlled. The memory of Afghanistan had long caused the Commander-in-Chief of such expeditions to be also the Government representative, and the chief political officer one of his heads of departments. But the same symptoms in a harmless degree could be discerned.

on his return road to India, the unfortunate Khan, who had refused to surrender, being killed in the defence. His successor, however, in the spring of 1840 had attacked Quetta, and all the Baluch tribes were giving trouble, necessitating some vigorous action at the hands of General Nott. In and round Kandahar itself Prince Timur, the heir-apparent, had not been successful in gaining the goodwill of the chiefs, and British troops found themselves engaged in several encounters, in which, however, the Sepoy regiments usually gave a good account of themselves. Nevertheless, the essential goodwill and devotion to the Shah was conspicuous enough by its absence. In the spring, too, the Dost had escaped from Bukhara and returned to Khulm, and from thence advanced with a large Usbeg force towards Bamian. Brigadier Dennie of the 13th Foot took out a considerable force and dealt faithfully enough with them; but now came rumours of the tribes in the Kabul Kohistan being up in the Dost's favour. In November Brigadier Sale led a force against them also. Here he found that the Dost was present in person, and that he had run into a hornet's nest that was rather more than he could smoke out. Matters were complicated by the notorious action of Parwandarra, where the 2nd Bengal Light Cavalry, ordered to charge as part of a successful action, failed to follow their officers, leaving them to gallop alone among a mass of Afghan swordsmen. The operations were vexatious, the tribes ubiquitous, and Burnes, who had accompanied Sale, went so far as to advise the Envoy to recall the force and order the immediate concentration of all the troops. Then, however, an unexpected stroke of fortune befell. Sir William Macnaghten, riding outside Kabul, was approached by a solitary horseman, and was told, to his astonishment, that it was the Dost come to surrender. And so it was. Weary, apparently, of his wandering life, sick at heart at the fickleness of the tribesmen, who fought for their own hand rather than his, he had thrown up the sponge.

In doing so he had struck a note that at once echoed in British hearts, especially since public sympathy was with him rather than with the ineffective Shah. Treated as an honoured visitor, he was escorted to India by Sir Willoughby Cotton, who was giving up the command, and went into an honourable exile as the guest of Britain.

And now indeed there seemed no obstacle to the success of British policy, and all Sir William Macnaghten's fears vanished. Everything was *couleur de rose* in that upland garden. 1840 closed in peace and harmony, and the Shah and Envoy repaired once more to the lower levels of Jalalabad for the Afghan winter.

One irreparable mischief had the Envoy done. He had insisted against military advice in withdrawing the garrison from the commanding security of the Bala Hissar and erecting an ordinary cantonment in the open, outside Kabul, amid the fortified residences of the nobles, vineyards, and ancient tombs. It was just such a cantonment as had been built outside Delhi or Hyderabad in the Deccan. And the British set themselves to live exactly the same carefree life, as if they had been in British India, holding the Afghans as a military proposition in supreme contempt. The Envoy sent for Lady Macnaghten, installed her in a bungalow of Indian type, from which she dispensed the hospitalities of a *burra mem.*[1] To India the officers were encouraged to send for their families, Lady Sale among them, and also some of the families of the soldiers of the British units. And all the while the Punjab was not even British, the Khyberrees were giving trouble, and there was not a mile of railway in the whole of India!

In addition to this, the old Lion of the Punjab was dead at Lahore these twelve months gone, and all was turmoil and anarchy in his capital. Nevertheless, the British force in Kabul proceeded to give every hostage to fortune that the occasion was capable of admitting.

The Crumbling of the Edifice

1839 we have seen pass into 1840 with some show of peace, and 1840, after a disturbed year, had waned in

[1] An important lady.

Lady Sale

Afterwards a prisoner in Afghan hands

good omens into 1841, the year of trial. It is generally admitted that Sir William Macnaghten, one of those extremely able public servants which, among many types, the Indian services produce, was entirely unsuited for the rôle for which he had been selected. He was a secretariat man pure and simple, and in service jargon had "never held the baby," had never been called on to handle men and affairs on the spot, however ably he might control and dictate from his seat in the secretariat. He had never seen men face to face, and he had no experience of the handling of Orientals; had neither the sympathy with the chiefs of old lineage and fierce record as had Henry Lawrence, nor had the knowledge of the astute, intriguing Eastern mind which men such as Malcolm and Elphinstone had developed, or in latter days such men as David Barr and Harold Deane, men who combined knowledge with their sympathy.

In his desire to give the Shah a legitimately free hand he had allowed him to do the most dangerous of all things —surround himself with *émigrés* who had returned with him. His vizier or chief minister was his old friend the Mulla Shikore, of whom it has been said that "He had lost both his memory and his ears, but had sufficient faculty left to hate the English, to oppress the people, to be corrupt and venal beyond all conception, and to appoint subordinates as flagitious as himself." "Bad ministers," wrote Burnes, "are in every Government solid ground for unpopularity, and I doubt if king had ever worse set than Shah Shujah."

When British officials brought complaints to notice, those who brought the complaints were punished. At Kandahar Prince Timur had surrounded himself with venal and incompetent *émigrés* also. In Eastern lands, when revenue collectors and officials are too oppressive, rebellions take place. Here in Afghanistan, under this unhealthy diarchy, rebellions, the natural outlet of the oppressed, were suppressed by British bayonets at the call of the politicals. And so at last everything connected with the British was tainted with the evil of the Shah's myrmidons. That it should have been so was a tragedy and a folly, for on the balance of evidence it would seem that the Shah, better served by his officials, might well have made good.

Then it must be remembered that our presence prevented the Shah preserving himself by Oriental methods. Had he been alone he would doubtless have removed by the axe, the cannon's mouth, and the rope, all those who stood in his way, but typical Afghan measures of authority of this nature were forbidden him.

Then when local chiefs had stood aside, the Envoy devised a policy which, while sound enough under other conditions, deeply stirred the chiefs. Since it would not rally to its king, the Envoy decided that the country must be governed by means of royal troops and royal armed levies. All over the country extra forces were raised to keep it in order, which, paid by the Shah, would, it was hoped, be loyal to him. It was a policy which would have held good in British India, where a newly acquired province of unruly folk had been occupied, and where a military force was engaged in disarming the people and turning sword into ploughshare. It might have been an admirable policy had Afghanistan been a less warlike and lawless and more accessible country. As it was, the *janbaz* [1] and local horse but more and more exasperated those whom they were supposed to cow.

Earlier in 1841 there had been more risings, both of Ghilzais and Duranis, though these were dealt with successfully enough by General Nott; and the fatuous Macnaghten wrote to a correspondent: "From Mookoor to the Khyber Pass all is content and tranquillity, and wherever we Europeans go we are received with attention, respect, and welcome. I think our prospects are most cheering. . . . The people are perfect children, and they should be treated as such."

Old General Nott, with whom was the able "political" Major Rawlinson, took by no means the same view. He wrote with more than a fair share perhaps of contempt for the system, but this is what he said:

[1] Militia. Lit. life-savers, *i.e.* "guards."

"The conduct of the thousand and one politicals has ruined our cause, and bared the throat of every European in this country to the sword and knife of the revengeful Afghan and the bloody Balooch. . . . Shah Shoojah is certainly the greatest scoundrel as ever lives."

But as late as September 1841 the Envoy was all cheerfulness. He had just been appointed Governor of Bombay, and Burnes was shortly to take over from him. Nevertheless, the dying year was destined to be more than stormy, and the first trouble was engendered by the not unnatural policy of the British Government, who were now feeling acutely the strain of the expenditure in Afghanistan, which still remained at a high figure. The Envoy received peremptory orders that the allowances to the tribal chiefs must be reduced. This immediately resulted in the Ghilzais closing the passes between Kabul and Jalalabad. At the same time, Akbar Khan, the Dost's son, was now in Khulm stirring up strife, and the indignant chiefs were well enough inclined to listen.

General Cotton had been succeeded in command by Major-General Elphinstone of the British Service, advanced in years, a martyr to gout, and quite unwilling and unfit himself to proceed to a country of which he had no experience, and command a force likely to require great energy. A further misfortune was that the troops in Kabul were due for relief. The 13th Light Infantry, who were *au fait* with every inch of the country, and whose relationship with their comrades, black and white, of the Indian Army had always been most cordial, were due for Europe. The experienced 35th and 37th, with efficient commandants, were also to go. The 13th had been relieved by the 44th Foot, whose conduct in India had been entirely opposite, and had been marked by a disinclination to fraternise with the Indian Army, and who were disliked in consequence, which bore its ill fruit in time of danger.

As General Sale and his brigade were to go down to the Punjab, it was a good opportunity for opening the passes and chastising the Ghilzais, and towards the end of October the brigade started. It got down to Gandamak after prolonged and severe fighting, in which it was not well handled, for it lost a good deal of baggage and had a good many casualties, including the General wounded. Further, it certainly did not, save on one occasion, chastise the Ghilzais, though in actual fighting it made a good enough account of itself. So heavy had been the transport losses that Sale had to leave the 35th with some guns at Khabbar Jabbar in dangerous isolation. At Gandamak it found a regiment of horse and a battalion of *jezailchis* [1] of the Shah's Contingent in their cantonment under British officers, but a day or so later the former deserted to the rebels.

[1] Musqueteers.

CHAPTER X

THE BURSTING OF THE STORM AND AFTER

The Murders at Kabul · Jalalabad and Kandahar · The Avenging Armies · The Finale at Kabul · The Return to India · The Commander-in-Chief's Comments

THE MURDERS AT KABUL

THE trouble at Kabul which had made the Envoy send a recall [1] to Sale now suddenly arose; but from the entries in Lady Sale's diary (a singularly direct and uncompromising compilation) there was nothing but calm up to the end of October, and the entries refer to her great regret at leaving her snug Kabul bungalow and her flower and kitchen gardens, both much admired by her Afghan sisters.

On the 2nd November, however, the storm broke. Without warning a truculent crowd surrounded Burnes' house, and in a very short time he and those with him were hacked to pieces, and his small guard, which also guarded the treasury, massacred. But paralysis seized those in authority.

Little that was effective was done by the British. Brigadier Shelton of the 44th marched to the Bala Hissar with a portion of the force, and the Shah sent one of his own levy corps under Campbell [2] to see what could be done, who made a reckless attempt to get into the city and was driven back. Shelton did nothing except cover Campbell's retreat. The 37th, left by Sale in the passes, were at once ordered back, and came through in fine soldierly style. But a blight seemed to have fallen on the military authorities, who could but quarrel, disagree, and convene that weird conception, which seems to have grown up under the strange

[1] Which Sale was unable, owing to state of his transport, to obey.

[2] The Eurasian officer already referred to. He became a Moslem and settled in Afghanistan, living to an advanced age as an Afghan General (*v.* p. 120).

situation, viz. Councils of War. Rarely before did a British commander need a Council of War to help him command; but we see the exotic growing freely in Afghanistan.

The story of how by gross military inefficiency a bad civil situation became a military disaster—an entirely unnecessary military disaster—is too long and heart-rending to be told here; how commissariat stores were lost by folly; how daring junior officers, only too anxious to lead and to fight, were thwarted by incompetent or timid or quarrelling seniors. No staff work, no courage, and no enterprise, and indeed no common sense, produced an appalling situation. The soldiers, who could have gone to the Bala Hissar and stayed there in security, insisted, against the wish of the Envoy, in concluding a treaty of evacuation with the rebels. Akbar Khan, the son of the Dost, was now the leader of the hostile Khans. The Envoy, not without courage himself, lost heart. Riding out to a Durbar with some of his staff on 23rd December, when seven weeks, seven precious weeks of moderate weather had been lost, he was murdered and his assistants seized and carried off. It was the hand of Akbar Khan that did the deed, but it is not improbable that the murder was done in a sudden gust of anger during a struggle, when seizure alone was intended. The unfortunate envoy was last seen holding Akbar Khan's arm and saying, "*Az barai Khuda!*"—"For God's sake . . ." Trevor, who was with him, was also killed, Lawrence and MacKenzie being taken prisoners.

With the loss of the Envoy things hurried on to an inglorious capitulation. A treaty was signed in which the Afghans guaranteed safe-passage through the passes. But the heavy frosts had already arrived, and were destroying the hearts of the Indian soldiery and followers. Because the force would not give up its baggage and waited for carriage, it was not till 6th January that it started forth in the snow from its comfortable cantonments,[1] 4500 fighting men, of whom 690 were Europeans, 2840 Indian infantry, and 970 cavalry. All guns, except six of the

[1] On which vast sums had been spent.

By courtesy of the Royal Artillery Institution

The Bengal Horse Artillery galloping through Afghan hordes, 1842

From a painting by Colonel Seccombe

horse artillery and three mountain guns, were given up, and General Elphinstone sent orders to Nott and Sale to evacuate also, which, however, both those independent commanders refused to accept. Through the prolonged agony of the passes we will not follow the pitiful story of soldiers thrown away by their leaders. Akbar Khan could not compel, even if, as seemed possible, he wished to, the promise of safe-conduct. The frost-bitten, wind-swept force, with many thousands of followers, perished in the defiles. A few officers and ladies were taken as hostages or for protection by friends, a few were preserved as they fell into Afghan hands. The bulk died on their tracks, the last effort being when the last remaining horse artillery guns galloped at the last barrier in the Jagdalak Pass. Small parties of the fittest struggled towards Jalalabad, but fell to treachery, and at last only a weary doctor, Brydon,[1] on a dying pony struggled into Jalalabad.

There was no getting away from the fact that a well-equipped British force of 4500 men had been destroyed by the tribesmen in alliance with *Général Janvier*. In a letter from Lady Sale at Kabul, written to her husband, she speaks in the most unmeasured contempt of the Envoy just killed, and the incompetent control of the military chiefs, which would assuredly result in the loss of the whole force.

Jalalabad and Kandahar

But though a force had been destroyed at Kabul, it did not mean that the whole British Army had gone, and it is desirable to keep this fact clearly before us. The force in Southern Afghanistan was intact under the stout Nott. When the first trouble threatened he had stopped M'Laren's brigade from marching to India, and at Macnaghten's request, on the murder of Burnes, had sent it up the Kabul road. Compelled to turn back by winter weather, it rejoined Nott, and left that commander with a strong force whose *moral* was high.

[1] Curiously enough he was later to go through the protracted evil of the defence of the Residency at Lucknow.

It consisted of Skinner's Horse, the 40th Foot,[1] and seven Sepoy battalions, with a regiment of the Shah's Horse. Kelat-i-Ghilzie was also garrisoned, as was Ghuzni. At Jalalabad, Sale, whose *moral* had collapsed, was eventually persuaded, chiefly by the energy of Captain Broadfoot, of the Shah's Sappers, to stay where he was till relieved from India. Once the old man's mind was made up he did it well enough; but a curious period of defëatism supervened on the arrival of Dr Brydon.

Eventually his force defied all attempts to capture the town, and in the spring sallied forth and heartily defeated the besiegers. For once again the adage should be remembered that an Afghan attacked and an Afghan attacking are two very different things.

Ghuzni, garrisoned by the 27th Bengal Infantry under Colonel Palmer, held out for three and a half months, surrendering on the 6th March 1842 under a promise of safe-conduct ruthlessly broken. The Sepoys, much deteriorated by the winter, were mostly massacred, and only the officers kept as prisoners, among them the lad John Nicholson. They had better have held out. Palmer was tortured to reveal the whereabouts of treasure. Kelat-i-Ghilzie, under Craigie, held out till the arrival of the original orders to Nott to withdraw to the Indus, when his force [2] was relieved and brought in to Kandahar.

At Kandahar Nott held his own with ease and determination, while an ineffective commander, General England, was endeavouring to put supplies in from Quetta. Against the General's determination the mass of Durani chiefs and tribes round Kandahar were powerless, and when the full meaning of the risings was clear, General Nott still further established his position by bringing in any of the Shah's troops who held the country around, and he was now prepared to carry out effectively any policy that the wavering Governor-General should indicate.

[1] The difference in the numbers of regiments in the formations at various stages of the campaign are due to movements in relief.

[2] The 3rd Shah's Infantry, who formed the major part of the garrison.

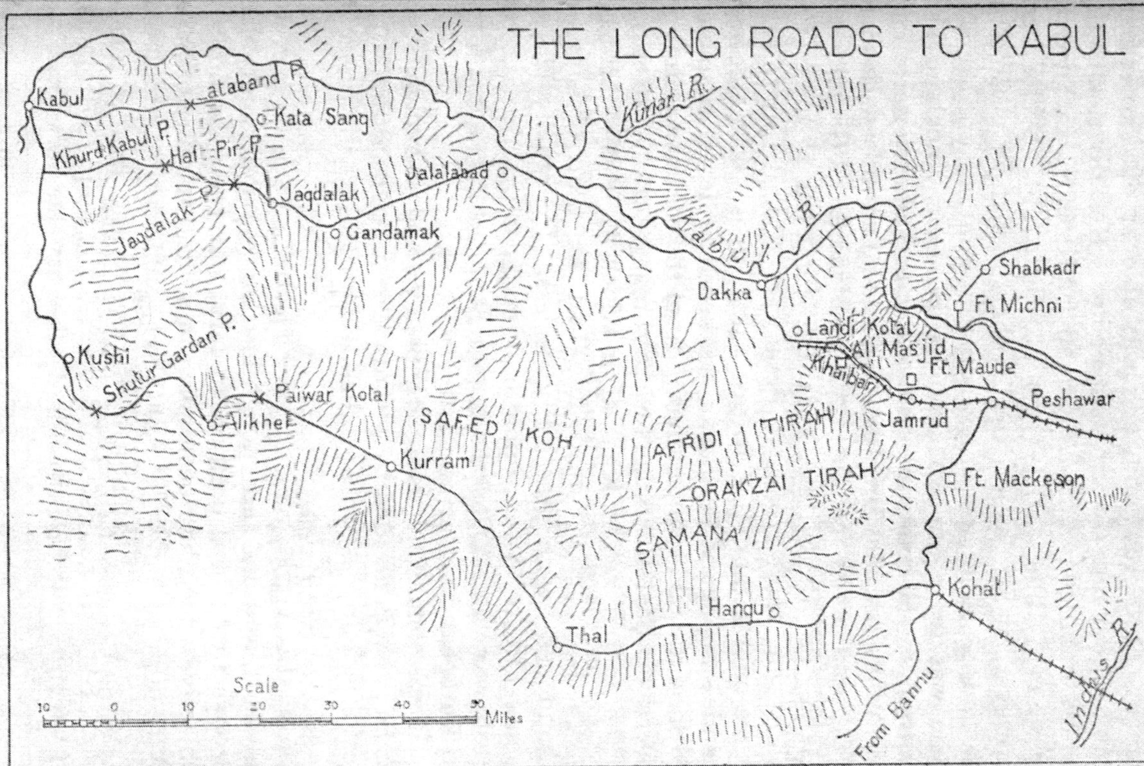
THE LONG ROADS TO KABUL
Kabul
Lataband P.
Kata Sang
Khurd Kabul P.
Haft Pir P.
Jagdalak
Jagdalak P.
Jalalabad
Gandamak
Kunar R.
Kabul R.
Dakka
Shabkadr
Ft. Michni
Landi Kotal
Ali Masjid
Ft. Maude
Khaibar
Peshawar
Jamrud
Kushi
Shutur Gardan P.
Paiwar Kotal
Alikhel
SAFED KOH
AFRIDI TIRAH
ORAKZAI TIRAH
Kurram
Ft. Mackeson
SAMANA
Kohat
Hangu
Thal
From Bannu
Indus R.
Scale
10 0 10 20 30 40 50
Miles

J. H. Astle.

The Avenging Armies

Early in 1842 Lord Ellenborough arrived in India to replace Lord Auckland, and was able at once to impart some vigour into Government policy. Heartily sick of the whole imbroglio, Lord Auckland had seemed inclined to leave everything and everyone to their fate. Stimulated, however, by Sir Jasper Nicolls, the Commander-in-Chief in Bengal, a soldier who knew something of hill warfare and who was by no means a nonentity, Lord Auckland had authorised the collection of four Bengal Infantry battalions at Peshawar under Brigadier Wilde, and another with some European units behind under Brigadier M'Gaskil. Mr Clerke, the British agent at Lahore, tried to make the Sikhs send more troops to Peshawar. But it was to take more efforts than this to put things on a better footing. Wilde's Sepoys at Peshawar, weakened by fever, tampered with by the Sikhs, and suffering from the cold feet that soon overtakes Eastern soldiers when things go wrong, after one attempt to force the Khaibar, in which Ali Masjid, held by levies, was first occupied, and then for want of supplies abandoned—were practically useless. Eventually Major-General Pollock [1] was appointed to command, and arrived at Peshawar with M'Gaskil's brigade, and behind that a force of European cavalry and artillery.

It was some time before any policy could be evolved, but at last it was decided to withdraw from Afghanistan, after restoring our prestige, and then leave the Afghans to settle their own affairs.

By 5th April Pollock had collected sufficient men to advance, and had put enough heart into Wilde's enfeebled Sepoys to be in a position to carry out the very limited objective which had been given him, viz. the relief of Sale. With him was now a Sikh force, sufficiently stimulated also to make the attempt by his side on the dreaded Khaibar. His force consisted of 8000 men, in all nine battalions, of which two were British and three cavalry corps, viz.—

[1] Of the Bengal Artillery. The first "gunner" to command a force of all arms.

9th Foot.	31st Foot.	3rd Light Dragoons.
6th Bengal N.I.	30th Bengal N.I.	1st Bengal Lt. Cavalry.
26th ,, ,,	53rd ,, ,,	10th ,, ,, ,,
33rd ,, ,,	60th ,, ,,	
64th ,, ,,		

But he had not yet had the instructions which he and all worthy soldiers wanted, viz. to wipe out the British defeats at the point of the bayonet, to avenge at Kabul the murders and entirely unnecessary treacheries, and to release the prisoners as well as the officers and soldier families, including the widowed Lady Macnaghten and Lady Sale. Pollock, when ready, marched on 5th April and forced the Khaibar with little loss, arriving at Jalalabad to find that the garrison had never been in any real danger, had defeated the Afghans in style a few days before, and by so doing had reopened for themselves the sources of supply. In fact, there were many who said that had Sale stayed at Gandamak instead of hurrying down to Jalalabad in the autumn, not only would British influence have been preserved, but the total destruction of Elphinstone's force would not have occurred.

Sale's force was a strong one, and was capable of holding its own anywhere so long as its supplies of food and ammunition [1] could be obtained; and food was to be obtained, so far as essentials went, by its own initiative.

Lord Ellenborough, who had issued a stirring manifesto, was not quite so prompt as he sounded, but it was evident that there would be difficulty in finding a satisfactory policy to follow. The Shah still sat on the throne of Kabul, and was saying, not without some show of reason, that the worst of our disasters were due to our failure to follow his advice. He was, however, murdered near Kabul on the same day as Pollock entered the Khaibar.

Once at Jalalabad, Pollock found difficulty in getting

[1] It is an interesting fact that when Sale marched from Kabul the 13th were armed with flint locks which were so worn that large numbers could not be fired. Sale had asked for a re-equipment from 4000 percussion muskets that had recently come up. This Elphinstone had refused, in spite of the fact that the 13th had to chastise the Ghilzais and put down their rebellion.

further instructions. The Governor-General had issued to him and to Nott, as well as to Mr Clerke at Lahore, a masterly enough résumé of the position, with a general explanation of the policy of the British Government, without, however, any very definite orders. At Kandahar, Nott had been put in command of the troops under England in the Quetta area, and ordered that dilatory individual to come at once to Kandahar with supplies.

Pollock, anxious to avoid descending into the Punjab at the worst season of the year, was reluctantly granted permission to remain at Jalalabad till the autumn. But still no orders of policy were issued. On the 4th July, however, Lord Ellenborough wrote to Nott that he might withdraw to India *via Kabul*,[1] but withdraw he must. Pollock was told that he might advance to support Nott's withdrawal.

This was licence enough for the soldiers, and the two managed to get into communication. Nott would advance to Kabul; Pollock would go thither to support him; the unfortunate prisoners, regarding whom no orders had been issued, should if possible be rescued.

On the 20th July Nott received the Governor-General's letter of 4th July sanctioning his withdrawal via Kabul, and on the 7th August his force and that under General England, which was to withdraw to the Indus, left the city and camped outside. On the 9th Nott started for Kabul with the 40th and 41st Foot and his own "beautiful sepoy" battalions,[1] and England took back three of the Shah's regiments and the Bombay Infantry, the Shah's Artillery and the Bombay Horse Artillery. Prince Timur, who was quite useless, was sent with him, and the Government of Kandahar handed to his younger brother Safdar Jang, as more likely to make good and be more acceptable to the Durani sirdars. On the 30th a large force of Ghilzais were defeated at Gohani, and shortly after Ghuzni was found evacuated. On the 17th September Nott arrived in the vicinity of Kabul, to find the Union Jack floating on the Bala Hissar. General Pollock had marched in two days earlier. His

[1] See Appendix to this chapter.

Field-Marshal Sir George Pollock, G.C.B., G.C.S.I.

From an engraving

By courtesy of A. Pollock, Esq.

force had defeated the Afghans, and especially the Ghilzais, with ease after some sharp fighting, having started from Jalalabad on the 20th August.

Nott, in spite of his success, was in no manageable spirit, and practically refused General Pollock's request to send a brigade to Bamian to support Sir Richmond Shakespear, who had taken 600 Kizilbash Horse to the prisoners' release. British enterprise had, however, seized the opportunity—the prisoners freed themselves! The Afghan in charge of the captives was a soldier of fortune who had been a subahdar in one of the Shah's regiments, and eventually, for a consideration of a sum down and a pension, agreed to assist them to freedom.

They hoisted a British flag on their fort, and Pottinger, the senior political officer surviving, summoned the local chiefs to come in and tender allegiance. The bluff held good, and in a day or so came the welcome news of Shakespear's approach, when the party, with 250 musketeers of Salih Muhammad, went forth to meet them, and triumphantly returned from the fastnesses of Bamian and the Hindu Kush to meet Sale with a brigade coming out to succour them. And a memorable and a joyful reunion it was. Poor Elphinstone had died in confinement on the 23rd of April, broken in mind and health, and a few others, but the remainder were in fair circumstances.

The Finale at Kabul

The sight at Kabul was a magnificent one. The British Army now camped in the valleys round was far larger than the Afghans had yet seen. Six European corps were on the ground, with several troops of horse artillery and innumerable Sepoy battalions. Streets of tents as far as the eye could see, and masses of men in scarlet coats and black shakos paraded and marched in every direction. Brass helmets flashed in the sun, guns peered from every corner of vantage, and the pomp of an efficient British Army of early Victorian days was never more in evidence. The Afghan sirdars were overwhelmed with anxiety as to what would be the consequences, and had no real illusions as to their power when it came to a serious conflict.

It is not perhaps out of place to glance at what the conditions really were in Kabul after the departure of Elphinstone's force. Shah Shujah, not devoid of resolution, conscious that the British troubles were of their own making, and due to some extent to their disregard of his advice, for he had urged them even at the last to come into the Bala Hissar to face the storm, had decided to remain. The massacre of the army had come as a great shock to him, who still relied on British support. It must either mean collapse or a renewed occupation. For some months he tried to ride the storm and play in the proper Afghan manner, one faction against another and one chief against the next. On 5th April His Majesty was proceeding in a litter with an escort of Hindustanis near Kabul to review some troops going to join Akbar at Jalalabad, when he was ambushed by one of the sirdars and murdered with many of his party. Other factions at once brought Prince Fath Jang, his son, to the throne, where, bullied and browbeaten, he remained till September, with Ghulam Haidar Khan Populzai as his vizier. But on learning of the approach of Pollock he escaped, and arrived at the latter's camp in a bedraggled condition.

Lord Ellenborough had had the wisdom to place General Pollock in supreme political charge, so that the earlier evils should not again arise. He was joined by the senior surviving political officer, Major Rawlinson, who had come up with Nott, and they were of opinion that an Afghan crown was an essential for the progress of business. With the acquiescence of all the leading chiefs who had "come in," Fath Jang was therefore replaced on the throne amid pomp and ceremony, the Union Jack, however, having been hoisted with equal ceremony on the Bala Hissar a few days earlier.

It was now necessary to decide what actual punishment should be inflicted on the guilty city of Kabul. The Afghans in arms had themselves been heavily defeated and had lost considerably, while punishment on certain individuals who had fallen into the avengers' hands had been carried out. The Kohistanis in the valleys behind Kabul were still in arms, and had been specially active against the British. It was decided to raze Istalif and Charikar, where the Shah's Gurkha regiment had been so mercilessly and needlessly massacred. This was done by a force under Sale. Towers and fortifications were destroyed, but reprisals in a cruel form did not, with a few exceptions, take place, despite the fact that the troops were hard to hold. They had marched for miles through the remains of their comrades, they had seen the barrier at Jagdalak derisively piled with their skeletons, and around them flocked the maimed and frost-bitten beggars who had once been not merely the followers of the unfortunate army, but Her Majesty's Sepoys[1] themselves.

For their succour and withdrawal Pollock had appointed a special officer with allotted transport; for they were many and pitiful, and more were known to be slaves in the interior.[2] Now and again, too, in later years some European child would emerge, carried off as an infant to some fastness and brought up by Afghans.

But against this must be set the treatment of the captives, which for the most part had been reasonable, while in their journeys under durance they had met with many instances of kindness and sympathy; in fact, there was throughout many parts of the country a recognisable appreciation of the attempts that the British had made for the country's good.

The only public punishment decided on was the destruction of the Grand Bazaar of Kabul, the Chahar Chauk, through which the mutilated body of Sir William Macnaghten had been dragged and exposed to insult. And this was formally done by the Engineers after the inhabitants had been removed.

When the time came to leave in the autumn, Shah Fath Jang's resolution failed him, and he begged to abdicate and accompany the British.

[1] The E.I. Company was really but another form of the Crown.
[2] See the story of Subahdar Sitaram in *Sepoy to Subahdar*.

The Return to India

The return was soon to take place by echelons, Pollock leading, followed by M'Gaskil and then General Nott, the first move being on 12th October. To Pollock, who thoroughly understood the art of piqueting, the march was uneventful enough. M'Gaskil, however, was harried, both by Ghilzais and Khyberrees; while Nott, whose experience was of the opener plains of the Kandahar district, got an even severer handling, losing more men and animals than should have been permitted.

Nevertheless, the operations had been an unqualified success. The British had defeated every combination, and had carried their colours whithersoever it pleased them. Vengeance, but not ruthless vengeance, had been taken, and though the policy underlying the whole venture had ended amid dire failure and contumely, British military prestige was restored. The chatter and the underground muttering in India died away, and the British officer felt that he could look Indians in the face once again.

Leaving Shah Shapur at Kabul, a gallant lad and younger son of Shah Shujah, to whom the sirdars had offered the precarious throne, the British Government had serious thoughts of handing the province of Jalalabad to the Sikhs, and had told Pollock not to destroy the defences of that city. These instructions, however, came too late; and in any case the Sikhs themselves, of whom a brigade had actually been induced to accompany Pollock to the ancient Indian province of Kabul, were not prepared to accept the grant. It was then offered to the Rajput chief, Gulab Singh of Jammu, who had military forces quite equal to the work. But this also fell through, and so Jalalabad, with its old Hindu remains, is Afghan and Moslem to this day.

The passage through the Punjab was uneventful. The attitude of the Sikhs, and indeed of India generally, *vis-à-vis* the Kabul disasters, had been one of the causes in both Lord Auckland's and Lord Ellenborough's minds that had delayed prompter action in regard to the avenging armies, as Pollock's and Nott's forces were now called. Indeed, Lord Ellenborough had wisely assembled a considerable army of reserve at Ferozepore in case of trouble with the unsettled Sikh Durbar.

This force, with the Governor-General and the Commander-in-Chief, was now waiting to give an enthusiastic and triumphant welcome to the returning armies, which were marshalled so that the defenders of Jalalabad should first cross the bridge of boats at Ferozepore and be received with military honour.

With Nott came the gates of Somnath, which he had wrested from the weeping priests at Ghuzni, and for which Lord Ellenborough was so ridiculed. Their arrival had indeed been notified in a somewhat flowery proclamation, for Somnath itself was ruined and in Moslem hands. But, as has been pointed out, it was Ranjit Singh of Lahore who had originally bargained for their return and started the idea.

So ended in honours and rejoicings this "Great Adventure," which had had such phases of sunshine and storm, and which had wrought such unintended havoc in Afghanistan. Better managed, even if not wisely conceived, it might have had far less deplorable results. Yet nevertheless its results for good are by no means indiscernible as we study the warp and weft of the modern and, until 1929, stable, Afghan kingdom which we eventually succeeded in establishing.

THE COMMANDER-IN-CHIEF'S COMMENTS

It is the modern vogue to endeavour to point the moral and adorn the tale by deducing lessons from events that have passed, and to minister to that desire it may not be out of place to read the reasons assigned for our failures in Afghanistan by Sir Jasper Nicolls, the Commander-in-Chief of Bengal, who had succeeded Sir Harry Fane, the Chief at the outset.

He wrote as follows:—

"The causes to which I attribute our failure in Afghanistan are these:

1st. Making war with a peace establishment.

2nd. Making war without a safe base of operations.

3rd. Carrying our native army out of India into a strange and cold climate where they and we were foreigners and both considered as infidels.

4th. Invading a poor country and one unequal to supply our wants, especially our large establishment of cattle.

5th. Giving undue power to political agents.

6th. Want of forethought and undue confidence in the Afghans on the part of Sir William Macnaghten.

7th. Placing our magazines, even our treasure, in indefensible places.

8th. Great military neglect and mismanagement after the outbreak."

These comments not only sum up very tersely all that has been related and that happened, but are points of which the neglect in later campaigns has always produced the same results. They are, moreover, points which Governments and optimistic planners of campaigns will do well to have before them for all time.

APPENDIX

Major-General Nott's Force

3rd Bombay Light Cavalry.
Skinner's Horse.
1st Shah's Cavalry.
41st Foot.
42nd ,,
2nd Bengal N.I.
16th Bengal N.I.
38th ,, ,,
43rd ,, ,,
44th ,, ,,
3rd Shah's Infantry.

CHAPTER XI

AFGHANISTAN UNDER DOST MUHAMMAD AND SHERE ALI

The Dost back in Afghanistan · The Afghans and the Sikh Wars · The Indian Mutiny and the Lumsden Mission to Herat · The Death of Dost Muhammad and Succession of Shere Ali · Afzal Khan as Amir · Shere Ali again Victorious · Shere Ali and the Russian Approach

THE DOST BACK IN AFGHANISTAN

THE withdrawal of the victorious avenging armies did not immediately settle the question of the throne of Afghanistan, where Prince Fath Jang had sat uncomfortably after his father's murder, at the instance of the Barakzais, for want of a better. But he was not prepared to remain a minute after the British finally withdrew. He and all the family of Shah Shujah would accompany the British to India, including poor blind Shah Zaman, at whose name for a while even the great Marquis Wellesley had paled. But a king of some sort under whose name the pot could seethe was necessary, and a younger Saduzai scion, Prince Shapur, the child of a Populzai lady, was, as stated, offered the throne.

In the meantime a proclamation by the Governor-General gave permission to all Afghans in India to return to their own land. Dost Muhammad in Calcutta showed no eagerness whatever to avail himself of the situation. He disclaimed the least knowledge of what had been happening in Kabul, declaring that the Saduzai intrigues must have produced the troubles. He was, he said, the prisoner or the guest of the British as they might ordain, and he had been more than handsomely treated. Disgusted probably by the ready falling away of his supporters in 1839, he seemed to be void of any desire to return. Nevertheless he eventually did so, quietly and informally, to be installed in his unstable seat by the predominating influence of his son Akbar Khan and general consent.[1] The former Barakzai governors returned to their provinces automatically, and he was soon able to take up the old ground. The Afghans themselves had had enough of fighting either internally or with invaders for some time to come, and the Dost's seat was a fairly easy one.

He was nevertheless but Amir of Kabul, Ghuzni, and Jalalabad, and it was some ten years before he was able to conquer Afghan Turkistan and occupy Balkh, to which he appointed his son Afzal Khan (the father of Abdurrahman) as governor. In 1853 he recovered Kandahar on the death of his brother Kuhn Dil, and in 1854 Herat for the first time was added to his kingdom.

The Afghans and the Sikh Wars

In spite of the heavy strain on their military and financial resources after the prolonged operations in Afghanistan, which in their final stages had called for such large efforts, the British in India found themselves in a series of campaigns within the Peninsula itself. The future of Sind was a direct legacy of the war. It had been made quite clear in the final settlement with Afghanistan that Sind reverted to its position as a province of Mogul and not Afghan India, and that the British would settle its affairs themselves. The Amirs of Sind were not prepared to come to any reasonable arrangement, and Sir Charles Napier, who was in command there during the last phases of the Afghan War, was put in supreme charge. The attitude of the Amirs and the subsequent annexation is outside this story, save as it refers to what was once a province of the Durani Empire. Shikarpur,[2] the scene of Shah Shujah's battles

[1] Young Prince Shapur slipping quietly away.

[2] Until quite recently one of the most remarkable trade centres in Central Asia, to which folk came from all the world, and whose Hindu merchants had branches far beyond the Oxus, now dying because of the railways.

in 1834, came of course into British hands, and a frontier force in Sind restrained the wild Baluch tribes of the hills from their raids into the plains.

The rights and wrongs of the Amirs have been much discussed, but the complete prosperity of the province since its annexation, compared with the barrenness of the earlier period, is justification enough for the British having insisted on their right to do what was suitable with a province of Delhi. Public opinion in India is none too favourable to the régime of impossible princes, and such a condition of affairs as existed in Sind could not long have been tolerated.

The disasters in Afghanistan, despite their retrievement, had grievously shaken British prestige in India, and had no doubt brought about the frame of mind which induced the army of Gwalior in 1843 to defy its own authorities and stand up to a British Army in two pitched battles.

But far worse than this was the state of affairs in the Punjab. That was not due to the Afghan War, save so far as the loss of military prestige may have affected the views of the Sikh Army towards engaging the British. The old Lion had died in 1839, and there had ensued a period of debauchery, murder, and licence at the Sikh Court which beggars all description. The heirs and pillars of the State had all suffered massacre in succession, and it is perhaps a chapter fuller of lessons as to what an Eastern Court and power can come to in modern times when the magic control has been broken, than anything that could be written. It concerns this history only so far that the disorders ended in bringing the British frontier up to that of Afghanistan.

The Sikh Durbar, fearing the licence of its vast forces, of which the main part had been organised by Europeans, thought it better that the British should deal with them, and let the army, more or less of its own accord, throw itself on British India. It crossed the Sutlej in December 1845, and after severe battles was practically destroyed at Sobraon, while the Afghans clamoured to be led to India, asserting that their mere presence on the Sutlej would result in our destruction. But the Dost restrained their zeal and bravado. Then the British endeavoured to re-create a Sikh dynasty and to introduce a system of reform into the justice and revenue. An untoward series of events produced an unexpected rebellion at Multan, and the old Sikh sirdars and soldiers flew to arms again. Once more in desperate battles the Sikh Army was broken.

This concerns Afghan history for two reasons: first, because already had our officers, on loan to the Sikh Durbar, been brought into close contact not only with the Afghan frontier and with the tribes in the Sulaimans, who from time immemorial had owned no effective master, but it also brought us into close touch with provinces recently clipped from the Durani Empire by Ranjit Singh, as already described. During the Afghan War we had naturally discovered all there was to know about the Khaibar, but had not been concerned with the tribes in the Peshawar valley and overlooking hills. Now from 1846 our officers were in close touch with Multan, the Upper and Lower Derajat, Bannu, Kohat, and Peshawar. Further, the Afghan province of Kashmir, which had been in Sikh hands for twenty-five years, was now given by us to Rajah Gulab Singh of Jammu, the great-grandfather of the present Maharajah, a Dogra Rajput of courage and address but still more of cunning and ruthlessness. He it was who had practically been offered the renewal of the old Hindu control of the Khaibar and Jalalabad already referred to. To this day Afghan settlers are to be found in Kashmir, having lost, happily, the endless desire for war which still permeates the hillmen of the wilder hills.

When the Sikhs rose in 1848 against their Durbar and British tutelage at Lahore, the desire to be in it was more than the Afghans could stand. They had held their hands during the first war, neither endeavouring to recover any of their lost provinces nor siding with the Sikh Army. In 1848, however, an Afghan sirdar in Peshawar, a brother of Dost Muhammad, who had received much kindness at British hands, helped to take the British political officers in the citadel of Peshawar prisoners by stratagem, and then, it was said, sold them to the Sikhs, that the old Persian saying should not be wanting: "*Afghan! Afghan! Be iman! Be iman!*" which may be translated: "Fie! Fie! Faithless Afghan!" The excitement of this second war they could not resist. The Dost, who still retained the liveliest sense of all that had been done for him in the way of courtesy and consideration while a *détenu* in Calcutta, was not probably much concerned. But feeling ran too strong for him. The Afghans generally felt that to have the British in full possession at their doors was more than they could bear, and Akram Khan, a younger son of the Dost, brought down five thousand Afghan horse to join the Sikh sirdars.[1] They did not arrive till after the Battle of Chilianwala, but were on the field at the "Crowning Mercy" of Gujarat, fought outside the village of that name in full view of the glorious snows of Kashmir on 27th February 1849, and saw defeat for their pains.

The Punjab proverb of the lady who went to Lala Musa might well have reference to this venture. The retreating Sikhs, handsomely beaten at their own game of big guns, fell back in confusion before the vigorous pursuit of General Sir John Gilbert and the cavalry of the force. The Afghan horse were little engaged from start to finish, and when the Sikh Army laid down its arms under the Buddhist stupa near Rawalpindi, showed a clean pair of heels in their endeavour to get safely through the Khaibar as soon as could be. They were pursued with the utmost vigour, and it was hoped to catch them at the Indus, but as the British arrived at Attock the Afghan rearguard was burning the bridge of boats. The damage was soon repaired, and the unfortunate Afghans were bustled through the Khaibar in ignominious haste, or to quote the Sikhs, "like dogs," their rearguard exchanging shots with the eager pursuers at the very portals of the pass. It was not a venture of which Akram or his host need have any pride, nor is it clear why they should have endeavoured to succour their hereditary enemies. The incident did not impair our good relations with the Dost. In the Multan area the Afghans

[1] Intending, *inter alia*, to seize Peshawar if opportunity offered.

of the Derajat rallied eagerly to confront the Sikh at the call of young Herbert Edwardes, the frontier political officer.

It is perhaps well to remind ourselves that even in these populous days the Sikhs, man, woman, and child, but number three million in a population of forty million, and that the army we fought was full of Moslem and Afghan descended troops, native to the Punjab; so that in some sense Akram Khan had come to the assistance of a Moslem force and, at any rate, an indigenous rule.

The Indian Mutiny and the Lumsden Mission to Herat

Shortly before the Indian Mutiny a party of British officers found their way into Afghanistan on a mission to that country, from causes that are part of the age-old story of Herat. The Mutiny itself, which so changed the orientation of things Indian, has also prevented the affairs of the twenty years preceding it from receiving anything like the amount of general notice that they merit. The long story of events in the Punjab which induced the British policy with regard to Afghanistan, the desperate wars with the Sikhs, the events in Gwalior, and the British mission to Afghanistan of 1857, have all received a film of oblivion by reason of the great Mutiny of the Bengal Army.

In 1854 Dost Muhammad succeeded in conquering the province of Herat and adding it to the Afghan state. But he was not to keep it for long, for the next year the Persians again invaded the province, killing Yusuf Khan, the Afghan Governor, and threatening to advance on Kandahar. Afghanistan invoked the aid of the British against Persia, and when diplomatic measures failed, a British expedition was sent to the Persian Gulf early in 1857 under Sir James Outram, to add force to the political remonstrances already made. The expedition had the required effect, and the Persians withdrew from Herat. The British action was much appreciated in Afghanistan, and did a good deal to restore confidence in Britain's point of view towards that country, but was overshadowed by the excitement engendered during the troubles in India of 1857.

In 1855, largely owing to the enthusiasm of Herbert Edwardes, Dost Muhammad actually came down to Peshawar to have an interview with the Chief Commissioner, Sir John Lawrence. The relations engendered were very amicable, for the Dost's recollections of Calcutta, added to the effect of his interview, had the most far-reaching results in the British hour of trial.

Akbar Khan, the eldest son of the Dost, had died in 1848, and a younger son, Ghulam Haidar, had been nominated heir, and educated to hold that situation. In 1855, on behalf of the Dost, he signed a treaty of amity, when the British promised to help against Persia, as the result of which the Amir undertook to maintain a regular army while he was in danger from Persia, and the British agreed to contribute a sum of one lakh of rupees per annum (£10,000) towards it if British officers were received in Afghanistan to assist in the expenditure. This was agreed to, and in March 1857, before the shadow of the coming Mutiny had been noticed, Major H. P. Lumsden of the Guides, Lieutenant Lumsden of the Quartermaster-General's Department, and Surgeon Bellew, with a small escort from the Guides, set out from Peshawar, reconnoitring for the first time the Shutur Gardan and Spin Gawi passes on the road from Kurram to Kabul and Ghuzni, arriving at Kandahar on 26th April.

Hardly had they reached there than the great outburst of the Indian Mutiny fell on a Government that was quite unprepared. Wild excitement prevailed in Afghanistan. Public opinion there generally was in favour of a descent on India—an opinion which the mullahs eagerly fanned. For this reason, coupled with the demand for British troops farther south, John Lawrence at one time seriously considered making a favour of necessity and offering Peshawar to Dost Muhammad. Happily that step was not necessary, and Dost Muhammad most staunchly abided by the agreement he had entered into in 1855. But for some little time matters were very critical. The

Barakzai sirdars, known as the Peshawari brothers, Sirdar Sultan Muhammad Khan and Pir Muhammad Khan, fanned the flame to the utmost, and called so fiercely for the Green Standard to be unfurled that the Dost nearly gave way. It was his son, Azim Khan, who reminded him of his relationship with Sir John Lawrence and his goodwill to the British, pointing out that the latter had never failed to recover from their troubles, and that the Peshawari brothers really aimed at getting the Dost into trouble.

The heir-apparent, Ghulam Haidar, who had visited Bombay, Madras, and Calcutta, was of the same opinion, and was at Kandahar with Lumsden. A stream of *cossids* [1] sped on their way to carry his persuasion to that of Azim Khan, so that the Dost recovered his balance and turned a deaf ear to the roll of the drum ecclesiastic and the demand for the unfurling of the Standard of the Faith.

Nevertheless, the fact referred to should be remembered —viz. that Lawrence, knowing the ferment that was going on, and knowing too well the demand for the British troops at Peshawar to go down to Delhi, actually contemplated for a while making a virtue of necessity and handing over Peshawar to the Dost once again.

In the meantime Lumsden, seeing that affairs were getting very complicated again with the Persians, and that he might be involved in a struggle for Kandahar, withdrew the mission safely in the spring of 1858, after having materially contributed in upholding British interests and prestige among the Afghans while the situation in India hung in the balance.

The Death of Dost Muhammad and Succession of Shere Ali

In 1863, while the British in India were in the throes of their first serious frontier tribal troubles of Ambela, the good Dost Muhammad was gathered with his fathers, passing away at Herat on 9th June. He left sixteen sons behind him, of whom five aspired to the throne, while a

[1] *Cossid* or *kasid* = a mounted messenger.

number of the others hoped to be rulers of provinces. The typical Afghan war of succession then ensued, fierce and fanatical, in the struggle for the throne. But from 1841 to 1863 (the considerable space of twenty-two years) the British policy of a strong and prosperous Afghanistan had been maintained under Dost Muhammad. The country but wanted peace, for there was, it must be remembered, a long tradition of more or less ordered government that had been transmitted from Mogul and Persian governors, and there were plenty of the clerkly class fitted by education and tradition to carry on the machinery if only folk would let the machine run. There was also a large and highly organised trading class, but the struggles of the later sixties tended to plunge the country back into economic disorder.

Dost Muhammad, five years before his death, had nominated his third surviving son,[1] Shere Ali, as his successor, passing over the two elder sons, who were uterine brothers, on the grounds that their mother was a lady of inferior birth, being of the Bangash tribe, who live near Kohat, and not as Shere Ali's mother, an Afghan proper, a lady of the Durani race and royal house. Abdurrahman in his autobiography challenges the propriety of this reason, practically saying that marriage raises the wife to her husband's status. Yet these matters are of much account in Kabul as elsewhere. The brothers passed over were Afzal and Azim, the former the father of young Abdurrahman, then nineteen years of age. Afzal had been Governor of Balkh for many years, a province of which the head had long been almost independent of the Amir in matters other than fealty, and young Abdurrahman had held various high offices from his early days in his father's principality.

Both the elder brothers professed acquiescence in the amirship of Shere Ali. Herat had been taken from the Persians once again, by the Dost, a fortnight before his death, and Azim was with him, but he left the royal forces at once and withdrew to one of his own fastnesses, while

[1] Ghulam Haidar died in 1858.

Afzal at Balkh prepared to make a descent on Kabul. In January 1864 Afzal proclaimed himself Amir, while Azim had written to the British that he and Afzal were resisting Shere Ali's claim. Shere Ali had, however, also reported his accession, and had received in December 1863 a letter from the Governor-General acknowledging him as the Dost's successor

Azim, who was the Governor of Kurram, was there collecting an army, while the Amir's full brothers, Amin Khan and Sharif Khan, were also collecting forces in Kandahar on their own account. The forces of disorder and disruption were now to be rampant for six years.

Shere Ali was able to defeat Azim, who fled to the British. There he was well received, his services during the Mutiny being well remembered. The long struggle that followed is told with much wealth of detail in the Abdurrahman's own autobiography. Afzal and Shere Ali met in battle at Bajgah, some sixty odd miles north of the pass of Bamian, without any great decision, and after that a reconciliation was affected, the Amir swearing to leave Afzal in possession of all that his father had given him.

It was not long before Shere Ali had cause to think that young Abdurrahman, the commandant at Takhtapul, was intriguing against him, and summoned him to Kabul. He refused to come, and the Amir therefore sent to Balkh and brought his father in fetters to the capital, while the young man fled across the Oxus to Bukhara. Then the Amir, oblivious of his oath to Afzal, gave Balkh to his nephew, Faiz Muhammad, son of that Akbar Khan who had murdered the British envoy, Sir William Macnaghten, in 1842.

This treatment of Afzal was much condemned by the Afghans, but it is typical enough of the Afghan ways and the Persian proverb.

Afzal Khan as Amir

Even his own full brothers opposed Shere Ali, and in May 1865 marched northwards against him from Kandahar, while from Bukhara Abdurrahman was trying to raise a force to support his father's claims and rescue him from durance. Shere Ali's army from Kabul met that of his brothers, Amin Khan and Sharif Khan, between Ghuzni and Kandahar at Kajbaz on 5th June. Shere Ali commanded in person, and apparently taunted his son and heir at his listlessness. The lad then led a charge, meeting his uncle Amin face to face, who shot him through the head. The footmen were able to dispose of Amin Khan and the charge won the day, but the death of his heir left the Amir broken-hearted, and he was not even to enjoy the fruits of victory.

His enemies were closing on him, and on 24th February 1866 Abdurrahman and his uncle, Azim Khan, entered Kabul while Shere Ali was absent at Ghuzni, but having with him Abdurrahman's father, Afzal Khan. On 10th May Shere Ali and his nephew met in battle, and the latter was victorious, bringing his father back to Kabul and installing him as Amir, while Shere Ali, who had lost guns, elephants, and equipment, galloped for Kandahar.

The Government of India, determined not to be drawn into the fray, merely told their agent at Kabul to offer congratulations, and the Eastern world watched the fissiparous fratricidal tendency at work. Truly the policy of maintaining a strong and prosperous Afghanistan was not to be easily attained, especially by a *laissez-aller* attitude.

But during this period John Lawrence was Viceroy of India, and held firmly by the policy of no more intervention with Afghanistan, and the necessity for only dealing with the *de facto* ruler of the country, when that country had made up its mind. In 1866 we find him writing his views and those of his council freely to the Cabinet:

"It is difficult enough to foresee what may be the turn of events in Kabul. The Amir Shere Ali may recover his power. He has shown that he in many respects possesses the qualities of a ruler, but he also has considerable defects; there can be little doubt that he has alienated most of the influential chiefs. His conduct towards his brother, Sirdar Muhammad Afzal Khan, whom he treacherously imprisoned after the most solemn promises and oaths of full security, shows that no faith can be placed in him. Still, Afghan chiefs are not to be judged by the principles of Christendom, nor can we be sure that the nobles and people will not again rally round the Amir if he shows resolution and vigour."

So much for Shere Ali as a man and a neighbour. Sir John went on to enunciate our policy, which has all along governed our actions since 1842: "It should be our policy to show clearly that we will not interfere in the struggle, that we will not aid either party, that we will leave the Afghans to settle their own quarrels, and that we are willing to be on good terms with the nation and with their rulers *de facto*."

The policy of leaving the Afghans to "stew in their own juice" was no doubt wise enough after our previous experience, and might have held for all time had it not been for the steady absorption of the Central Asian Khanates by Russia. That absorption was in its way all to the good of mankind and civilisation, for the Turki and Usbeg Khans had little to contribute to the well-being of the world. Had it not been for our policy of maintaining Turkey in Europe and in Asia, and therefore getting at loggerheads with Russia, we might have had a settlement which would have relieved us of much of our anxieties. As it was, Russia was well aware that we had a weak spot, and on that she could play at will. Such being the case, for good or for evil the policy of "masterly inactivity" (Lawrence's famous catchword) could not hold the field for ever.

The Amir Afzal was not long to enjoy his seat on his father's throne. Shere Ali at first fled to Kandahar, and in 1867 Abdurrahman drove him to Herat, where he remained, while Afzal held Kabul and Kandahar with Ghuzni thrown in, and we find the Governor-General in pursuance of the *de facto* policy writing to both Amirs. To Afzal he wrote that since Shere Ali held Herat and had friendly relations with the British he would be recognised, while he was prepared to recognise Afzal as Governor of Kabul and Kandahar, and in fact he congratulated both on their God-given dominions! Perhaps we may feel that the situation in 1867 has a strong resemblance to that of 1929.

Shere Ali again Victorious

Afzal, the Amir, however, was rapidly drinking himself to death, having, in Eastern metaphor, "opened the door of enjoyment to strong waters." He leant greatly on his brother Azim Khan, and in vain Abdurrahman implored his father to nominate him his successor. He would not move without Azim, who was absent in Kandahar as the end drew nigh. On the Amir's death intrigues and excursions took place, but eventually Abdurrahman agreed to serve his uncle, though the latter also signified his willingness to stand down. Indeed it is probable that Abdurrahman realised that he had not enough personal influence to take up the amirship.

Afzal died at the age of fifty-six, after reigning sixteen months. In the meantime more trouble was brewing from the north. Faiz Muhammad, Governor of Balkh, who had played Shere Ali false by allowing Abdurrahman to advance on Kabul, and had been confirmed in his governorship by Afzal, anticipating displacement, returned to his original allegiance. It has been said that in Afghanistan, statesmanship consists of changing sides at the right time. If so, Faiz Muhammad failed to satisfy the test, for not only was he defeated by Abdurrahman, but was killed by a cannon-shot, while Shere Ali, who was with him, fled back to Balkh. Nevertheless the latter's star was ascending, for Yakub Khan, his eldest son, succeeded in retaking Kandahar while Abdurrahman was attacking Maimana. This delay at Maimana, where Abdurrahman is said to have buried alive two chiefs of Akcha as a warning against rebels, prevented his attacking Shere Ali in Herat.

While these matters were in progress Sir John Lawrence had written to Azim Khan, addressing him as Wali of Kabul and Kandahar, and congratulating him on coming to an agreement with Abdurrahman as to the succession to the amirship. Azim, however, had made himself greatly disliked at Kabul, and matters were going agley. In June 1868 Shere Ali was back in Kandahar, and so changeable is public opinion or so susceptible to victory, that within a fortnight he was also in possession of Ghuzni.

It was at this time that Sir Henry Rawlinson wrote his famous memorandum on Afghanistan, and pointed out that we should have done much better in supporting Shere Ali than in allowing the country to fall into disorder and civil war.

At the end of July Azim marched out of Kabul to meet Shere Ali, and had got as far as Ghuzni, when news reached him that a Barakzai sirdar, one of his own supporters, had seized the Bala Hissar in Shere Ali's name. The latter, avoiding Azim, slipped into Kabul and was gladly hailed as Amir once again. Azim and Abdurrahman made one more attempt to save the situation. They failed, and fled to Waziristan. Here, owing to some misunderstanding, Abdurrahman did not, as he wished, enter India, but fled away through Baluchistan to Meshed, being plundered *en route* by the Kakar tribes. Eventually Abdurrahman made his way to Russian Turkistan, where he remained in exile for many years, while Azim Khan died shortly after at Shahrud between Meshed and Tehran.

Shere Ali was now firmly established, and in March 1869 came down to Ambala to meet the new Viceroy, Lord Mayo, at another of those brilliant gatherings for which India is so famous. Already had Lord Lawrence [1] followed the advice of Rawlinson and given him six lakhs of rupees and 3500 stands of arms.

The rightful Amir was now on the throne, rightful in so far as under Islamic law he was the nominated heir of Dost Muhammad; rightful, too, in so far as it appeared that Afghan people as a whole confirmed that nomination. His most important brothers were dead, and for a while the barometer seemed set fair. Further, Shere Ali had entered into definite friendly relations with the British in India—relations, however, much exaggerated in Russia—and was apparently willing to abide by British advice, so

[1] Sir John had been made a baron.

far as his fickle mind would let him. Indeed it seems probable that had it not been for the loom of the advancing Bear and the Russian efforts, which our share in European affairs in 1877–78 had stimulated, Shere Ali might have ended his life on the throne at Kabul.

Shere Ali and the Russian Approach

That, however, was not to be, for while Shere Ali was consolidating his kingdom, the steady absorption of the Khanates of Central Asia by Russia continued, and brought Afghanistan into world politics. General Kaufman, the Russian Governor-General, wrote in 1870 to Shere Ali that though his nephew Abdurrahman had arrived at Tashkent and had received hospitality, no assistance whatever would be given him to act against the Amir. "The Tsar's possessions in Turkistan do not border on the countries at present under your rule. . . . No collision or misunderstanding can take place between us. . . . Though distant neighbours, we can and ought to live in concord," wrote he.

At this time the relationships between England and Russia were extremely cordial, and Abdurrahman was repeatedly told that he could look for no assistance. The British desire for a peaceful and prosperous Afghanistan seemed to be coming true, though Abdurrahman was keeping in close touch and intrigue with his adherents south of the Oxus. He not unnaturally represented to his Afghan correspondents that Shere Ali as a friend of the English would bring them all to ruin. In 1873, when Yakub Khan was in rebellion against his father, Abdurrahman was keenly on the look out for a chance to take part. In the meantime Russian civilisation, in many ways very genuine civilisation, was approaching. In 1870 Michailovsk, on the eastern shores of the Caspian, was captured. In 1873, however, Russia agreed with Great Britain that the Oxus should be the boundary of Afghanistan for a great part of its length, and the independence of Yakub Beg of Kashgar was recognised. In May 1873 the Russians captured Khiva after many difficulties and disasters, and released some 15,000 slaves of all races, including many Russians, and in 1875 they annexed the Khanate of Khoqand, making it a province under the name of Ferghana. In 1877 Yakub Beg of Kashgar died, and China reoccupied that province. Then the inexorable march of events foreclosed on the Amir. The following year, when the Russo-Turkish War was in progress and the British fleet watched events in Besika Bay, and when an Anglo-Indian force was at Malta, Russia must needs send an envoy to Kabul and commence, not unnaturally, her anti-British propaganda. And this was the undoing of the unfortunate Shere Ali.

CHAPTER XII

THE SECOND AFGHAN WAR

The First Phase · Kurram, Ali Masjid, Kandahar The Treaty of Gandamak · The Massacre of the British Mission · General Roberts' Advance on Kabul · The Great Afghan Rising · Sir Donald Stewart's March to Kabul

THE FIRST PHASE

IT is not the purpose of this volume to provide a military history of either the First or Second Afghan Wars, or to do more than outline the course of military events. But as in the first war of 1839–42, so in that of 1878–81 there was more than one separate phase, and it is important for the reader to get the sequence of events set before him in some sort of panorama. The Second Afghan War is in reality the story of two distinct wars and historical episodes, and at one time it was the custom to speak of them as the Second and Third Afghan Wars. The first war ended with the Treaty of Gandamak, when the British attained for the moment the objects they had set before themselves. It is merely by chance that the massacre of the British mission sent to Kabul as the result of that treaty followed so close on the treaty itself. The campaign that ensued was a separate one, and had the space of a year intervened between the treaty and the massacre, as might easily have been the case, the two wars would have been recognised as separate for all time. As it is, it has become the custom to speak of these two adjacent wars as one, and we now use the term Third Afghan War for that impudent and fatuous venture of the Amir Amanullah Khan in the year of Grace 1919, and of the Hegira 1337 in the calendar of Islam.

The Amir Shere Ali having received a Russian mission under the circumstances related, the British Government decided to send one also, and selected the veteran General Sir Neville Chamberlain, then Commander-in-Chief of the Army of Madras. Sir Neville was one of the few survivors of the First Afghan War still serving with the active army, a war in which he and his brother had served with much distinction, and he was also a personal friend of the Amir.

Shere Ali, however, was now persuaded on his suicidal course, believed that an affront was intended, and obstinately refused to allow the mission to enter Afghanistan. In fact, Sir Neville's party was courteously but firmly turned back from the Khaibar, which was then in Afghan hands, by a threat of force. This was more than the British and Indian Governments were prepared to swallow. The tension with Russia elsewhere over the war with Turkey was acute, and it was decided to bring the Amir to his senses by force of arms.

So once again the Indo-British forces were to find themselves marching by the old, well-known roads to Kabul and Kandahar, though perhaps Sir Neville Chamberlain was the only man who knew them personally, and he was not to go into the field. Horse, foot, and artillery, guns heavy and guns light—for mountain artillery was now an understood thing—the twenty yoke of the forty-pounder train alongside the jinketty-jink of the pack guns, were to swing up the Khaibar once again.

Kurram, Ali Masjid, Kandahar

The British were to enter Afghanistan in three directions: General Sir Donald Stewart would march by the ancient ways to Kandahar; General Roberts, the Quartermaster-General in India, was to command a force in the Kurram valley and enter by a new way, that of the Shutur Gardan, a pass first surveyed by the Lumsden mission in 1857; while General Sir Sam Browne was to force the Khaibar and capture the old mountain fortress of Ali Masjid *en route* to Dakka.

Mindful of Sir John Keane's experience at Ghuzni, heavy guns drawn by elephants and long yokes of powerful bullocks were to go both to Kandahar and into the Khaibar. At this period, however, the army in India was singularly unprepared for war. At the fighting of Ali Masjid, for instance, there were no medical arrangements other than the regimental medical personnel, and field ambulances and hospitals did not exist, though they were, of course, soon improvised and formed. Transport for the army there was actually none, except with the units of the actual frontier force.

The three columns were to enter Afghanistan simultaneously, Sir Michael Biddulph at Quetta leading the advance on that side till joined by Sir Donald Stewart with a division assembling at Multan. The railway communications of 1878 were very different from what they are now. On the northern line railhead was at Jhelum, below Rawalpindi; on the southern line it but reached to the Indus. The forces for Kandahar were therefore destined, as before, to a trying march over the desert of Kach Gandava, and through the Sulaiman mountains to Pishin, but with this advantage, that Quetta was already a cantonment, and therefore an organised milestone on the long road.

Sir Sam Browne's Khaibar column consisted of 10,000 men with 30 guns, General Roberts had 6500 with 24 guns, and Sir Michael Biddulph would start from Quetta to Kandahar with only 6000 men and 18 guns, with Sir Donald Stewart behind him with as many more.

Reserve divisions were formed at Hassan Abdal on the northern line under General Maude, and at Sukkur on the southern line under General Primrose. The supreme command was to be exercised by the Commander-in-Chief in India from the headquarters of Government.

As no answer had been received from the ultimatum sent the Amir, Sir Sam Browne crossed the frontier on 21st November 1878. The General advanced himself direct on Ali Masjid, but had detached two brigades overnight by the northerly passes to come in on the flank of a position held by the Afghans. By noon the main force came under the guns of Ali Masjid, and was engaged all along the line held by the Afghans; but the turning force had not got in.

After two hours' bombardment Browne advanced to the attack in the belief that his turning movement must by now have got into position. The facilities of modern armies for intercommunication did not then exist—the lofty mountains of the Khaibar mouth prevented any visual signalling—and as there was no sign of the turning troops, the frontal attack, after some sharp fighting, was ordered to halt. But next morning when General Browne was about to resume, it was found that the turning pressure had been too great and the Afghans had gone in the night. Browne then advanced through Dakka to Jalalabad without further fighting other than continual tribal molestations of his communications, which were now held by Maude's reserve division.

In the Kurram General Roberts also crossed the frontier on the 21st and marched promptly up the Kurram valley, the Afghan troops retiring before him in confusion to the Paiwar Kotal to take up a position four miles long amid the pine and cedar forest on the hilltop. A brilliant capture of the position followed, in which the 72nd Highlanders and 5th Gurkhas especially distinguished themselves, and the Kotal was duly crossed and held.

The force then pushed on to Ali Khel on the road to the Shutur Gardan, to which point but fifty miles from Kabul a reconnaissance was pressed. Transport difficulties, however, forbade further advance for some time.

The advance of Generals Stewart and Biddulph on the southern line was long and arduous as to distance and terrain, but uneventful, and Sir Donald Stewart rode into Kandahar on 8th January 1879 to meet with a reasonable welcome. Merchants and traders had vivid memories of the money to be made from feeding the troops, while even the chiefs were cognisant that allowances were to be had for those who would keep the countryside in order. The Governor had fled with the Afghan cavalry towards Herat, and the Deputy Governor made over the city. Biddulph marched on to the Helmand to facilitate supply, and there had a sharp engagement.

With the occupation of Kandahar, the storming of the

By permission of Macmillan & Co., Ltd.

The attack on the Paiwar Kotal, 2nd December 1878

From Lord Roberts' "Forty-one Years in India," by Vereker M. Hamilton.

Paiwar, and the capture of Ali Masjid, for which two actions clasps were awarded when an Afghan War medal came to be issued, the first phase of the second war came to an end. Shere Ali had fled the country, writing to the British as he fled that he was on his way to St Petersburg to report their action to the nations of Europe. Death soon after terminated his misfortunes.

The Treaty of Gandamak

Sir Sam Browne had reached Jalalabad by the 20th December, and there paused to consolidate his communications before pushing on to Gandamak, the ill-omened site of cantonment of the Shah's contingent in the old war. But before he marched from Jalalabad he had to report that the Amir Shere Ali was no more. On 10th December the last Russian had disappeared *quam celerrime* from Kabul, and his chiefs had told the Amir that he could not oppose the coming of the British. Shere Ali in despair, for he had put his trust in the Russians, now released his eldest son Yakub—who, before his heart had been broken by his father's treatment and his long captivity, had been a man of promise—made him regent, and then fled towards Tashkent on the heels of the Russian mission. But General Kaufman would not have him across the frontier, so, broken-hearted and sick unto death, he returned again to Afghan Turkistan, and died near Balkh on 21st February.

Lyall, whose Afghan verses the Amir Abdurrahman knew so well and often quoted, makes the latter soliloquise:

> "And yet when I think of Sher Ali as he lies in his sepulchre low,
> How he died betrayed, heart-broken, 'twixt infidel friend and foe,
> Driven from his throne by the English, and scorned by the Russian, his guest,
> I am well content with the vengeance, and I see God works for the best."

The rule of Yakub Khan was no great matter, and as in the days of yore, the chiefs deserted him and slipped away to the British camps. In February the new Amir made overtures, and shortly after reported his father's death and his own actual accession to the throne. Major Cavagnari, Sir Sam Browne's chief political officer, wrote to him the terms under which the British were prepared to negotiate a peace. More of his sirdars left him, and the British concentrations towards Gandamak steadily went forward, so that he thought it best to come down himself to see the British commander. The Amir and his Commander-in-Chief arrived dressed in Russian uniforms, were received with due ceremony, and by 26th May a treaty of peace was signed and ratified.

The treaty contained the most important provisions, and was specially framed with regard to the general apprehension then felt as to the ambitions of Russia. Great Britain definitely undertook to protect Afghanistan against Russian aggression, and in return for this Afghanistan was not to have direct dealings with other powers. The practical corollary of this was to have a British representative at Kabul who could act, and this was agreed to. The British, of course, undertook to have nothing to do with any internal questions, but for purposes of the outside world Afghanistan was to be a part of the Indian Empire, as she had been in the halcyon days of Delhi. But there was one new point. Instead of, as in Mogul days, Kabul paying tribute to Delhi, the British would make an allowance to the Amir to enable him to put his army on a better footing!

For some time the Government of Lord Beaconsfield had aimed at having a scientific frontier whence the Afghan borderland could be kept quiet and the Russian menace met, and this is fully discussed in a later chapter. To satisfy that aim and to make the British position in Baluchistan effective, the Amir agreed to surrender any of his ancient but nebulous claims to the districts of Sibi on the plain of Kach Gandava; to give up the Kurram valley, which was inhabited by the Turis;[1] and lastly, to abandon his claims to the country on either side of the Kabul and Michni passes. That meant control of the Afridis, who had always declared that Kabul was nothing to them, and

[1] Who were of the Shiah persuasion, very antipathetic to the Afghans, and had urged this step on us.

who had been such friends of Shah Shujah, and those of the Mohmand clans whose dealings had always been with Peshawar, and whose constant raiding of our border could but be a source of trouble to an Afghan Government. That the treaty was an admirable one and useful to all concerned could not be denied; but the memory of 1842 was still fresh, and many there were who shook their heads and said that harm must surely come of it. Nor did Yakub Khan seem to be man enough to bend his peoples to the new conditions, for they too had memories of 1842, recalling the loot but not the punishment.

Major Louis Cavagnari, quite the most remarkable frontier officer of his day, half British, half Italian in origin, who fully understood the wishes of Government, and who had brought the treaty to a successful issue, was appointed the British Envoy at the Afghan Court. No one probably knew better than he the hazards that he might be running in this half-savage capital, ruled by a crazy ruler. But frontier officers are of a breed that take risks, and the great game was well worth playing. So, accompanied by Mr William Jenkins of the Civil Service, Dr Ambrose Kelly, and seventy-five men of the Queen's Own Corps of Guides, commanded by Lieutenant W. R. P. Hamilton (who was awarded a posthumous V.C.), Sir Louis Cavagnari[1] rode confidently into the Bala Hissar on 24th July 1879, where he was received with high honour, and conducted to the Residency prepared for him not far from the Amir's palace. In India, however, his friends were full of apprehension.

That the Afghan public disliked the arrangement there was no doubt, but the presence of a British minister in Kabul was obviously going to be so good for trade and the general advance of amenities, that there was always a strong party who approved. For a few weeks all went well enough, and then there marched into Kabul from Herat regiments of Ayub Khan's force, the other son of Shere Ali who had lately secured the province of Herat and whose hatred of the British was widely known. They passed through the Kabul streets shouting abuse of the

[1] He had just been made a K.C.I.E.

Envoy. On 2nd September, however, Cavagnari still reported to the Viceroy that all was well.

The army of Sir Sam Browne had been marched back to India. It will be remembered that General Pollock in 1842 had refused to cross the Punjab in the summer, but the coming of the railway to the Indus, and the hill barracks awaiting the troops, made the old arguments apparently inoperative on the northern line. The army marched home, and with it marched in its worst form that evil genius of Eastern armies, Asiatic cholera. The cholera morbus, known to the army as "Corporal Forbes," fell among all and sundry, and the home-coming was known as the "Death March." The British medical services of those days did not understand sanitation and their responsibility for it; the staff neither knew how to exact proper care from the medical service, nor how to help the efforts of those medical officers who had ideas on the subject. Devoted doctors toiled and died, but there was neither system nor service worthy of the name. It was a deadly and bitter period that cast a gloom over all the successes of our arms.

On the southern line Sir Michael Biddulph, after his success on the Helmand, had marched to the Punjab in the spring by the unknown route of Thal Chotiali, leaving Sir Donald Stewart in Kandahar. This force was now to remain there on sanitary grounds till the autumn.

In the Kurram a force was to remain for the summer in an admirable climate, while the new state of things was adjusted with the tribes.

The war was at an end, and had the new régime in Kabul endured a little longer, the second phase would have supervened, in the general sense of history, as a fresh war. Unfortunately, the edifice was to topple so promptly that the two wars became but two phases, as already explained.

The Massacre of the British Mission

It was on the 2nd September that Cavagnari had sent his confident message to Simla. On the morning of the

3rd some Afghan regiments were parading without arms in the Bala Hissar for their pay, of which considerable arrears —no new thing in army life in Afghanistan—were due. The arrears were refused, and the men betook themselves to the Residency to present a demand to the envoy. Some among them threw stones, and the troops rushed to the arsenal hard by for arms. The Residency gates had been closed at once, and ere long it was necessary to open fire on the rabble. The house was not planned for defence—it was merely a residence within the palace precincts. The city, hearing of the disturbance, poured out by the thousand. Cavagnari had at once sent word to the Amir of what was happening, and the Amir sent his Commander-in-Chief, Daud Khan. Whether he showed any energy or not is questionable; even a Commander-in-Chief was useless at that stage, but a couple of hundred disciplined soldiers might have emphasised his action. The Amir sat in his palace helpless and useless.

In the meantime matters in the Residency, surrounded by a yelling mob, were getting desperate. Time after time the British officers sallied forth at the head of the Guides and the Afghans fled like sheep, only to surge back as the desperate men retired within their gates. From the adjacent arsenal the Residency was commanded on all sides. One by one the defenders were picked off, and the swordsmen crept to the walls. Hamilton and Jenkins alone made one last sally, and then a Sikh subahdar. After that no more, and by noon the gates were forced, the building was fired, and the last of the little band were massacred.

The forward policy had tumbled for the moment in blood and ruin, and the British world stood aghast.

General Roberts' Advance on Kabul

The news first came to Simla in a curious way. The East has long been famous for its news system, faster even than the electric telegraph, and it has never quite been explained. The story has been told that General Roberts, who had just returned to his post in Simla, after dining quietly with another officer, was chatting to a fortune teller in the verandah. He had promised to give them both high command at once, and the usual chaff was in progress, but the man said, "What I am telling you is true, and you will know ere long." That very evening came a telegram from the Kurram with the bad news from Kabul, and all was consternation.

Fortunately Lord Lytton, the Governor-General, however aghast he might be at the collapse of his own structure, and the apparent justification of all that Lord Lawrence had urged about masterly inactivity, saw at once that only one course could be taken. The British must go forthwith to Kabul, and General Roberts hurried off down the hill to take command again of the troops on the Kurram line.

In the Kurram the British force was a small one, but admirably situated for a dash on Kabul. Brigadier Massey, who was in command on the spot, was ordered to seize the Shutur Gardan, only fifty miles from that city, while the rest of the troops available for this line were concentrating. But in accordance with our age-old custom, which has landed us in so many troubles in the past, notably in the two Sikh wars, the army had been so severely demobilised that carriage was practically non-existent, and some 6500 men was all that could at once be laid hands on. The troops available for General Roberts to lead to Kabul were the cavalry brigade under Brigadier Massey, and two infantry brigades under Brigadiers Macpherson and Baker, with three batteries of artillery and a company of sappers. Some 4000 more men would be collected to protect his communications, and a force under Major General Bright would be assembled at Peshawar to advance up the Khaibar. It was proposed to supply Roberts by the Kurram line till it was closed by the snow, by which time Bright should have been able to open the Khaibar line right through. A reserve force would be gathered in the vicinity of Hassan Abdal, again under General Ross. But the outstanding fact remained that there was no "carriage," that all the arrangements made for the first phase had been scattered,

Lord Roberts

From a painting by R. H. Sylvester; the property of the East India United Service Club, London, by whose permission the portrait is published

and that it would be some time before they could all be recast. Further, General Roberts would have to advance with only half the transport required to move his troops, which meant they would have to go by detachments.

On the southern line Sir Donald Stewart was directed to recall any troops who had left him that were within reach. His force would be brought up to 9000 men, while General Phayre was to keep his communications open.

The important rôle had fallen to Roberts, much to the satisfaction of the army, he then being but forty-seven, and full of fire and activity. He and MacGregor arrived at Ali Khel on 12th September, but it was not till 1st October that he was able to concentrate his force by detachments at Kushi in the Logar valley, forty-eight miles from Kabul. Even collecting the transport for this force and the line of communications had taken all available transport from Peshawar, and thrown back the date on which General Bright could move forward on the northern line.

In Kabul things were in a bad way. The murder of the accredited envoy to a court was a different matter from the murder of Burnes and Macnaghten by the party other than that of Shah Shujah, whom they were supporting. It put the Amir and all his folk out of court for any of the usual diplomatic treatments. The sirdars urged the Amir to raise the green flag and shout "*Jihad*"! But Yakub Khan had no inclination for such a course, and no doubt felt his position keenly. So he packed up his court and presented himself at the British camp the day before General Roberts arrived, coming there, ostensibly at least, as an ally whose peoples had deserted him.

Feeling in British India and in the army ran strongly, and the sight of the reception accorded him was not pleasing to the forces. Nevertheless, whether his faults were only those of feebleness, or whether to save his own throat he had acquiesced in the fall of events, will never probably be known. It was only patent that in no sense could he possibly ride in the saddle of Dost Muhammad and Shere Ali.

Roberts at once paid him a visit, and was met with the

request that the British advance should be delayed. This was peremptorily refused, and the Amir remained an honoured guest under surveillance until such time as opinion as to his deserts could crystallise. The General was anxious enough to get forward, but it was not till 2nd October that he felt able to cut himself from his communications and head for Kabul.

Students of military science have always held that this march of a force which has been described about the size of a Prussian brigade on a war footing, moving to a capital which was seething with enmity and which we had not seen for thirty-seven years, by a road we had never yet traversed, was a far more striking feat than the dramatic march from Kabul to Kandahar.

On the 5th October the main body of the force, in this case Baker's brigade, and the cavalry with the 92nd Highlanders from Macpherson's, camped south of the village of Charasia, before a ring of hills which divide the Charasia valley from the plain of Chardeh outside Kabul, and through which runs the road by the Sang-i-Nawishta Pass.

Reconnaissances showed no signs of the enemy, though information imputed to them the determination to make a great effort to prevent the British reaching Kabul. At dawn on the 6th October the General, anxious to secure the pass and make it practicable for his field guns, pushed on the Pioneers with a couple of mountain guns and a wing of the 92nd. A very different sight met their gaze as the sun rose. The pass and hills on either side bristled with Afghan regular troops and tribal standards, while large bodies on the nearer hills threatened the camp. The troops in Baker's brigade, added to the 92nd, were some of the finest corps in the army, and General Roberts had no hesitation in attacking, knowing well the difference between an Afghan attacked and when allowed to take the initiative. He was entirely victorious, defeating the whole army of Kabul and capturing all its guns. Baker bivouacked that night on the Kabul side of the pass, and next morning the whole force passed through and camped within sight of the Bala Hissar of Kabul, in time to hear the Afghans blow up their magazine in Sherpur.

Brigadier Massey led his cavalry forthwith into the cantonment, to find a park of seventy-five pieces of artillery deserted. The Afghan troops, reinforced by three regiments from the Kohistan and a rabble from the city, still occupied the Asmai Heights. Baker was ordered to attack, but the difficulties of the terrain prevented his getting in touch, and by morning the enemy were gone, abandoning their camp and equipment.

The city environs were at once occupied, Massey leading the cavalry through the streets unmolested; and on the 11th General Roberts himself visited the scene of the tragedy in the Residency, which, to the great shame of the Amir, had never been cleared up. The scorched remains of the defenders still lay unburied amid the debris of Cavagnari's quarters and in the Guides' barracks among the bullet-dented walls. Next day formal entry was made into the Bala Hissar, and the British flag again was hoisted where Pollock had once before put it on the walls of that ancient fortress. There a Durbar of chiefs was assembled, and orders proclaimed that Kabul would be disarmed and fined. Three of the sirdars were arrested, the others dismissed, and on the 3rd the force marched through the city with its bands playing.

An unexpected explosion in the Bala Hissar, by which many lives were lost, determined General Roberts to move to Sherpur, sending a force back to the Shutur Gardan to bring in the detachment under Colonel Money which had been beset by Ghilzais, and roll up that line of communications. The whole of Roberts' force was concentrated at Kabul by the 3rd November, and was isolated. The serious state of unreadiness for war of the Indian Army had made it impossible for General Bright's force yet to make progress. This meant that the force at Kabul had to rely on supplies obtained from the country round, which was a difficult matter, and led to trouble with the tribes, who feared starvation if they sold more than a small portion of their store.

Fortunately Shere Ali, who had been intent on raising

a trained army and had a considerable arsenal and gun factory, had built a cantonment for a division at Sherpur under the Behmaru Heights, fortified and bastioned, but not quite complete. In this were lines of defensible barracks, and it was a ready-made habitation for the winter for the whole of the force, easily protected in quieter times. It was not far from the site of the old British cantonments and Envoy's residence of tragic memory.

The splendid weather of the late autumn was enjoyed in the beautiful setting of the Kabul hills in peace and calm, but no one knew better than the General that a storm of some kind was brewing. At the great Durbar the Amir had refused to be present and had tendered his resignation.[1] This had to be referred to India ; but by 28th October assent had come, and General Roberts issued a proclamation stating that the Amir had voluntarily resigned, and that the country would be governed by the General until such time as, after consultation with the chiefs and sirdars, a new Amir could be found. This caused consternation. The sirdars had anticipated punishment, which their own laws and customs told them well enough they had earned. They had expected something similar to General Pollock's doings of old—some punishments, some destruction, and a swift withdrawal rather than prolonged occupation.

Some punishments, indeed, there were. The Mayor of Kabul, who had taken Cavagnari's head in triumph through the city, and two other important officials concerned in the outrage, were executed, also about fifty of the mutinous soldiery concerned in the attack on the Residency, while the Bala Hissar was partly demolished to complete the buildings in Sherpur.

The Great Afghan Rising

In the meantime the tribes were gathering under Muhammad Jan of Wardak, an able leader, aided by the

[1] The correspondence between General Roberts and the Amir is given at length in *Forty-One Years in India,* and is a curious commentary on Afghan mentality and the question of Yakub Khan's true position.

old Ghuzni Mullah Mushk-i-alam. On all sides the drum ecclesiastic had been frantically beaten and the old cry raised, "Glory for all and heaven for those who bleed." In vain had MacGregor been sent down with a brigade to help open the road to India. At Kata Sang, two miles from Gandamak, MacGregor had met for a few moments General Bright with Charles Gough's brigade, pushed forward for the purpose, and then want of supplies had compelled Bright to withdraw again. Jenkins with the Guides, however, was left at Gandamak, and MacGregor returned.

The position of the British in the old wars had been described as a war of sentry-boxes, and that still more applied to the present position. The Afghan sirdars, who had accepted the governorship of provinces at the British hands, had been expelled with ignominy, and in some cases murdered. The British could at any moment drive the Afghans like chaff before them, only for the wave to close again when the troops had passed by.

On the 8th and 9th of December General Roberts had planned to defeat the gathering forces of Muhammad Jan. Macpherson and Baker had taken out their brigades in different directions in a converging movement, with which Massey's cavalry, some three squadrons and four guns, was to co-operate in the Chardeh valley as occasion offered; but the tribal gatherings in the various valleys were found to be enormous and the movements were delayed. Muhammad Jan appeared in front of the cavalry, unsupported in the Chardeh valley. Gallant but ineffective charges of a hundred sabres or so against tens of thousands were made, and the mounted troops only extricated by Roberts himself, who, luckily, had summoned a wing of the 72nd Highlanders from Sherpur to cover the retreat on Kabul. The cavalry were, with difficulty, extricated. Sherpur stood to arms, and the outlying brigades were summoned to return at once. Then followed several days' stout fighting round Kabul, in which the troops usually drove the Afghans from any position, but could make no real headway.

On the morning of the 15th Baker went out from Sherpur and successfully cleared the Asmai Heights, when a huge mass of some 20,000 fresh tribesmen were reported pouring down on the cantonment from another quarter, on which the troops were got back with difficulty within the defences of Sherpur.

Fortunately, Roberts had been able to summon to his assistance, after an adventurous forced march, Colonel Jenkins and his superb Guides, who marched into Sherpur as the troops were withdrawing to the cantonments on the evening of the 11th.

The British division of 6500 men was now closely invested by a force which at times must have swollen to 100,000 men. The tribesmen were, however, for the first few days chiefly concerned in looting Kabul, the Hindu and the Kizilbash quarters suffering severely. Mushk-i-alam became the Governor of Kabul, vice General Hill. On the 17th and 18th the Afghans threatened an attack in force but did not press it home, and then Muhammad Jan, with some memory of older days, offered General Roberts a safe-conduct to India, saying that the tribesmen were like wolves around his encampment.

As there were no symptoms of anything but contumely in the British reply, the threatened Afghan attack in force took place on the night of the 23rd. All night long the Afghans fired and screamed, working themselves up to a furious rush, led by ghazis in the early dawn, which withered before the steady fire of the defenders. Later, as the attack died away, a counter-attack was led out by a gap in Behmaru Heights, which swept on to the Afghan flank. That was the end of it, and huge masses of Afghans broke away, pursued by the cavalry. Muhammad Jan had shot his bolt and failed, and the cavalry rode far afield, lashing the fugitives, whose dead lay thick across the fields. Kabul and the Bala Hissar were reoccupied the same day. That evening also marched in Charles Gough's brigade, and the force at Sherpur was now fully able to shift for itself, while the line of supply from Peshawar was at last open.[1]

A Durbar was called which many chiefs attended, and an amnesty was proclaimed for all except a few of the more

[1] See the sketch map on p. 145.

implacable leaders. The force now settled down to improve its military position, while the political situation was studied and developed, and the search for an Amir continued. By March the troops had increased to 11,500, organised in two divisions, and on the 2nd May Sir Donald Stewart rode in from Kandahar, while Mr Lepel Griffin had come up from the Governor-General to act as chief political officer in making the final settlement. Sir Donald now took over the command in Northern Afghanistan, three divisions in all, leaving General Roberts in command of the original two divisions at Kabul. The presence of this large force quieted the more turbulent forces of the countryside while negotiations were in progress.

Sir Donald Stewart's March to Kabul

Sir Donald Stewart's march to Kabul, with two brigades of infantry and one of cavalry,[1] was an important one, up the historic road that no British officers had seen since Nott's last march in 1842. It was not particularly eventful till he got near Ghuzni. He was supported in a nondescript manner, and proportionately embarrassed by a horde of friendly Hazara tribesmen who were eager partisans and marched on the flanks, looting the villages whenever they could. But outside them on the western side, beyond parallel hills, also marched a large body of fanatical Afghans, chiefly Duranis from Zamindawar, waiting an opportunity to attack the column.

At Ahmed Khel, some thirty miles from Ghuzni, the hills in front were reported occupied, and the leading troops deployed for battle. Almost before the ranks were formed hordes of ghazis swarmed on both flanks and to the front, amid the exhortations of frantic mullahs and the wild beating of tom-toms, while all along the left flank of the lengthy column of route the corps formed to a flank or hurried to the front. Both the cavalry regiments, the 2nd Punjab Cavalry and the 19th Bengal Lancers, were involved

[1] See Appendix to this chapter.

in desperate charges as the ghazis surged round the flanks of the guns, while even the general commanding and his staff had to draw their swords. The 59th Foot with the 2nd Sikhs and the 3rd Gurkhas beat back the attacks, till the remaining troops coming up completed a crushing defeat, in which the Afghans lost severely, and which enabled the force to reach Ghuzni and move on unmolested toward Kabul. The Ghilzais themselves had been pretty severely handled already at Kabul, so that Sir Donald Stewart now joined Roberts to take over the chief command as already related, without further fighting.

APPENDIX

ORDER OF BATTLE OF SIR DONALD STEWART'S FORCE

Brigadier Barter	60th Rifles. 15th Sikhs. 25th Punjabs.
Brigadier Hughes	59th Foot. 2nd Sikhs (F.F.). 3rd Gurkhas.
Brigadier Palliser	A/B R.H.A. 1st Punjab Cavalry. 2nd Punjab Cavalry (F.F.). 19th Bengal Lancers.
Artillery	G/4 R.A. (Field). 6/11 R.A. (Heavy). 11/11 R.A. (Mountain).

CHAPTER XIII

THE END OF THE SECOND AFGHAN WAR

The Future of Afghanistan · The Coming of Abdurrahman · His Acceptance of the Amirship · The Evacuation of Kabul and General Roberts' March to Kandahar The Battle of Maiwand and the Investment of Kandahar The Battle of Kandahar · The Departure of the British

THE FUTURE OF AFGHANISTAN

THE search for an Amir presented many difficulties. It was a comparatively easy matter for the British to occupy Kabul, as the past had shown, but it was also known that it was quite another matter to find and install a ruler who could fill the rôle. The death of Shere Ali, the failure of Yakub Khan, and his recognition of his own unfitness had now placed the British in a quandary. The age-old British policy of a strong Afghanistan still held, but there was now the question of such a position as would enable a war to be fought against further Russian aggression.

Afghanistan was an enormous country; Kabul, Afghan Turkistan, Ghuzni, Jalalabad, would leave a fine kingdom. Kandahar, which had so often been detached from the Afghan kingdom and from the Afghan provinces at Delhi, might very well be detached again. With the student of strategy, Colonel Colley, at his elbow, Lord Lytton was of opinion that Kandahar should be made into a separate state under British protection; while the kingdom of Afghanistan should be as before, all that Dost Muhammad had bequeathed to Shere Ali, less the old Gandaric province of Kandahar.[1]

If this policy were carried out, the whole British frontier

[1] For a short time the Governor-General entertained the idea of handing Herat back to Persia.

would be put on that "scientific" basis that the strategical consideration of the frontier demanded. The arrangements of the Treaty of Gandamak would remain : the Khaibar and the Kurram within the British sphere, Pishin a portion of British Baluchistan. The coming of the railway had changed the old problems. Already was the line creeping up to the Indus at Attock, and far across the Indus in Sind, was steadily climbing the passes on to the high plateau of Khurasan, the plain of Shawal, and Quetta. Already had Lord Lytton appointed another Shere Ali—a first cousin of the Amir Shere Ali, son of Mihr Dil Khan, a younger brother of Dost Muhammad—as Wali of Kandahar, as a prince tributary to British India. The next thing to do was to find an Amir for the rest of derelict Afghanistan, and for this purpose the Governor-General's thoughts had been turned to Abdurrahman, son of the Amir Afzal Khan, who for so many years now had dwelt in exile in Russia, but whose reputation for staunchness and capacity still remained in people's mouths. The same idea, moreover, had, not unnaturally, occurred to Abdurrahman himself; while Russia also, approaching the matter from a different angle, thought that a chief so long given honourable asylum might not only help to cook the British goose, but might attain to power with the strong bias towards Russian influence that they had hoped to attain over the Amir Shere Ali.

In March 1880 the Governor-General had telegraphed to the Cabinet that it was most urgent to find an Amir, and that there was no one in Kabul or elsewhere in Afghanistan who at all filled the rôle. He advocated early recognition of Abdurrahman as the legitimate heir of Dost Muhammad. He also proposed that Kandahar should remain a separate principality under the Wali Shere Ali, supported as long as necessary by a British garrison there. To these proposals the British Conservative Government agreed. In May 1880 it was announced in Durbar by the chief political officer in Southern Afghanistan (Colonel St John) that Shere Ali should be Wali of Kandahar, should have the much prized right of coining money, and that the *Khutba* should be read in his name; and the proclamation also ran: "Under the just Government of Wali Shere Ali Khan, and under the protection of England, Kandahar will, if it please God, remain free from foreign oppression, and will rise to such a height of wealth and prosperity that will be the envy of the whole of Islam."

But the best laid plans gang aft agley, and this policy, which, as the song ran, gave "a splendid jewel in her crown, Kandahar . . ." [1] was destined to fall to pieces under the stress of events that were yet to come.

The Coming of Abdurrahman

For close on thirteen years Abdurrahman, son of Afzal, had eaten the bread of exile, a refugee to Russian hospitality, while his uncle, Shere Ali, had ruled in Afghanistan. But the dramatic death of the latter, and the eclipse of his sons, Yakub and Ayub, had brought Abdurrahman's chances uppermost on the wheel of fate. During his sojourn in Russian Turkistan he had received kindly and courteous treatment at Russian hands, after seeking from them advice in his affairs.

With the British once again at Kabul, with the Amir Yakub Khan abdicating and gone to India, with Ayub in arms, defying all and sundry, there was considerable room for another candidate in the field, a candidate who might adopt the rôle of friend of the English, or the deliverer of his country from their dominion, as circumstances should dictate. Abdurrahman, at all times an Afghan patriot, longed to be on the scene of action, and persuaded the Russian authority at Tashkent to allow him to start for the Oxus with a hundred other refugees. General Kaufman, the Governor-General, was absent in Kabul, but his deputy had an interview with Abdurrahman and gave him leave to depart.

Russia was naturally little enough pleased with a British occupation of Kabul, and was only too glad to let loose a claimant who must have absorbed considerable sympathy

[1] A parody on the music-hall song of the day, "Lah-di-dah."

and feeling towards his hosts of thirteen years. So Abdurrahman received some small gift of arms and money, and at the end of 1879 started for the Oxus.

Early in February 1880 the British in Kabul heard that he had crossed that river at Rustak and had occupied Ghori, and further, had been joined by Sultan Murad Khan of Kunduz, Chief of the Kallaghan Usbegs, an old ally of Abdurrahman in the wars of 1863–68, but who had eventually been bribed by the grant of Kunduz to come over to Shere Ali's side.

Something of a time-server, the Sultan had already written in 1879 to Sir F. Roberts to the effect that he was most cognisant of all the British had done for India, and that he too was now a servant of the British Government.

He was also the first adherent of Abdurrahman, who, no doubt, was letting it be known that he was the champion of the Afghans against the British. Such conduct would in any case be but the natural Oriental outlook on what was a very complicated position.

Abdurrahman was soon to be gratified by a cordial response to his inroad. His father's control of Afghan Turkistan, and the son's early reputation, both preinduced support. There was no Amir, and if a real Amir was to be forthcoming, here might be one of the stock of the Dost ready to hand. The Chiefs of Turkistan almost all rallied to his support. His appearance also was a godsend in disguise to the British, and gave some prospect of establishing a stable Government. Mr Lepel Griffin, the chief political officer now attached to Sir Frederick Roberts, wrote to him on 1st April, by the hand of a confidential messenger, who was charged with communicating more than the written message.

That message in itself was but the prelude to a wrestle of diplomacy. "It has become known that you have entered Afghanistan, and consequently this letter is sent you by a confidential messenger in order that you may submit, to the British officers at Kabul, any representations that you may desire to make to the British Government with regard to your object in entering Afghanistan."

The messenger was charged with intimating that Abdurrahman's long intimacy with Russia did not influence the British, who wished him well, and that it was to his own interests to enter into friendly correspondence.

Abdurrahman consulted with the Afghan chiefs who had joined him, who all wished to send a blood-and-thunder answer. But the wiser leader asked what good could come of that at this stage, and showed how wise it would be to hear more. He accordingly wrote, in a cordial and statesmanlike manner, acknowledging the letter written in a spirit of justice and friendship, spoke of the disgrace brought on Afghanistan by the perverse folly of the Amir Yakub Khan and his evil advisers, of the need for Afghanistan to dwell in ease and tranquillity between the great empires. He ended by suggesting that Russia and England between them should guarantee Afghanistan's integrity.

The messenger also brought an account of his cordial reception, and a verbal message from Abdurrahman to the effect that for twelve years he had eaten the Russian's salt, and he would be loth to accept conditions that would appear ungrateful. He wished to be friendly with both Powers, but especially with the English, who would, he hoped, secure him independence. He would gladly come up to Charikar with 500 horse to discuss matters.

From this reply Sir Frederick Roberts and Sir Lepel Griffin [1] inferred that he was willing to come to Kabul. Lord Lytton had already made up his mind that Abdurrahman was the only candidate for the throne that could fill the bill, viz. control and develop a strong and friendly Afghanistan.

His Acceptance of the Amirship

Abdurrahman appeared to have a shrewd idea of the difficulty in which the British were placed in Afghanistan. In colloquial language, they were looking for someone to whom they could "hand the baby." He was in no hurry to offer to take it. It was also probably patent to him that

[1] He had now been made a K.C.I.E.

with so much hatred of the stranger in men's minds, it would not serve his cause to display undue alacrity. Further, every Afghan is by instinct an acute bargainer, and by hanging back he might get more—that more being the whole kingdom as ruled by Dost Muhammad.

Also, a change of Government had taken place in Great Britain, and Mr Gladstone's Government had come into power. In those days most Eastern potentates flattered themselves that they knew the length of the Liberal foot. He would dally, and dally he did. He probably knew that the Liberal Government wished to clear out of Afghanistan as soon as possible.

The summer was coming on, and Sir Lepel Griffin on 30th April wrote urging Abdurrahman to come to Kabul. On 16th May, after Sir Donald Stewart had taken over command, he replied in friendly and general terms. What conditions, he asked, do the British make, so that I may consult my chiefs before I come? Will Kandahar be included in my kingdom? What responsibilities shall I have?

The amirship seemed to be hanging fire, and it now began to be felt that General Roberts had been premature in removing Yakub Khan. But with a Liberal Government in power had come also a new viceroy, Lord Ripon. The Home Government had suggested that the retention of Kandahar by the British might not be necessary. On 14th June Sir Lepel Griffin wrote to Abdurrahman the reply to his query, that since Russia and Persia had disclaimed any intention of interfering with Afghan affairs, Afghanistan must have no relation with foreign powers except through the British; that all Kandahar would be placed under a separate ruler, except Sibi and Pishin, which would be retained in British possession; that the provisions of the Treaty of Gandamak, as regards the rest of the frontier, would remain; and that a British Moslem agent would be stationed at Kabul. Herat, could he expel Ayub Khan, was to be his. The promises made to Shere Ali in 1873 of support in case of unprovoked aggression were renewed.

To this communication Abdurrahman gave a general reply, making no mention of Kandahar, and the feeling was strong in the minds of Generals Stewart and Roberts and their advisers that Abdurrahman was playing false. General MacGregor in his diary repeatedly reiterated this view. The Afghans in Kabul said that he would never take the amirship at British hands, and would not come to Kabul while the British were there. He was no doubt a little uncertain of our good faith, but on 20th July 1880 arrived at Charikar in the Kohistan, north of Kabul. General Roberts immediately summoned a Durbar of Kabul notables, and in the presence of his representatives proclaimed Abdurrahman Amir of Kabul.

Then, as if to complicate matters and lessen our prestige, came the untoward news of a disaster to British arms in Southern Afghanistan. A British force of some size, under General Burrows, had been practically annihilated at Maiwand at the end of July. As the news came, Sir Lepel Griffin was starting out to meet the Amir at Zimma, sixteen miles north of Kabul. It was now more than ever important to settle matters, as Sir Frederick Roberts was to depart for Kandahar with a body of picked troops. The Amir and the British commissioner met on 30th July at a striking conference or Durbar, in a wild and picturesque setting. The Amir especially asked for some formal undertaking in writing, and this was vouchsafed him in the following terms, and he appeared satisfied:

"After compliments, His Excellency the Governor-General-in-Council has learnt with pleasure that your Highness has proceeded towards Kabul in accordance with the invitation of the British Government. Therefore, in consideration of the friendly sentiments by which your Highness is animated, and of the advantages to be derived by the sirdars and people from the establishment of a settled Government under your Highness's authority, the British Government recognises your Highness as Amir of Kabul. I am further empowered to inform your Highness that the British Government has no desire to interfere in the internal government of the territories in possession of your Highness, and has no wish that an English resident should be stationed anywhere within those territories. For the convenience of ordinary friendly intercourse, such as is maintained between two adjoining states, it may be advisable that a Mohammedan agent of the British Government should reside by agreement at Kabul. Your Highness has requested that the views and intentions of the British Government with regard to the position of the Ruler of Kabul in relation to Foreign Powers should be placed on record for your Highness's information. The Viceroy and Governor-General-in-Council authorise me to declare to you, that since the British Government admits no right of interference by Foreign Powers within Afghanistan, and since both Persia and Russia are pleased to abstain from all interference with the affairs of Afghanistan, it is plain that your Highness can have no relation with any Foreign Power except the British Government. If any Foreign Power should attempt to interfere in Afghanistan, and if such interference should lead to unprovoked aggression on the dominion of your Highness, in that event the British Government would be prepared to aid you to such extent and in such manner as may appear to the British Government necessary in repelling it, provided that your Highness follows unreservedly the advice of the British Government in regard to your external relations."

The foregoing may be said to be the charter and rehearsal of the policy which was to guide the two countries for the next forty years, and it also enabled the British to evacuate the country with a clear conscience and a feeling that their policy of a strong and prosperous Afghanistan was in a fair way to be attained.

The Evacuation of Kabul and General Roberts' March to Kandahar

Apart from the general desire of Mr Gladstone's Government to close the book of Afghanistan as speedily as might be, the situation in Southern Afghanistan that had ensued after the defeat of General Burrows at Maiwand was serious, and called for reinforcement and relief.

General Primrose, commanding in Kandahar, was now invested in that city by Ayub Khan, reinforced by the fierce Durani tribesmen of Zamindawar and the country around. With him, his province in uproar, was the Wali Shere Ali, no more popular or influential than the British themselves.

Sir Frederick Roberts was to lead his picked force—a force without wheels, equipped for rapid movement—on Kandahar via Ghuzni and Kelat-i-Ghilzie; while General Sir Donald Stewart was to bring the rest of the force down from Kabul to the Khaibar, rolling up as he came the line of communication. Within a week of the durbar at which Sir Lepel Griffin had met the Amir, General Roberts had started on his march, and a few days later, on 10th August, Sir Donald Stewart evacuated Kabul. Just before the start Abdurrahman came into the British lines at Sherpur to say farewell, after despatching a high official of his own with Roberts' column to assist in obtaining supplies, and generally to endeavour to prevent the Ghilzais and other tribes from impeding the British. Indeed, in Abdurrahman's eyes the British were now fighting the former's own battle, since Ayub was as much in arms against Abdurrahman as against ourselves.

The disappearance of General Roberts and his light-moving column appealed immensely to the dramatic sense of the British public. Without a line of communication the force disappeared, as it were, into "the blue," and for some days was out of the public ken. In these days of wireless how different would the position have been! In 1880 the force passed from view, marching through a hostile country, to meet a victorious Afghan Army at the other end. As a matter of hard fact, it was by no means the most adventurous of undertakings, for General Stewart himself had just led a force from Kandahar to Kabul, and had administered a severe defeat to the tribes, marching in April 1880 by a road untraversed since General Nott had led his army by the same way thirty-eight years before.

Further, Sir Donald Stewart had allowed General Roberts to take with him the pick of the Kabul force.[1] As a military feat, General Roberts' advance from Kurram to Kabul in the autumn of 1879, with a far smaller force and inadequate transport, over the Shutur Gardan Pass to face a Kabul seething with excitement after the murder of Cavagnari and his escort, has always been awarded the palm.[2]

The two marches were uneventful enough, Sir Donald Stewart reaching Jamrud in peace by October, leaving for some months a garrison at Landi Kotal, and Sir Frederick Roberts Kandahar by 30th September, picking up *en route* the garrison of Kelat-i-Ghilzie, but finding Ayub Khan and his army waiting to receive him close to Kandahar.

Before recounting the defeat of the latter, it is necessary to hark back to that day in July in Southern Afghanistan which had been the cause of all the pother.

The Battle of Maiwand and the Investment of Kandahar

Of all the many fights between Briton and Afghan, the battle of Maiwand stands out as the one British defeat, the one battle lost in open fight, the one real blot on the scutcheon of military fame. Disasters there had been, as that to the frost-bitten Kabul force of aged Elphinstone; contemptible little incidents, such as the failure of the 2nd Light Cavalry at Parwandarra, or England at Haikalzai, and the wave of defeatism which suddenly came on forces for no fair reason; but nine times out of ten all collisions were victorious, and the élan of the soldiery, European or Indian,[3] was greater than the élan of the Afghan. But at Maiwand a force was defeated in the open, a large force, by bad staff work, bad weather, and bad soldiering—bad soldiering, too, on the part of some of the weary soldiery.

[1] If the truth be told, there was not much competition to share the honour.

[2] See p. 182.

[3] The idea that the Bengal Sepoy of 1841 was inferior is not borne out by facts. Well led even in shako and cross-belts he could tackle the Afghan.

And it came about in this wise. Incidentally, it very nearly upset the British apple-cart at the critical time when sufficient prestige was needed to induce Abdurrahman to accept the amirship on our terms and not his.

Ayub Khan, the exiled brother of Yakub and second son of the Shere Ali, had appeared at Herat from exile in Persia and been welcomed there as an anti-British leader. Before long he had brought an army down to Kandahar to fight the British and the new Wali Shere Ali. The Wali had troops at Girishk, seventy miles out from Kandahar on the Herat road, and reported that Ayub was advancing towards him, and asked for British support. In Kandahar it was known that the Wali's troops were none too staunch, and to support him a force under Brigadier G. R. S. Burrows was despatched, consisting of one British and two Indian infantry battalions, and part of Brigadier Nuttal's cavalry brigade, *i.e.* a battery of horse artillery and a portion of two Indian cavalry regiments.

The total strength of the force was 2600 fighting men, consisting of—

The 66th Foot.	E/B R.H.A.
1st Bombay Grenadiers.	The Sind Horse.
Jacob's Rifles.	3rd Bombay Light Cavalry.

By 11th July Burrows had reached the left bank of the Helmand and joined the Wali. Two days later the Wali's infantry, 2000 strong, mutinied and went off, taking with them a smooth-bore field battery. His cavalry behaved rather better, but his force was no longer in being. The mutineers, however, were severely handled by Burrows, the guns were recovered and manned by infantry detachments, superintended by a few gunners from the horse artillery.

Ayub's force was reported to number 4000 regular horse, 4000 to 5000 regular infantry, besides the Wali's troops, and some thirty guns, many of them rifled, and a large body of irregulars.

In view of the changed situation and the defection of the Wali's force, Burrows fell back to Kushk-i-Nakhud, forty-five miles from Kandahar, where several roads from the

Helmand fords converged. There he remained in observation from 16th to the 27th July. It should be realised that General Stewart's march to Kabul had left but a comparatively small force at Kandahar—two infantry and one cavalry brigades.

Before long it appeared that Ayub was trying to get between Burrows and Kandahar, and was moving on Maiwand, a village whence the latter got much of his supplies.

Somewhat tardily Burrows moved to Maiwand early on the 27th, but too late in the day for a summer march with a fight in prospect.[1] Four miles from Maiwand the force practically ran unexpectedly, in the heat-haze, into Ayub's force, marching on the same objective. Two guns of E/B under Lieutenant Maclaine precipitated events. Burrows hurried up his infantry brigade, who formed front on ground of little tactical value, and after some time the closer action was commenced by an attack of ghazis. The enemy's guns, contrary to expectation, were well up, and the British line was subjected to considerable pounding, in which twelve inferior British guns, 6–9 pr. R.M.L. gun of 6 cwt. (a feeble weapon), and six of the Wali's smoothbore guns manned by infantrymen, were opposed to thirty Afghan ones, many being of superior calibre.

The day grew hotter as high noon passed, water was very scarce, and the cavalry had suffered severely from the pounding, when ghazis in large numbers attacked the 66th on the right and two companies of Jacob's Rifles on the left. The latter broke after a feeble resistance, crowding in on the Grenadiers and the rest of Jacob's Rifles. These two corps, heavily assailed, broke badly and became as sheep to the slaughter. The Bombay Cavalry regiments failed to charge home as ordered, and all became despair. The 66th, formed in squares, eventually fell back sullenly, making a magnificent last stand at Khig, where Colonel Galbraith and many others fell. Then it became a rout, the retiring guns of E/B, supported by a small party of the 3rd Bombay Cavalry, being the last point to which stragglers

[1] Orders to march were issued late, and the troops were half the night packing up their kit, which was that of a standing camp.

could reach and survive. The Afghans pursued for four miles, the remnant finding the various villages and gardens on their route full of ghazis. The survivors struggled onwards to Kandahar, without discipline and almost without

THE DEFEAT OF BURROWS' BRIGADE AT MAIWAND, 27TH JULY 1880

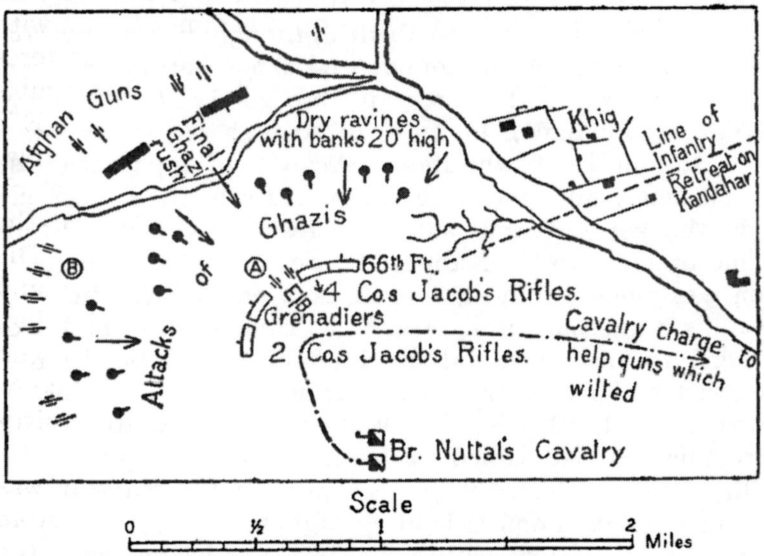

Ⓐ 6 Guns of E|B. The advanced pair (Maclaine's) were captured. The 6 smooth bores with ammunition exhausted had been withdrawn earlier.
Ⓑ Afghan Armstrong guns.

hope, supported only by the resolution of the Royal Horse Artillery[1] and Lieutenant Geoghegan's party of Bombay Cavalry. Tortured for the most part by an enduring thirst, the straggling column, some six miles in length, crossing a waterless desert of sixteen miles in extent, reached Hauz-i-Madat at midnight, where water was found. It was not till midday on the 28th that the exhausted remnants of the force staggered into Kandahar, spreading alarm and

[1] Major Blackwood commanding had fallen, and Captain Slade commanding the smooth bores had rejoined.

consternation. Out of 2476 fighting men engaged, 964 were killed with 331 followers and 231 horses; 167 wounded combatants were got in.

The remnants of the brigade and the garrison in Kandahar did not now number much more than 4300 men. The Afghan cavalry reached the cantonments on the 29th, which had been abandoned on the evening of the 28th when the whole force moved within the walls of Kandahar, from which it was necessary to expel the inhabitants. The city was invested forthwith, though it was not till 8th August that Ayub commenced a bombardment. Nor was the spirit of the force any too good. The Bombay Army, which had held its head so high for many years after the mutiny of the Bengal Army, had apparently lost its efficiency and soldiering tradition for a while. On one side the gardens and walled enclosures of Deh Khojah came up close to the Kabul gate, and from here the garrison was much annoyed, as well as from the attentions of Ayub's numerous guns. General Primrose, who had succeeded to the command in Kandahar when Sir Donald Stewart had marched northward, now decided to make a sortie against Deh Khojah. Eight hundred infantry led by Brigadier Brooke sallied forth on the 16th August. The village was reached, but no headway could be made among the massive mud houses held by Afghans, and the force was compelled to retreat within the city after losing 106 killed and 107 wounded. After that, General Primrose was feign to sit down and wait for assistance that was coming to him from two directions: that from the direction of Quetta by a force of Bombay troops under General Phayre, much hampered by want of transport, and the more hopeful advance of the admirably equipped force which General Roberts was leading down from Kabul itself.

The Battle of Kandahar

As has been related, General Roberts and his splendid force left Kabul on 8th August—10,000 fighting men, and not a wheel in the whole column, its transport consisting of between 8000 and 9000 mules, ponies, and donkeys. By 28th August the General had reached Robat, 303 miles from Kabul and 17 miles from Kandahar, after marching for twenty days, with only one day's halt at Kelat-i-Ghilzie, whence the garrison from the Kandahar force was withdrawn *en passant*. No hostilities had been met with, for Sir Donald Stewart had given the Ghilzais as much as they wanted, and the agent of Abdurrahman with the force had smoothed its way as far as possible.

At Robat General Roberts learnt that Ayub had taken up a position close to Kandahar on the road to Herat, and that transport difficulties would prevent General Phayre's force from marching in for several days yet. So he decided that with General Primrose's force he would attack the Afghans as soon as possible.

On the morning of the 31st the Kabul column reached Kandahar, and found the enemy entrenched on the foot-hills in front of the Baba-wali Kotal and Pass by the village of the "Forty Daughters."

The Afghans appeared full of fight, and General Roberts decided to attack early next morning (1st September).

The battle was simple enough, the defenders being driven from their hills, with the loss of all their guns and camp equipage and about 1000 men killed, though the prepared pursuit by the cavalry did not come off, so seldom do enemies escape by the line expected.

It was a dashing though easy victory, and a fitting enough ending to our last war in Afghanistan. General Roberts' loss was astonishingly slight, and British prestige was fully restored.

One tragedy dimmed the glory, for Lieutenant Maclaine, R.H.A., who had been taken prisoner during the retreat from Maiwand, was found outside Ayub's tents, his throat cut by his rascally guards.

The Departure of the British

Thus ended in victory and efficiency the Second Afghan War. On 9th September General Roberts led part of his division off to India, followed by the Bombay troops, while a force under General Hume remained in Kandahar itself in support of the Wali Shere Ali for the best part of a year more, when it was decided to offer Kandahar also to Abdurrahman, as will be related in the next chapter.

Kandahar had been in continuous British occupation since the autumn of 1878, and was now to continue so till August 1881—for nearly the same length of time as in the first war, which endured from the spring of 1839 till that of 1842.

Of the final results of the campaign, and all it stood for, more will be said hereafter, but it may be urged here that, in light of the knowledge we now have, the results of our policy of 1880 gave us thirty-nine years of a strong and friendly Afghanistan, and brought us through the World War without any untoward incident, roll the drum ecclesiastic of Islam never so loudly.

CHAPTER XIV

THE AMIR ABDURRAHMAN

The New Amir · The British hand back Kandahar · Master in his Own House · The Panjdeh Incident · The Ghilzai and Other Rebellions · Yaghistan and Passes of the Hindu Kush · The Roof of the World

THE NEW AMIR

THE chain of events which had brought the exiled Abdurrahman to his grandfather's throne after his years of exile is a remarkable one—romantic in its occurrence and most fortunate in its results. To have been put on the throne with the acquiescence of the more influential of his countrymen, and to have at his back British goodwill and the British purse, was as good a start in its way as Ahmad Shah Durani had received. From this return dates the real existence of Afghanistan as a homogeneous kingdom, and as a realm bordering on the modern conception of such. Since the first Durani had passed away in 1773 Afghanistan had gone from bad to worse, and, as has been related, had been the scenes of struggles, murders, blindings, fratricides, and every horror that man unto man can do. Even under Dost Muhammad peace and permanence were, at best, but chastened phrases.

Writing from Kandahar in 1858 of Dost Muhammad, then staunch in his regard for the British, Lumsden wrote of him and his people thus: "A despotic tyrant . . . but a master-spirit over such a barbarous, superstitious, and discontented race as the Afghans have shown themselves to be." And Lumsden knew them intimately and had a great regard for many of them. The Persian proverb has already been quoted: "*Afghan! Afghan! Be iman! Be iman!*" "Fie! Fie! Faithless Afghan!" It was now the master-spirit of the Dost's grandson who was to try his hand in taming this mixture of peoples and make them into a nation. And wisdom was coming also to the British. Shere Ali had said : "The friendship of the British is a word written on ice." The cold aloofness of the scalded child which had animated British policy in the days of John Lawrence had now changed, and we were prepared to see that the Amir we had put on the throne should have adequate support in staying there.

But it was a rough road that His Highness had to travel, and one which perhaps only he could have safely wended. We had given him Kabul, Ghuzni, Jalalabad—the old Western Afghanistan—Balkh he had secured himself, and we had told him he was welcome to get control of Herat, and this he now proceeded to do, while we hedged on Kandahar. Fortunately he had money and arms. It has been stated that one way and another, including refunds on account of Afghan revenues we had collected during the occupation, we paid him in the first two years some thirty-six lakhs of rupees, and that is a sum with which a good deal could be done in Afghanistan.

The story of His Highness's reign, a story which lies within the memory of many of our older soldiers and statesmen and frontier officers, is a most interesting story of consolidation, of the settling of the difficult questions of Russian frontiers and Russian views, and also the delicate matters of cleaning up the fringes of our frontiers between Afghanistan and the meeting-points of Afghanistan, Russia, and China. All along these borders, especially in the more inaccessible hills, lay many small states and khanates, whose orientation towards one powerful neighbour or the other had never been settled, and up to now had hardly called for settlement. The squaring up of these matters, now needed in a modern world of travel and commerce, called for much diplomacy, and involved us in many little campaigns of interest and romance which will be touched on. Further, the time had also come when it was necessary, in the interest of civilisation, that some dividing line should be agreed on in which India and Afghanistan should admit responsibility towards those tribesmen in the Sulaiman mountains, the Rohillas of Ruh, who had always been within the Mogul and Durani Empires, but had never kissed the hem of any skirt could they avoid it, and had lived at ease for thousands of years on the tolls of passing caravans.

THE BRITISH HAND BACK KANDAHAR

As soon as the British had left Kabul the new Amir commenced to gather up the threads of government. His long sojourn in the comparative efficiency of Russian Turkistan had produced in his mind some very definite ideas of the administrative system needed. Ayub Khan, defeated by Sir Frederick Roberts, was still a power in being, aiming at a kingdom of Herat for himself such as Kamran, nephew of Shah Shujah, ruled in 1838–42.

Abdurrahman's first act, after the manner, and probably the wise and prudent manner, of his race, was to round up and hunt down all partisans of Shere Ali who were at all likely to oppose him. Across the Hindu Kush his cousin, Ishaq Khan, governed Balkh in his name. Farther north, Badakhshan and Wakhan were held in his interests; but the Ghilzais near Kabul were restless and hostile, and the new throne was far from a bed of roses. The British had left thirty of Shere Ali's rifled guns at Kabul, had handed the Amir, perhaps the most important factor of all in Afghanistan, several lakhs of rupees as aforesaid, and promised more.

The policy in the matter of Kandahar was to be reviewed in London, for a Liberal Government pledged to retrenchment was not likely to look with favour on our occupation of that province, whether as a possession or in support of a subsidised Wali. The defeat at Maiwand had left the Wali without an amirate, and had shown how low was his prestige. Nor, indeed, had he evinced capacity or a desire for a principality, and gladly enough accepted the British offer of a home and a pension in India, when orders were issued to the Governor-General to hand the province to Abdurrahman. Public opinion in Great Britain was strongly in favour of its retention, while military opinion in India held that Afghanistan and India could not be defended against Russia unless we had Kandahar as a position in a district full of supplies, from which we could base our forward operations. Sir Garnet Wolseley, however, took the view that we should secure no military advantage by holding Kandahar, while we should incur considerable risk of renewed war by remaining there. He said: "Whenever the Russians march up on Herat we must certainly occupy Kandahar, unless we intend to give up India or allow it to be taken from us; but the longer we postpone the occupation, the better we shall be able to incur the vast expenditure it will necessarily entail upon us, as we can always get there with the greatest ease. I would deprecate, in the strongest terms, our going therein until the necessity for doing so actually arises, and I am therefore of opinion that the sooner the troops now there can be withdrawn from it with safety and honour, the better it will be for the true interests of our Indian Empire."

This clinched the view of Mr Gladstone's Government, amid a chorus of contumely in the British press and music-halls; yet, viewed by the light of subsequent experience, there can be no question as to the correctness of Lord Wolseley's considered opinion. The carrying of our broad gauge railway from Quetta and Pishin by tunnel through the Khojak range has removed any obstacle to the covering of the seventy odd open miles intervening between our own railhead and Kandahar in the shortest time when necessary.

The province of Kandahar, which in the past had alternated between Delhi and Persia, as has been related, but which since 1747 had been part of the Afghan kingdom, was now offered to Abdurrahman. That astute prince, who had so cleverly avoided acquiescing in stated terms in our severance of this province from his kingdom, now feigned to hold back, pleading want of arms, ammunition, and transport to meet so great an addition to his liabilities. But at last the rendition was accepted, and on 15th April 1881, under a salute of thirty-one guns, the British flag was hauled down and, accompanied by the Wali Shere Ali, the British force marched away to the east of the Khojak.

Master in his Own House

But Abdurrahman was not destined to complete his kingdom too easily. Ayub Khan, *pro tem.* independent prince of Herat, aimed at adding Kandahar to his dominion, and in June 1881 appeared in that province and defeated the Amir's Governor not far from Girishk, occupying the city of Kandahar at the end of July. Abdurrahman, although still but loosely seated in the saddle at Kandahar, was statesman enough to realise that the prestige would not survive such flaunting, and despite the hostility of the Ghilzais and the people of the Kabul Kohistan, led such troops as he could muster southward along the road that General Roberts had traversed the year before. Some of the Ayub's troops rallied to the Amir's side, no doubt for due consideration, and the former was then defeated at Kandahar on the 22nd September 1881. While advancing on Kandahar the Amir, realising that Herat must be weak, directed Ishaq Khan to send a force from Balkh under Abdul Quddus [1] to seize Ayub's capital. This was taken easily enough even before Ayub was beaten at Kandahar. The latter, beaten in the field and bereft of his capital, took refuge in Persia. This victory now left the Amir master of all Afghanistan, except the small Usbeg state of Maimana held on behalf of Ayub. But the Amir could afford to let this wait, while consolidating his power and modelling his administrative system, and it was not till 1884 that Ishaq Khan, after much urging, sent his force to capture the town and bring its chief in chains to Kabul.

During these years, and indeed the first ten years of his reign, Abdurrahman was making his name a holy terror to all who dared lift a voice against him. His kingship was clearly enough shown to all and sundry as he entered Kandahar after his victory over Ayub. A mullah had reviled him as *kafir*, an unbeliever and an associate with unbelievers, and, to escape the Amir's wrath, had taken

[1] Said to be the grandson of Akbar Khan, son of the Dost, and to have a negro mother.

shelter in a shrine where a relic, a robe of the Prophet, was held in high veneration. The Amir tells the story in his own autobiography. He had him hauled forth, and then "I slew him myself that such an impious dog might not pollute the world." The impiety of calling your ruler an unbeliever and a dog was thus expiated; but it is only strong and ruthless men who will thus ride the storm. And so he pursued his way, purging the administration to the end that rough justice should prevail, and that the King's revenues should find their way to the King's coffers. And woe betide any who said the Amir nay. The knife and the rope, the cannon's mouth and the poison bowl, between them rid the land of all who, in Abdurrahman's opinion, were inimical to the interests of Afghanistan as personified in himself. And it cannot be said that the British were always proud of their new friend. But a friend he remained for his own sake and theirs, and British wisdom and foresight in Afghan matters were for the first time justified.

But of that iron rule many stories remain, and they have been inimitably told in the verses of Sir Alfred Lyall, who knew the Afghan, and had been Foreign Secretary, and equally in the songs of Mr Kipling in the "Ballad of the King's Mercy" and the "Ballad of the King's Jest."

" Before the old Peshawur Gate, where Kurd and Kaffir meet,
The Governor of Kabul dealt the Justice of the Street,
And that was strait as running noose and swift as plunging knife,
Tho' he who held the longer purse might hold the longer life."

The King's Mercy.

THE PANJDEH INCIDENT

In 1885 there happened the first serious clash with Russia, which gave the start to great military expenditure in India. Under the Treaty of Gandamak and the agreement with the new Amir, it will be remembered that we had insisted that foreign relations between Afghanistan and the outer world should be conducted by ourselves. It was that which had made the presence of a British mission at Kabul seem imperative, so that there could be someone on the spot to deal in the first instance with local Russian communica-

The Bala Hissar

The ruins of the historic fortress which frowned down on the city of Kabul

tions. Indeed, without such, the position of Afghanistan as envisaged by ourselves had something incongruous, if not ridiculous, therein. The understandings of the early seventies with Russia had passed in Shere Ali's last years, and now a game of catch-as-catch-can was in progress. There was much unsettled borderland at various ends of Afghanistan, as has been described. The first trouble came over the question of Shignan and Roshan. Up to now the Amir's activities had been concerned in gaining control over those lands which were undoubtedly within the patrimony of Dost Muhammad. Shignan and Roshan, however, were two small hill khanates high up on the Oxus and close to the Pamirs. They had hitherto been allowed to live for generations in inaccessible independence, and, like many of the chiefs of these mountain pockets, claimed descent from Alexander of the Two Horns and his Macedonian colonists. Russia claimed that the Mir of Shignan was a vassal of the Khan of Khoqand.

The convention between Russia and England that made the Oxus the limit of the Afghan territory cut across Shignan. The Mir of Shignan had invited a Russian visitor, and the Amir, incensed thereat, took a strong line—sent a governor of his own and brought the Mir to Kabul. The Afghan claims were that these states were part of Badakhshan. Eventually the Amir was allowed to have his way on all territory on the hitherside of the Oxus or Ab-i-Panja, as it is here known. And hard though the conditions may have been to the Mir, the coming of the Afghans was a great boon to civilisation, for the former had but traded his people and his beautiful maids as slaves and was worthy of no real consideration, so that a great amelioration of conditions followed.

But the Amir did not confine his attention to the statelets on the Oxus. There was much uncertain area held by small chiefs of nebulous allegiance up the valley of the Kunar River and stretching up to Chitral and Bajaur. The Amir, knowing that ere long Great Britain was bound to put responsibilities on a firmer basis, was now making such occupations as he could to strengthen Afghan claims, of which more must be told later on. Before these problems became acute a far more serious matter arose.

As we come down the Oxus it is obvious that the river trending away to the north must cease to be the boundary of Afghanistan, and that some land-line from a point on the river to the Persian frontier must be recognised. However much the Government of St Petersburg might be anxious to avoid trouble with Great Britain and the Amir, the somewhat lightly controlled Russian frontier officers were not unnaturally out to do the best they could for their own country in debatable lands. It is a trait with which British frontier officers can sympathise and can understand. So long as the Merv Turkomans were independent, the frontiers were merged in grazing grounds, which perhaps did not need too sharp a definition. But early in 1884 Russia had decided to accept the offer of the roaming tribes to become a Russian people. The question of the frontier of Afghanistan at this part then became important. A joint Russo-Afghan-British boundary commission was created, on which General Sir Peter Lumsden was appointed the British Commissioner and General Zelenoi the Russian. But neither British nor Afghans were waiting for the arrival and decisions of the commission. *Mulk-giri*, the seizing of lands, was in progress. Various rival claims were put forward. The Afghans were in occupation of Panjdeh, and the neighbouring Russian and Afghan commanders were engaged in vituperation. The Amir talked of sending a big force,[1] and did not believe that an amicable settlement, such as Great Britain naturally wished for, could be reached.

General Lumsden arrived at Sarakhs at the end of November 1884 and visited Panjdeh. He told the Afghan General very straightly that there was, in his opinion, little chance of the Russians sending troops to any place where they had been prohibited, that, therefore, more Afghan troops were not required at Panjdeh, and that in any case he was at hand, to whom all disputes could be referred. But in early 1885 tension was very great. Earl Granville

[1] Which he had not got.

actually wrote to Lumsden that, though the Russians were at Zulfiqar Pass, Aq Robat, and Qizil Tepe, and could not well be attacked there, pending negotiations, he thought that any further advance, subject to military considerations, should be resisted by the Afghan troops. He was firmly of opinion that Panjdeh itself did belong to the Afghans, as well as the whole district of Badghis.

In the meantime, Russian and Afghan troops scowled at each other across very short distances, and the situation grew more and more tense. The actual Afghan troops at and near Panjdeh were about nine hundred horse, two battalions, a few hundred matchlock men, and eight light guns; but the whole equipment was miserable and archaic.

Their tactical positions were weak, and they had, without authority, crossed to the debatable left bank of the Kushk River. The Russian Commander-General, Komarov, ordered a withdrawal, sending an ultimatum, which the Afghan General, Shams-ud-din, refused to obey. The Russians then attacked the Afghans, whose ignorance and arrogance had brought about the collision, and the Cossacks inflicted heavy losses on the miserably armed Afghans. Around this incident at the time there arose an immense mass of invective and controversy long ago out of date. With the Afghans was an officer of the Lumsden mission, who very probably felt that he must not be involved in a collision. He removed himself very hastily, and incurred the undeserved derision of the unthinking part of the Indian Army and of the Afghans, and many good stories of the time abounded in the British frontier cantonments, which were all agog.

The collision was in every way unfortunate. But it stirred British public opinion and complicated the process of diplomacy. Great Britain considered that the Russians had gone beyond the limit of decent behaviour in attacking when a boundary commission was on the spot, and mobilised the field army of India. Whether or not this act did produce the disposition to climb down, which Russians evinced, is a matter of opinion, but it may well be remembered that those were the days when British

Imperial policy was a matter of party politics. Mr Gladstone's Government repudiated much of the foreign policy of their predecessors, and when a Liberal Government was in power, our more aggressive neighbours usually thought the British lion's tail could be twisted. When it came to bed-rock the tail usually proved untwistable. But the result of this would be that the overdue stiffening of the British attitude produced the paradox that it was the peace-loving Liberal politicians who usually found themselves involved in wars, which their previous policy had made it harder to wage satisfactorily.

During the Second Afghan War the necessary railways on to the edge of the Central Asian plateau at Quetta, where our troops now were, had been discontinued. The mobilisation of the field army ordered in 1885, to the command of which Sir Frederick Roberts was appointed, was grievously hampered by want of this railway, and the troops flocking up the passes to the frontier on the road to Kandahar suffered severe outbreaks of cholera and the like from the conditions on the communications.

But it was evident to Russia that Albion meant business, with the result that eventually the boundary was delimited with the consent of all concerned.

Fortunately, the Amir Abdurrahman was in India at the time of the Panjdeh incident, on a visit to a gathering of brilliance presided over by the Governor-General, Lord Dufferin, and the whole circumstances could be discussed and explained under conditions of amity not otherwise possible.

The Ghilzai and Other Rebellions

The completion of the labours of the boundary commission in 1887 did not inaugurate that rule free from alarms and excursions which the British at any rate had hoped for. Fear of an immediate war with Russia was happily over, but the internal forces of disruption, so long a curse to the progress of the country, were fermenting below the surface.

In 1886 the Amir had to face a serious rising of the Ghilzai tribes, and it served to bring home to the British Government, and no doubt to the Amir, that the Ghilzais are the most important section in the countryside. It is as true now as it was in 1841 and in 1887. For reasons many and various, possibly injured vanity of chiefs, possibly the inherent fissiparous tendency, possibly undue zeal on the part of the revenue commissioners, and partly because the Amir had curtailed the pensions of the son of the old mullah, Mushk-i-alam, "The Fragrance of the World," he who had led the great rising against Sir Frederick Roberts, and no doubt for a dozen other causes, the Ghilzais, and especially the Hotak Ghilzais, rose in rebellion, and a very serious rebellion it was. So much so, that the Amir gave out that the British had collected seventy-two battalions to come to his assistance. Once again the inherency of the British paramountcy was recognised by a petition from the Ghilzais to Queen Victoria, sent to Sir Oliver St John, praying her to come to their aid without delay if ever she intended to come to "benefit and cherish the distressed people of Afghanistan." It was some time before the Amir could collect sufficient troops to deal with the situation, and ere long 30,000 Ghilzais were said to be in arms. The tribesmen won several victories, and Shah Khan, of the Hotak clans, proclaimed himself Amir. He was a descendant of that Mir Wais who established the Ghilzai dynasty in Persia, as has been already told. General Ghulam Haidar Orakzai and his father, Sikandar, were in charge of the principal operations, but it was not till August 1887, after varying fortunes and mutinies of sympathising troops, that the Amir's forces were victorious. The scantiest mercy was shown to captured leaders. The Amir was determined to have no more rebellions if he could avoid them. The rebel mullah fled to British territory, and vengeance was wreaked on the grave of his father, the old Mushk-i-alam, whose body was exhumed and the grave ploughed with asses. Timur Shah, an army officer who had joined the rebels, was stoned to death in Kabul, the rebel mullah's brother was tortured to death, and so forth.

By mutual agreement Ishaq Khan had been allowed to take up the governorship of Balkh, so long held by Abdurrahman's own father. It from time immemorial had been a province with a considerable amount of independency, and this the Amir had allowed in some sort to continue, but had annoyed Ishaq Khan by taking away from his control the smaller provinces of Maimana and Badakhshan. Ishaq Khan was a mullah rather than a soldier, though his mother was an Armenian Christian, and both he and his son lived austere lives of religious observances. He had, for this reason, considerable reputation with the devout and the old-fashioned Moslem party. Abdurrahman, however, was not the man to endure a would-be semi-king in his country, and as soon as he felt strong enough, sent for the Khan to give an account of his province. The latter did not obey, but sent a subordinate in his stead, whose head the incensed Amir cut off. This was a fair signal that the end was at hand, so that in self-defence Ishaq Khan, in the summer of 1888, raised the standard of revolt. And an even more serious matter for Abdurrahman than the Ghilzai trouble it at first promised to be, for during the Ghilzai rebellion he had with difficulty kept the greater part of his country in hand. Ishaq Khan, however, though he had regular troops of the same type as the Amir's, a good many breech-loading arms, and many supporters, had not a warlike population to fall back on.

Ayub Khan, who had been in exile in Persia, started for the Afghan frontier to join, apparently, this rebellion. The Amir, however, headed him off, and in despair he surrendered to General MacLean, the British agent at Meshed, and thenceforward became, like his brother Yakub, a sojourner in India, living on the bounty of the British Government, as his descendants are to this day.

Hardly had this second menace died away when Abdurrahman had to face the rebellion in Afghan Turkistan. The Turks of that country had lost to some extent their warlike proclivities in their more fertile valleys and plains. General Ghulam Haidar was again to the fore, and the Amir's Governor of Badakhshan was sent to join him, the former marching by the Bamian passes. A pitched battle took place on 17th September at Ghuzni-chak, three miles from Tashqurghan. One wing, that of the Governor of Badakhshan, was beaten, and fled in the direction of Kabul, but Ghulam Haidar attacked so stoutly that Ishaq's troops were utterly routed and their chief in full flight for the Oxus and safety with his old Russian friends.

But the fugitives of the beaten wing had reached Kabul, spreading news of disaster, and the Amir, much perturbed, appealed to the British to move troops to Chaman, Kurram, and Landi Kotal in his support, and even thought of asking the Governor-General to occupy Kandahar.

When better news arrived the Amir set out at once for the seat of rebellion, not only to reorganise, but to deal out a full measure of his vengeance; and very terrible it was, many leaders being sent to Kabul for public execution. So severe was the tally of his displeasure that the Governor-General felt bound to remonstrate, and the story of the punishments at Mazar-i-Sharif gave rise to questions in the House of Commons. But as the Amir was shrewd enough to remark, " Neither do the English like rebellions, and it is not so long ago since English and Scottish gentlemen who rebelled were publicly executed with appalling savagery. Indeed," the Amir went on, on one occasion, to remark, " he also was against rebellions, and did not pretend to be within one hundred years of the English in civilisation, nor his people either." He also found it necessary to suppress a rising in Badakhshan, where the old reigning family had been set up. This, however, was soon dealt with.

It was not till July 1890 that His Highness was able to return to his capital, and even then he was not yet to settle down to the task of governing a complacent kingdom. For some little time his attitude towards the British had been growing suspicious, and there were a good many minor points of misunderstanding. The Viceroy was anxious to send Lord Roberts, whose tenure of the Commander-in-Chiefship was drawing to a close, to Kabul to discuss affairs between them. The problem of the tribes on our border brought in its train many difficult points of contact. The actual precise division where they ceased to be tormentors of the British, and became the legal tormentors of the Amir, had never been laid down. They were no doubt a sort of buffer between ourselves and the Amir, as he was between ourselves and Russia, but a very unsatisfactory buffer without boundaries. Moreover, the march of progress had compelled us to take some portion of the trade routes through these hills under more definite protection. The splendid isolation of days gone by could not endure. The tribal chiefs who had got into trouble with the British at times would demand protection from the Amir, and this we could not countenance. But our actions, and no doubt malignant misrepresenters, who so flourish in the East, helped to make bad blood, so that it was very desirable to get back into some measure of *rapprochement*. As far back as 1888 the Indian Government, and the Amir himself, had been anxious for some such mission, but the various rebellions made the moment unpropitious. Nor, in the opinion of those versed in the Afghan problems of those days, did a mission then seem desirable. Abdurrahman was not a national Amir, they urged, but a sectional conqueror. It was important that Ghilzais, Duranis, and Hazaras should know that we wished them well, but not necessarily that we were on the side of an Amir they could not abide. This difficulty, then as now, is most truly illustrative of the fissiparous tendency running strong under stress exactly as it does in this Year of Grace 1929.

In any case, though plans for mutual action *versus* Russian aggression would, no doubt, have been discussed, a Commander-in-Chief who could hardly have had a small escort was perhaps not the best envoy, and a year later Lord Lansdowne was able to send Sir Mortimer Durand, the son of that distinguished engineer officer who had helped blow in the gates of Ghuzni, and had lost his life when Lieutenant-Governor of the Punjab. Sir Mortimer Durand, with Colonel Ellis of the Quartermaster-General's staff, Captain MacMahon, and Captain Manners Smith, Messrs

Clarke and Donald, and Major Fenn, started for Kabul in September 1893, and were received with great éclat and consideration. The envoy was able to settle the whole situation *vis-à-vis* the Amir, and obtained his concurrence as to the dividing line between the Afghan and the British tribes—a line now famous as the Durand Line. This line was actually demarcated, except near the Khaibar, where there were points of extreme nicety to settle, in the following years by a joint commission. In return for his amicable consent, the grant of money to the Amir was raised from twelve to eighteen lakhs. Durand also obtained the Amir's acquiescence in the status of the small states and khanates, the territory known as Yaghistan (the country of the unruly), under the Hindu Kush in the vicinity of the Pamirs, and of the Chiefs of Bajaur, while acknowledging on our part the Amir's right to Asmar, and to his having a free hand with the settlement of Kafiristan. It was not perhaps realised then that this entirely unique people out of touch with the world, and with a language, habits, and religion of immense interest to scientists, were being handed over to a ruthless conversion to Islam and enslavement. But the proselytising spirit was stirred at the idea of adjacent pagans handed over lock, stock, and barrel, and the Amir worked his will on them. It had been difficult to agree to any other course, although the Amir's drastic dragonades were not expected.

In 1893 some minor difficulties with enterprising Russian officers on the Herat border occurred, and Colonel A. C. Yate proceeded to see that no aggression was taking place, on which this and one or two other incidents of zeal passed off without serious trouble.

The Amir's own account of the British mission in his autobiography is entertaining. He did not want Lord Roberts and his escort to come, and sent Mr Pyne to represent his views, ordering him to dawdle on the way so that the time for Lord Roberts' departure from India should be overdue. Friends, he said, had told him, though he did not believe it, that Lord Roberts was looking for an excuse to prolong his appointment, and might not come as an emissary of peace. He took some credit for having countered this possible intrigue!

His excuse, however, for postponing the receiving of a mission was, with some show of reason, the war in progress between 1890 and 1892 with his Hazara subjects, who occupied the inaccessible highlands between Ghuzni and Herat, and who had always preserved for themselves some measure of independence. This the Amir determined to end, and since they were non-Afghan,[1] and Shiahs to boot, he had little scruple in doing so before he could feel himself really the ruler in a united Afghanistan. It took him some time to gain his object, and his troops were fully engaged, the Hazaras endeavouring to get Great Britain to intervene. As a people we had known them in Kabul, enlisted them in the Guides and Sappers, having known them first at Jalalabad with Broadfoot's Sappers, and had eventually, with the Amir's reluctant consent, raised a pioneer battalion from them, but it was not possible to support them against their lawful overlord. In disgust many thousands of families migrated to the vicinity of Meshed.

Yaghistan and Passes of the Hindu Kush

Reference has been made to the necessity that lay ahead of clearing up the status of the various small Moslem states of Yaghistan which lay tucked up under the mountains of the trans-Indus Kohistan and the passes that led from the Pamirs. The necessity of this was to be unpleasantly brought home to the Government of India when Colonels Gromochevsky and Yanov, on different occasions, led parties of Cossacks through the Baroghil, Dorah, and Darkot Passes into Hunza and Chitral. Unnecessary alarm was caused at the accessibility of these passes as routes for Russian aggression—alarm which was based on a singular misconception as to the use of the passes for a force of any size. They run to 13,000 and 14,000 feet above sea-

[1] Described in Chapter II, p. 27.

level, only open for a few short months of the year. But the mere rumour of Russians on the passes had set the whole of the bazaars in Northern India talking, and in time of war would inevitably cause excitement. So the Government of India decided to end the matter once and for all. The Amir had been putting out feelers as to the real ownership of these little states, and the matter did not brook delay. Happily, the state of Jammu and Kashmir, originally the state of the Jammu Rajah Gulab Singh, to which we had added in 1846 the former Afghan province of Kashmir, held by the Sikhs for twenty-five years, had in its early days an enterprising military career. The Maharajah had a large army trained and equipped by the same agency as had trained that of Ranjit Singh. The proposals to offer him Jalalabad in 1841 had not materialised, and he had used this army to enforce his authority on all the small mountain states that were not actually Chinese. Hunza and Nagar, Yasin, Chitral, Tangir, and Darel, had all fought his armies and acknowledged his superiority. The suzerainty of Kashmir in 1892 was sufficiently extant to be revived. The Jammu and Kashmir Army was thoroughly overhauled, and, with some British support, proceeded to make its frontiers secure. Hunza and Nagar had defied authority for some time, and was little but a nest of robbers. It was dealt with faithfully in 1892 by Colonel Durand and a joint British and Kashmir force. Chitral was similarly supported against further Cossack visitors, but the old Mehtar had died, and an attempt was made by an uncle, supported by local Afghan chiefs, to seize the state. The British Agent from Gilgit and a small escort were besieged for several days, and only rescued by the arrival of a force under Colonel Kelly after a most difficult march from Gilgit, and the advance of a large force from the Peshawar border under Sir Robert Low. It was a costly campaign, but once and for all this, and Durand's operations, settled the question of the Hindu Kush states. It is interesting to note that in this connection Jammu-and-Kashmir alone of the feudatory (the popular, if not quite accurate, phrase for the principalities of the ruling chiefs) states of India lies on the outer frontier, and marches with China, Russia, and Afghanistan through these sub-feudatories of hers. To this day the Jammu and Kashmir Army, largely Dogra and Gurkha, still finds the garrisons for this inaccessible portion of the British frontier at Gilgit, though Chitral, now under direct control, is held by a British-Indian garrison.

The settlement of these problems, without incurring any opposition from the Afghan side, was one of the happy results of the Durand mission.

Writing himself on this matter, Abdurrahman points out that he considered he would have made India much more secure by making the people of Yaghistan, and the other debatable parts of our frontier, his own faithful subjects, and therefore staunch allies of India, rather than the unwilling subjects of Great Britain, and he pointed, not without some justification, to the Chitral, Afridi, and Waziristan wars to illustrate the point.

The Roof of the World

There was still one more troublous problem to be settled before Great Britain could sit down to a period free from frontier problems and the Amir could enjoy the fruit of all his struggles.

Far up in the mountains, beyond Badakhshan, lay, as has been related, the district of Shignan and Roshan, of which the trans-Indus portion had been surrendered with the acquiescence of all parties in Russia. The portion left to Afghanistan, known as Wakhan, lay between the Oxus and the Hindu Kush. In 1893 Colonel Yanov, finding an Afghan post in Shignan, attacked it, inflicting considerable loss under circumstances that need not be entered into. The Russians, who had been getting active on the Pamirs, were out to get all the territory they could.

The Afghans were justly incensed at the loss of life to their frontier detachment, and the Russians were clearly in the wrong, even if the Afghan commander was within Russian territory. The matter was eventually, however, happily settled between the three Governments, and a joint boundary commission examined the country of the Pamirs on the spot, and included an agreement with China as to her precise frontiers in this region. The Amir was to withdraw all his troops from the right bank of the Ab-i-Panja (true Oxus), and in compensation the Amir of Bukhara was to hand over to Afghanistan a piece of Roshan, known as Darwaz, which lay in a curve of the cis-Oxus, and which had always been a matter of annoyance to the Amir. With this decision it may be said that all boundary questions that could possibly arise between Russia, Great Britain, and Afghanistan, and even China, were now happily settled. The Amir from henceforward was able to devote his energies to the development of the government and progress of his kingdom.

CHAPTER XV

THE DEFENCE OF INDIA AND THE NORTH-WEST FRONTIER

The Modern Phases of the Russian Advance to the Oxus · The Scientific Frontier · The Possible Course of a Russian Invasion · The Tribes of the Indian Frontier · The Kitchener Period

THE MODERN PHASES OF THE RUSSIAN ADVANCE TO THE OXUS

THE history of Great Britain's connection with Afghan affairs, and therefore the greater portion of the orientation of the present book, is concerned with the defence of India, so that a discussion of that problem in its modern aspect is essential to the completion of the history of Afghanistan from a British and an Indian pcint of view.

The alarms caused by the plans of Napoleon and the Tsar have been already described, and the measures taken in the early days of the nineteenth century to guard against them, and the disturbance due to the encroachment of Russia on Persia and on the Central Asian khanates. In this chapter it is proposed to describe the general policy adopted since 1885. The earlier wars with Afghanistan, as have been shown, almost entirely centred round this problem, while in the case of the first two wars the undue reception of a Russian agent or mission at Kabul precipitated the situation. During the seventies and eighties the absorption of the Central Asian khanates by Russia was going on apace, and the march of science had enabled the Russian troops to overcome the physical difficulties of cold and transportation which had so hampered the earlier attempts to tackle the deserts and endure the winters. The Russo-Turkish War of 1877–78 had brought the whole problem much nearer. Our policy with regard to Turkey, so directly opposed to

E. N. A.

The Jagdalak Pass between Jalalabad and Kabul, where the last of the Kabul Brigade was destroyed in 1842. (See p. 143)

that of Russia, our move of Indian troops to the Mediterranean, the presence of the British fleet in Besika Bay, all right and necessary actions, no doubt, not unreasonably developed, resulted in Russian counter-activity on the Oxus. She found that by working on British apprehensions as to the safety of India and the integrity of Afghanistan, she had an effective counter-irritant to our Near-Eastern policy of befriending and of maintaining the Turks on the Bosphorus.

When Lord Lytton came out to India as Viceroy he came specially primed with knowledge of the Russian advance through the khanates, and the designs at any rate of some of her statesmen on the Oxus and Afghan Turkistan, if not on India herself. He held the strongest views as to the necessity of facing facts and not letting the Central Asian problem go by default. Lord Lawrence's policy was that suited to his period and not necessarily one for all time. The control of Afghanistan, so that the country should not be Russianised, was one of the natural planks in any platform that resisted *laissez aller*, and where this policy led us has already been described.

The Scientific Frontier

To students of this period there are three phrases, almost catch-words which predominate in all arguments, discussions, and pamphlets, or indeed any writing of the time. These were "The Forward Policy," "Back to the Indus," and "A Scientific Frontier." The "Forward Policy" has a greater and a lesser intent. In its wider sense it applies to the conceptions of 1838, the active control in the affairs of Afghanistan as an *État Tampion* to India, and the general desire to make our influence and policy felt up to the Oxus, while the opponents thereof uttered as their tocsin, "Back to the Indus." The lesser intent refers to the absorption of the tribal hills between the administered territory and Afghanistan, as defined now by the Durand line and the exercise of our control right up to that line. Lord Lawrence in his age had been uncompromising. He would have none of it, neither the greater nor the lesser intent. But his policy applied to the age, to the days when India had been shaken by our failures at Kabul before, to the days when railway lines were only beginning to creep up from the coast to the plains of India, when Indian revenues were very exiguous for the thousand and one crying needs, and when the shock of the Mutiny had left us somewhat inert for outside enterprise. Added to this had come the experience of Ambela, and the knowledge that the reconstituted Indian Army had little stuff yet fit to contend with the tribesmen in a fanatical mood. The British Government had scrapped its hereditary Poorbeah army, that had risen against the hand that fed it, and it had not yet properly filled their place. So all may agree that Lord Lawrence was eminently wise and right in his generation, "Let the tribal hills be." "Keep your tidying hands off them and many other anomalies of our position in India, and let the matters solve themselves." Very good talk, Jan Lawrence *Sahib*. *Roshan-ki-bat!*

But there was always the question ahead of when this point of view, based largely on the requirements of the moment, should come up for revision. As regards the greater intent, Lord Lytton and the Tory Government thought the time had arrived.

The question of the "Scientific Frontier" was based on a somewhat different point of outlook. It was not necessarily concerned with the Forward Policy in its greater intent, and this is what its exponents said: "If you have to fight Afghanistan again, or if you have to resist invasion from an army organised and equipped on Western lines, you must be in a position to meet it. You cannot work, at any rate through the summer, with your bases on the red-hot shores of the Indus; you cannot expect to bring your troops into a field fit for their purpose if you have to assemble them in temperatures at which human nature can hardly even exist. You cannot march them over the wastes of Kach Gandava in summer, or through the Derajat, or keep them in the fever-stricken Peshawar valley, and then expect to fight and win. It is true that you can fall back beyond the Indus even and allow your adversaries to face the climate, but they would be in quite a different position, for they would assemble all the summer in the highlands and would advance on you in the winter. Further, you are too far committed trans-Indus to be able to adopt such a position and maintain your prestige.

"For climatic reasons alone you must cross the Indus valley and deploy your troops in the uplands with roads and railways behind them. It is from Herat and Kandahar that your dangers must come, and the elevated plateau of Baluchistan is the place from which you meet an advance in health and strength. The ancient routes into the Derajat need not worry you; they are dominated by Ghuzni, but troops in large numbers will only come to Ghuzni and to the old strategical road from Kandahar to Kabul by way of Kandahar. If you can dominate Kandahar you need not worry about the Derajat. Nor need you be excessively anxious about the routes from Kabul. Kabul can only be reached by invaders by way of the lofty snowbound passes of the Hindu Kush, closed for many months of the year. Otherwise Kabul also is only reached in numbers by the strategic road from Kandahar."

And what they said then is what the strategists say now. Lord Lytton had brought out with him as military secretary the ill-fated Colonel G. P. Colley, a shining light among the Staff College alumni, and one to whom strategical study had especially appealed. Those who were opposed to him would point later to his fate as General Sir George Colley on Majuba Kop, as proving the fallacy of his opinions on his own gallant person. But he fell at the actual head of a gallant tactical effort, which only the peculiar conditions of guerrilla war upset. His strategical acumen was not concerned, and he undoubtedly brought to India some much needed wider views at a very critical time.

Speaking generally, the views that he had put forward were eventually those which were adopted for the defence of India by those for whom he had demonstrated them.

It has already been related how the desire of the British Government and of Lord Lytton to occupy Kandahar in support of a detached Afghan state independent of Kabul was abandoned in 1881. It had been desired as a strategical point from which to protect India, and it was abandoned for the alternative of supporting an all-powerful Afghan Amir and developing Afghan powers of resistance —a policy which at any rate for forty years had borne good fruit.

But the Scientific Frontier produced many derivatives, and the most important ones were the controlling of the passes by which Afghanistan could be entered from our own side—passes lying in the No-man's-land of Ruh, and the making them so secure that our troops advancing to the succour of Afghanistan should not have the anxiety of a dog-fight with the tribes *en route*. Especially did this concern the Khaibar, which from time immemorial had refused all acknowledgment of authority from Kabul, the route by the Kurram, which the Treaty of Gandamak brought to our hands,[1] and the control of the wild yet not impassable tracts of Zhob. The importance of Zhob and the adjacent districts of Bori and Thal Chotiali will be evident from a glance at the map. From Multan, that old strategical centre from the earliest days, marching troops could reach Quetta and Pishin by a far shorter route than that of Sukkur and Kach Gandava, and by routes that were fairly accessible and passable. But this fact was still more evident when the conditions of a railway to Quetta and Chaman were fully understood. Those conditions apply just as much to-day, even when engines are more powerful and crossing stations more numerous, viz. that the ascent to the uplands from Kach Gandava and Sibi is close on 5000 feet, which must be climbed in a fairly short distance. Gradients are, therefore, more than steep, and trains must be very light and none too frequent. In other words, the railway to Quetta, even as now improved, and taking the Muskaf-Bolan alignment rather than the marvellous but somewhat uncertain alternative Harnai route, cannot take many troops and stores in the twenty-four hours. All that can march should march, and the plans of even Lord Kitchener's days

[1] A change especially acceptable to the Shiah tribes of the Turis, who occupy most of the Upper Kurram.

postulated the detraining of mounted troops and transport near Multan for a march, a useful hardening march, up the passes to the plateau by Zhob or Bori or Thal.

The general opening up and pacification of this country bulked very large in the last decade of the nineteenth century, but its vicinity to Waziristan, and to the Afghan frontier and the routes from Ghuzni, make it liable to excitement and disorder if its neighbours are in such condition.

The Possible Course of a Russian Invasion

The problem of the defence of India had then, and has now, two separate aspects: first, when we are defending the integrity of Afghanistan as her ally, and secondly, when Afghanistan is openly hostile or cowed into such neutrality as to allow free passage through her territories. It has long been realised that Herat must be the first objective of the invader, and for centuries Herat has been referred to as the "key of India." The meaning of that is that those who could secure Herat would acquire a jumping-off point within a most fertile valley, rich in stored supplies of grain and well watered, from which to advance towards India.

As our policy of strengthening the Afghan Army bore fruit, it seemed possible that Herat when attacked could hold out till succoured. British engineers at the time of the Panjdeh incident strengthened the defences of the city so that it could hold out against heavy guns of that period and put up a defence which would delay the advance of an invader. It was intended to return once again to Kandahar, carry on the railway from New Chaman to that city, and thence act as may be. It was believed that Afghan troops could always hold the high passes of the Hindu Kush beyond Kabul or Ghuzni till reinforced from Peshawar, and compel the decision to be made somewhere between Kandahar and Herat. But the second alternative had to be faced—that of a hostile Afghanistan supporting a Russian advance on India, or a situation in which the Afghans were beaten back and a Russian advance was moving over their bodies to India. To meet this, the Indian Defence Committee, which worked for so many years after 1885 and of which the late Field-Marshal Lord Nicholson was so long the secretary, arranged for a permanent fortification of the Indian frontier, on the assumption that Afghanistan was overrun. The policy decided on was to resist on the Quetta plateau, to make the crossings of the Indus impossible at Attock, and to compel the invaders to try to enter India by the routes of Khushalgarh and the Gumal, thus throwing them on to what in those days were the waterless ways of the Sind Sagar Doab and the Salt range, and which would compel them to cross the great rivers. To this end strong fortified positions were prepared, and remain to this day beyond Quetta and at Attock. In those days, the theory of entrenched camps and *places d'armes* at intervals, which an invader could not pass unless masked by a strong force, held the field as the best scheme of defence. An entrenched camp was placed at Rawalpindi on the main road between Peshawar and Lahore, specially designed to threaten the advance of an invader via Kurram or Ghuzni who tried to hug the better-watered area to the north, and would drive him on to the then impassable wastes farther south in the Punjab, thus impaling him on the horns of a dilemma—that of exposing a flank to the highly mobile force sallying forth from the entrenched camp within the circle of redoubts, or attempting a waterless waste that could hardly be negotiated. Times have somewhat changed, for the waste areas are now highly irrigated and supplies abound, while any interference with the headwaters of the canals would be practically out of the question, since Government could not deprive of water the large population that now exists. In any case, the theory of entrenched camps has probably seen its day, and Rawalpindi stands in its circle of obsolescent redoubts as an example of a strategical theory that has outlived its vogue. Nevertheless, should times change and Russian and Afghan join forces, we may easily see the whole position revert to its old conditions, and we may be glad to strike on the Helmand while holding the foe on the Indus.

Lord Curzon's frontier policy developed naturally *pari passu* with the general war policy of the Government of India, which Lord Kitchener had come East to develop, and the release of unnecessary troops from the great curtain of the Sulaiman mountains accorded well with the latter's plans to prepare the army for active operations in Afghanistan should the Russians encroach on the latter territory.

The Tribes on the Indian Frontier

By common fallacy it is the custom to speak of the north-west frontier of India as "the frontier" pure and simple, though there are a north-eastern and an eastern frontier which have seen plenty of rough-and-tumble work in the past. For convenience sake this custom may be followed here, and it is worthy of notice that even this one frontier is over a thousand miles long, and for the best part of that way faces Afghanistan. But only on the Baluchistan side and in the Khaibar does it actually touch Afghanistan for any practical purpose, since between the two runs that long stretch of tumbled mountains known in days gone by as Ruh, which has already been described. From the spurs of the Hindu Kush in the north to the mountains of Solomon in the south live our old friends the Pathans, that Pashtu-speaking people who claim, as we have shown, relationship to the Abdali, but who are in reality none other than the Aryans of India, modified by a very fierce form of Islam, and hardened to iron by the hills and the climate within which they live, as well as the devil life of savagery to which fate has condemned them.

Let us for a moment retell the age-old story, already described in the early chapters of this book. From earliest times the less accessible portion of the hills appear to have known no master. Mahmud of Ghuzni, Muhammad Ghori, Slave Kings of Delhi, Mogul emperors, have all owned sway over the lands which surrounded these mountains of Ruh, but rarely made their claim to the conclave effective. The routes through the Khaibar, the roads from Ghuzni to the ancient Dhankot crossing of the Indus, those through the

Derajat and Bori to Kandahar, have seen countless armies come and go, and the Rohillas by the way, swept aside by the passing, have swarmed on the straggling baggage and fallen on the isolated since time was. They have drawn their revenue, like other highland caterans, from private trader and caravan who paid toll, from kings who paid for peace, and they have "shot at the strong and slashed at the weak" long before Alexander of Macedon came through them. When, as occurred now and again, some king turned in wrath, they climbed away to the snow-level and hid in caves, to swarm on the skirts of the angry monarch when circumstances compelled him to withdraw—an old game long played to the great content of the caterans, and a game in which the aeroplane and the long-range howitzer are somewhat altering the conditions.

Some of the tribes own sway of chiefs, and some are little more than peculiarly ruthless and irrational soviets.

Neither Alexander of the Two Horns and his successors, nor Ghuznivide nor Ghoride, could hold or tame them. Mighty Delhi of the Moguls could but wink at their ways, and the Sikhs could but burn alive any that fell to their hands. The only principle that has ever been followed has been to block them into their hills to prevent their raiding getting past bearing. Wherever, as has been mentioned, the raiding paths entered the plains, and where armed police or military posts have been stationed by the Sikhs or British, and, no doubt, their more immediate predecessors, there are also to be found the ruins of Græco-Bactrian posts that obviously filled the same purpose. It is interesting to remember that it is not whence raiders come that matters, but it is the routes along which captured stock can be driven on the return journey that decides the blocking site.

When the British succeeded the Sikhs as their heirs-at-law in 1849 they were brought into touch with these tribes, whom indeed they had met earlier in the Khaibar and the Bolan during the First Afghan War. Where the Sikh border rested at the foot of the raw-red mountains, there for the time being lay the British border, and there for the most part it remains to this day. For the first thirty years or so the Punjab Frontier Force and the Border Military Police, familiarly known as the *Bardar*, kept the tribesmen in their hills, or saw that when they came to the market towns within the British line they first lodged their arms and came as one gentleman visiting another. When their crimes mounted high and could no longer be endured, then a military punitive expedition took place. Before the nineties those expeditions had been as a rule on a small scale. The tribes along the borders of the Derajat, Bozdars, Sherannis, Maris, Bughtis, and the like, kept the old Frontier Force busy. The opening of the Kohat Pass, that is to say, the road over the hills of the Jowaki Afridis which joined the Sikh fortress of Kohat with that of Peshawar, had to be effected in the early fifties. This tongue of tribal mountain running down between two settled and administered areas which the British had taken over from the Sikhs is one of the many curious and somewhat anomalous features of this frontier. In 1863, as one of the aftermaths of the Mutiny, it was necessary to penetrate the frontier hills and rout out that nest of fanatics maintained by refugees from Hindustan [1] that existed in the Yusufzai country at Sitana, and which had given Ranjit Singh so much trouble in the twenties. To it had gone those irreconcilables who had fanned the Moslem side of the rebellions which accompanied the Mutiny. But the whole of the adjacent hills and valleys thought it well to join in the fray, and at the Ambela Pass we learnt more about what tribes could do when a fanatical wave had set in, than ever we learnt in the First Afghan War.

After that we left the hill tracts severely alone, unless compelled by too many raids to make reprisals.

But time was rolling on. Railways threaded Hindustan, trade was increasing, modern goods were in demand everywhere. The traders wanted peaceful routes, and since trade and commerce is the British instinct, we were bound to endeavour to meet their needs. The Durand line had been settled by treaty, and the British Government decided that the trade routes should now be protected. These were, as

[1] See p. 97.

we have seen, principally the Khaibar, the Kurram, and the routes from Ghuzni, either by the Tochi valley to Bannu or by the Gumal to Dera Ismail Khan, and as a variant, from Pishin down to the Lower Derajat and Dera Ghazi Khan.

The steps necessary to protect these routes need not be described at length. They were reasonable and necessary. They involved such steps as holding the Samana range by military and police posts, which protected the road to the Kurram and our own tribesmen from Afridi and Orakzai. They included the tightening up of our responsibility in the Khaibar, and the general improvement of control in the Gumal, as well as the opening of the Zhob. But they raised fierce religious and tribal anger, which, added to the news of victories of Turks over Greeks in Europe, set the whole border ablaze. As soon as the snows were melting and the spring crop reaped in 1897, then the whole of our frontier blew up in a series of independent conflagrations. Seventy thousand troops had to be put into the field before they were quieted. When Lord Curzon arrived in India he found that a very large force was stationed across our administrative border as a result of these risings, and that the regular army, required to act for offence or defence in the case of serious war, was locked up in compulsory frontier garrisons. Further, he found that the Indian soldiers hated frontier garrisons, save for the expensive fact that they received rations and allowances in compensation.

He set himself to an improvement of an old policy. He realised that it was only needed to hold the forward positions at Peshawar and Quetta as the bastions where we would meet invasions or whence we would start a forward move. He knew that there were many among the tribesmen who wanted quieter times and less lawless days. So he devised a system whereby tribal militia, led by selected British officers, should hold the trade routes through their own country, and that there need be no more regular soldiers along the extended curtain between Peshawar in the north to Quetta in the south than was necessary to give some support to the militias. He also brought to fruition the long debated question of forming the Punjab frontier districts into a separate frontier province.

This policy was carried out, to the general improvement of the army as a better trained force. It met with difficulties, in that all the tribes, notably those of Waziristan, could not be trusted—as could the Afridis, for instance—to behave well as militiamen so long as the clans as a whole which furnished the levies wished for peace; but it held the field as a policy till the World War.

It has been explained how the Forward Policy of the "lesser" intent is distinct from that of the "greater." How the latter refers to an active military policy in regard to Afghanistan with a view to securing Herat and the line of the Oxus, but the former to the discussion as to whether or no it were best to occupy and administer the mountains of Ruh as Baluchistan is occupied and administered, viz. by a semi-tribal system of responsibility known as the "Sandeman System." The protagonists of the Forward Policy urged that we should go forward to the Durand line; older heads said, "Only go forward where you need. In spite of the cost of many frontier expeditions, the cost of occupation and administration will be more. There are little revenues to get for your pains, and it is ill taking the breeks off a Highlander."

Some talk of the allowances given to tribal chiefs for keeping their lads in order as *dane-gelt*; others show that it is wise to provide penniless men with a credit, and teach them to spend so that they may miss what may be withheld for misdemeanour. It is also urged that the valleys of Baluchistan are parallel and easily negotiated, and far different in formation from those of Tirah and Waziristan; and this is very true. It is also pointed out that in Baluchistan the chiefs were men of influence whom their clans were prepared to obey, and that in the other parts the clans were intensely republican. And so the discussion has swayed backwards and forwards, and in 1914 the "lesser" Forward Policy did not hold the field.

The Kitchener Period

The end of the South African War found everyone anxious that the Indian Army, like that in Great Britain, should undergo considerable overhaul in view of the experience of that campaign, and especially of the knowledge of the efficiency of modern weapons. Lord Kitchener was appointed with a mandate to reconstruct it thoroughly, and especially with regard to the meeting of a Russian army, in view of the fact that railways in Russian Turkistan were in direct connection with Russia in Europe, and that the Transcaspian and Orenberg lines were being linked. Lord Kitchener had the possibilities and logistics of a Russian invasion of Afghanistan very carefully studied, and presented to the Indian Government his estimate of what was required to bring the army in India up to the standard of modern requirements.

The Scientific Frontier, somewhat modified from its original conception, had long been occupied. We held the lines of advance to and from Afghanistan, and frontier tribal policy was being overhauled by Lord Curzon, as described above. Transport, that bane and bugbear of all Indian campaigns outside internal India, and the improvement of the railway lines that ran to the frontier, were among the important points of his programme. The Amir el Kebir [1] had long been established, and had just been gathered with his fathers in the fullness of years and of power. To the breaking of a time-honoured rule there was no disputed succession, owing no doubt to the wise measures of the Amir in recognising and having recognised the heir he had selected. The Afghan Army was now a respectable concern, very different from that of Shere Ali, in its discarded trappings of the Bengal Artillery and in travesties of Highland attire. Lord Kitchener was anxious that British officers should study tactical problems on the ground on which troops coming to the assistance of the Afghans might expect to fight over. This the Amir

[1] El Kebir=The Great, as Abdurrahman was called in his later days.

was too suspicious, or perhaps too afraid of his religious party, to allow, though one or two special missions were permitted to traverse routes hitherto unreconnoitred. Nor was it possible to think out any plans whereby Afghan and British officers could train together, but the whole set of plans were framed on the basis of a friendly Afghanistan needing succour. The old desire to occupy Kandahar and have the railway established there in peace time had been dismissed as unattainable. The country between Chaman and Kandahar was easy enough, and the rush forward of a line over the eighty-odd miles intervening could only be a matter of two or three months,[1] with railhead daily moving nearer as construction progressed. Kandahar and the Afghan troops on the passes between Ghuzni and Kabul and the Oxus could be reinforced long before any Russian threat would become effective, though distant Herat, four hundred miles from Kandahar, might fall before sufficient help could come.

The actual problem, therefore, had now, with our scientific frontier and bases, resolved itself into waiting events in a state of preparation, and for a while the signing of the Anglo-Russian Agreement of 1907 seemed to make trouble more remote.

The main principles of 1885 remained unchanged, viz. regular troops and *places d'armes* on that part of the frontier on which advance could be made, and the holding of the intermediate curtain with as few regular troops as possible, while in India improvements in railways and in transport organisation were kept in the forefront of all programmes.

[1] See p. 307. It should be remembered that the Indian line is considerably wider than standard range, and construction is therefore slower and material heavier to move. The distance in a straight line is between sixty and seventy miles.

CHAPTER XVI

THE STABLE AFGHAN KINGDOM

The Afghan Character · The Faith of the Prophet · The Ways of Abdurrahman · The Advice of the Amir el Kebir · The Accession of Habibullah Khan · Afghanistan and the World War

THE AFGHAN CHARACTER

A GREAT deal has been written of all the evil in the Afghan character—the barefaced, shameless treachery, the disregard of life, the want of the fighting courage save when maddened by religious zeal, and the ruthless cruelty to enemies even of their own people as well as to those of other races. It is therefore time that something should be said on the other side. Abdurrahman knew them thoroughly, and spoke of them forcibly enough: "You say I am an iron ruler. I rule an iron people." When Shah Shujah was asked to approve a proclamation, one of the typical hot-air British proclamations that a man of the Macnaghten type would evolve, talking of the rights of folk and the amenities of life, His Majesty openly scoffed that anyone could dream of putting forth such stuff as applying to Afghan peoples.

But Abdurrahman was equally strong on the potentialities of the Afghan race when he had made them into a people and had conquered their fissiparous tendencies and their fratricidal jealousies. We have seen how so many of their qualities appealed to the British in those happier days at the beginning of the Shah Shujah period when we came as allies and as friends. Their love of sport and games, their handsome, open, engaging mien even when covering a faithless heart, all pointed to a people that should have a future. Abdurrahman, without realising the parallel, saw that he had here what so many nations lacked—the small country gentry and chiefs innumerable from whom to draw, as the British have drawn, a faithful race of national servants both as soldiers and administrators as well as of professional men.

We may perhaps feel that those traits, which had been so brutally prominent since the break-up of the Durani Empire of Ahmad Shah, were due to the conditions of the times; the reaction, as it were, from a century or so of Mogul rule, in which the law apparently held good even in the Afghan provinces of Delhi. The parallel has often also been drawn, with some justice, between life in the Highlands of Scotland a few centuries ago and that in the Afghan hills. Except that the Highlands of Scotland are tiny instead of vast, the parallel perhaps applies, for we see the same conditions producing ruthlessness and ill-faith together with faithfulness and hospitality.

Abdurrahman aimed at taming these highland loons and bonnet lairds as well as the bigger chiefs, and, as we have seen, removed ruthlessly from his path all who opposed his purpose, as we have also known kings of England forced to do. From 1881 to 1919 (a period of thirty-eight years) his leaven has been watched at work. The roads were safe, administration was developing as fast as the aspirations of his people would accept, and the family life of the Afghan gentry and better classes, as well as the simpler life of the cultivating lesser clansman, was developing much that was human and good in their past customs and traditions. And indeed there was plenty of it to develop. In those rich valleys where "the vines on the upland swell" there was plenty of civilised, homely, happy life of a kind, and under the national system the scions of the countryside were going to the army and the public services.

All over the country, wherever the available water had given cultivation, where the almond and the peach tree flourished, and the vine gave its wealth, and the poplars and the mulberry raised their heads, there in the country castles of the gentry a happy life of squiredom has gone on. It is true that till quite recently it has gone on much in the way that it went on among the Jock Elliots of the Scottish border, for in the midst of it the cry to arms might come, but it was full of picturesque and admirable amenities and conceptions.

THE FAITH OF THE PROPHET

It is not out of place to write here something of the effect of Islam in the national life of the Afghan. The teaching of Al Islam, which means "The Submission"—submission to the will of God—has come out of a Semite mind which thought and taught on the wide-rolling deserts and pasture uplands of Arabia. Born to some extent of knowledge of the truths that Jewish and Christian teachers brought, it succeeded a romantic paganism that had long lost its hold. It filled in men's minds a great gap, or it would not have spread like wildfire over those parts of the East which Christianity had not touched, and it built up in an astoundingly short space of time a vast temporal power. In Persia as well as elsewhere it actually ousted Christianity from races seemingly unfit for it. In these days when theological thought is greater in its sympathy than in days of yore, it may even be held that Islam, a conception of dignity and purity, may in itself be something of a revelation, and that Muhammad may well have been a prophet, even if, as some say, he fell from grace in his old age. Indeed, some thoughtful folk there be who think that the way of "The Submission" may be but a half-way house to grim, uncultured minds on the road to higher things. Be that as it may, the teaching of the Prophet is in many ways the teaching of righteousness, and it swept away the idolatries, just as it appealed in India to so many for whom popular Hinduism contained no message and no hope.

It is to be noticed, however, that Islam is essentially the religion for Semitic tribes and races. It is with them that it runs in that fierce fervour that made the Arab Empire for a while one of the largest that the world has ever seen. The drum ecclesiastic banged and rolled, and the great cry swept north, south, east, and west for many a thousand miles: "*La Illah ha il Illah ho, O Muhammad*

Rasul il Illah." "There is no God but God Almighty, and Muhammad is his Prophet." The bitter struggle between Crescent and Cross was never a struggle of religion, but one of politics, beginning when the Turkish conquerors of the Arab empires began to oppress Christian pilgrims to the holy places in the days when places were taking undue value in mediæval minds.

It was Muhammad who said that "Jesus is truly the Son of God," and that "The Christians are always your friends." Never does a devout Moslem utter the name of Christ without the additional blessing, "*Alleh Salaam.*" "Peace be with him." The ignorant Afghan priest talks of the British as *kafirs*, or unbelievers, but no educated Moslem dare call the *Ahl-i-Katab*, the "People of the Book," such as Christian or Jew, an "unbeliever"; it simply is not done. Yet priests are ignorant, and the Crusaders were often worse, so that Cross and Crescent have long fought for supremacy when they should have combined.

But though Al Islam is a conception of Semite psychology and mentality, it by some strange chance fell partly among a race more suited by temperament to the far older faith, which millions of it still hold. The Turk, Tatar or Mongol, that race so different in all its characteristics, mental and physical, linguistic and tribal, from Aryan and Semite, has long been the home of Buddhism, to whom the philosophy spread, if, indeed, it did not there originate. But as the hordes of the Tatars came out of the crucibles of what is now the desert of Gobi and Mongolia, beat up against the Aryan bulwark at Balkh, and eventually swept over it, it met in time the Arab wave and "The Submission," till at length we see a large portion of them adopting that faith late in the Middle Ages. Samarqand, infected by Herat and Meshed, became, under Tatar protection, one of the great homes of Islamic culture and learning. But nevertheless the Faith never appears to have bitten deep into the Tatar mind and soul as it did into the Arab.

When the Turk captured Constantinople, and the Sultan of Rum became the Caliph by methods which are still the

16

subject of controversy, the centre of Islamic religion did try to become in Constantinople a rival of the religious centre at Rome.

When we study the story of Islam we see that the power temporal is an essential part of the system. The Turkish Sultan, the head of the Ottoman Turks, was accepted throughout the Islamic world as the successor in the realm of Islamic power to the Arab caliph. Church and State are inextricably mingled in Islam. We have yet to see whither the separation is to lead in Turkey. All the laws of Moslem life are ecclesiastical laws, and draw their force from the Sheria, the religious law, and that is why modernisation of system and marching with the times is so hard a feat in Moslem countries.

But though a Turk some centuries ago was recognised as the head of the Islamic kingdoms, and the Sheikh-ul-Islam resided at his seat of Government, it is very doubtful if the true Turk, the Mongolian whom we see in the Turk of Anatolia, and who so resembles the Hazara and even the Gurkha in appearance, is essentially a Moslem by nature. He apparently has not the instinct, and that possibly is why the new condition of affairs in Anatolia has been so easily accepted. His heart is more pagan or more readily adopted to the Buddhist philosophy than to monotheistic imperative Islam.

As the Indian Moslem sergeant told the Prussian staff officer at Beersheba when asked how he came to be fighting against the Caliph, "This is a war of politics and not a war of Islam."

In 1914 there were only two countries where Islam really flourished in something resembling its old austerity. Those countries were India and Afghanistan. India had, however, some knowledge of the world to temper religious zeal, and Indian Moslems who felt the call kept it in hand. In Afghanistan, where the mullahs are most fervent and the tribal mullahs the most ignorant, the most fanatic, and the most bitter of any, the call came with great force and appeal. Happily the Amir did keep it in hand to some extent between 1914 and 1919, but there has always been in the country a narrow and fanatical Islamic party, who put hatred of the British as one of their principal cults. Every Amir has had, to some extent, to bow to it, even the Amir el Kebir, the great Amir Abdurrahman himself. Its existence has always complicated his policy and that of his son Habibullah towards Great Britain, and finally induced the Third Afghan War, as well as the downfall of King Amanullah.

As things are in 1929, the mass of tribal opinion will not yield to the abandoning of the old customs, which are bound up so inextricably with the law of the Prophet. All aping, all genuine copying of the ways of the West, however much such copying is for the general convenience, are little tolerated by priestly classes and the masses whom they sway. There is in this matter no small leaven of self-preservation, for the Moslem clergy live by offerings. The spread of education has, as they have seen in many countries, meant lean times for that clergy whose stock-in-trade is priestcraft over the ignorant and fervid.

The Ways of Abdurrahman

Abdurrahman has described his policy with regard to the many chiefs and claimants who had at any time been hostile to his house, other than the really dangerous and implacable ones he had to get rid of—those for whom "stone dead hath no fellow."

This is how he writes [1] of his plans for peace and continuity in his group of principalities and provinces: "I have tried by every possible means to increase the number of rulers and chiefs of the neighbouring states of Afghanistan about my Court, as well as to gather together there the most influential followers of my rivals, either from Russia or from India. Most of these men are by my orders the personal attendants of my son, and their association is of such intimate character that many of them are his closest friends."

This showed both a statesmanlike outlook and also a

[1] See his autobiography.

human side. We have seen the kings of England try the same with the young Irish princelings and lords. He classed such folk into four classes: those expatriated or expropriated by Russia, those whose countries had been annexed by himself, those in the British sphere of influence who had not accepted their position, and lastly, those in exile from Afghanistan and supporters of rivals of the dynasty. "In this way," said His Highness, "no rival to the throne of Kabul exists to disturb my son's peace." In Britain we have seen it so with Jacobite supporters. Sir Alfred Lyall puts the rougher part of the pacification perhaps more bluntly when the Ghilzai chief was invited to Kabul.

> "High stands thy Kabul citadel, where many have room and rest;
> The Amirs give welcome entry, but they speed not a parting guest;
> So a stranger needs safe escort and the oath of a valiant friend;
> Whom shall I choose of those I know? Whom ask the Amir to send?
> Wilt thou send the Vazir Nur Ahmed, the man whom the Ghilzaies trust?
> He has long lain lost in a dungeon, his true bold heart is dust.
> Wilt thou send the Jasmsheedee Aga, who was called from the western plain?
> He left the black tents of his horsemen, and he led them never again.
> Shall I ask for the Mullah, in Ghazni, to whom all Afghans rise?
> He was bid last year to thy banqueting—his soul is in Paradise."

But those days of his tender ruth had passed, and firm in his seat he could and did turn to the more human side of life, and he makes a shrewd allusion to this.

"It is a curious thing that even well-informed and responsible Englishmen holding high official positions regard the Afghanistan of to-day in the light of twenty years ago. In illustration of this it is just as if a person were to say, 'Oh, the English Government is a cruel Government, because it had such a cruel law as to hang a man for sheep-stealing. . . .'" And he claimed, and with truth, that immense changes had taken place in Afghanistan in a very short time.

India was flooded with stories, however, brought often enough by those Europeans who returned from serving

Afghan tribesmen

'An eye for an eye, and a tooth for a tooth'

the Amir. The latter had vastly improved Shere Ali's first attempts at arsenals. English engineers came to erect and manage them. Indian artificers trained in British arsenals and gun factories took service with him. British medical officers at times visited Kabul to attend the Amir, and even to advise him on medical organisation.

Two stories are worth giving as showing how Abdurrahman kept his country in order. Sir Salter Pyne, the sturdy British engineer who stayed so long in Kabul, told the writer of a visit to the palace.

"The Amir sent for me to the palace, and was a-eating ice-creams in an upper verandah. Four hundred mutinous soldiers from Herat were marched in. The Amir scowled. 'Poke their eyes out,' he ordered, and they did it then and there. I couldn't finish my ice-cream, but the Amir gulped his."

One of the medical officers told the writer that riding one morning in Kabul attended by an Afghan orderly he passed a comfortable gentleman ambling on a pony wearing an Indian velvet cap, such as is often affected by Moslems in Bengal. "Who is that?" asked the doctor of his orderly. "Oh, that is the doctor *babu-ji*." So the British doctor rode alongside and passed the time o' day, wishing to chat with a brother of the profession. He found, however, that his companion was not very forthcoming, so he mentioned this to the orderly afterwards. "Well," said the latter, "perhaps not. We call him the doctor *babu-ji* because it sounds better, but really he is the official blinder."

The Amir well said, "You call me a hard man, but I rule a hard people." He claimed that he had made Afghanistan roads absolutely safe from robbers, and his methods were emphatic.

The British agent at Kabul was going to Peshawar, and had alighted to water his horse and drink at a stream. He had hung his belt on a tree and rode away without it. When next he passed, a man living hard by produced it and handed it to him. The other, delighted, urged him to come to Kabul, where he would be presented to the Amir in Durbar, who loved an honest man, and would reward him. Nothing loath, the other agreed, and was presented to the Amir, who listened to the tale. Then the Amir el Kebir smiled, and with a twitch of the mouth asked him which hand he had picked it up with. The man held out his right hand, expecting a *douceur*. The Amir roared: "Cut it off! Cut it off!" And then: "How often have I told you Afghans that I will not have you touch other folks' things!"

One more. The Amir el Kebir had answered the importunities of an elderly female relative by finding her a husband. She before long appeared at his Durbar to complain that the husband had no teeth; why should she, with a mouth full of teeth, be married to one with none! "Woman," he said, "teeth are given by God, but man can remove them, and you shall have no cause for complaint. Yours, too, will be removed."

"A hard man among a hard people." And whether it was good or whether it was evil, he had produced an ordered, prosperous country to which his son Habibullah succeeded. Something in his way after the manner of Napoleon did he reform the system so far as there had been one. In every province, revenue, public works, army, police, manufactures, trade, and justice, all received his competent attention and were duly administered under a definite procedure. Justice was the justice of the East, but it was understood and administered, though at times, as Kipling has written, "He who held the longer purse might live the longer life."

The country was ruled and administered with common sense, and with something of British and something of Russian systems; but never were any innovations allowed likely to upset the religious prejudices which in his heart of hearts Abdurrahman heartily despised, as those who held private converse with him well knew. And so, when he was gathered with his fathers, dying as he had never expected to die, in his bed, it was a consolidated and peaceful kingdom to which Habibullah Khan his son succeeded, though in every direction there were weeds likely to grow that needed watching.

The Advice of the Amir el Kebir

Before seeing how the great Amir's successor was able to follow in his footsteps for eighteen eventful years, it will be of interest to glance at some of the precepts for his successors which he wrote out carefully in his autobiography some five or six years before his death. He had very clear views on all matters of State, and among others, on the rate at which his country could be encouraged to develop. To-day, with the conditions of 1929 before us, we can realise the wisdom that lay therein.

Plenty of confidence had he in the Afghan future, but this is how he envisaged it. First of all, he pledged his opinion in the integrity of British intentions towards Afghanistan, and was equally insistent on the evil intentions of the Russians, although, as he frequently says, he had nothing but gratitude for their kindness to him for the many years that he sojourned with them as an exile.

"The British are showing that they have the interests of Afghanistan in their hearts, not only by their words but by their actions, in trying to use all the means that they can to give help in money, in arms and machinery, and in several other ways, for the safety, strength, and protection of Afghanistan, in which they see that the welfare of their own Indian Empire is so closely bound up. British ministers have not only shown their willingness to help Afghanistan, but they have gone a step further in guaranteeing the safety of my kingdom against any foreign aggressor, which enables me and my successors to devote all my attention to the progress of the internal affairs of my kingdom, leaving the anxieties of its external dangers and responsibilities to its true friends in England."

To his successors he writes :

"The first and most important advice that I can give my successors and people to make Afghanistan into a great kingdom, is to impress upon their minds the value of unity.

Unity, and unity alone, can make it into a great power. All the Royal Family, nobility, and people must have one mind, one interest, and one opinion to safeguard their homes."

He frequently inveighs against the mistake made by amirs and shahs in the past of making their sons governors of various distant provinces, surrounded by their own flatterers, each dreaming of succeeding to the throne. "I have arranged matters during my lifetime in such a way that all the members of my family, and the Afghan people, acknowledge the supremacy of my eldest son. . . . The Russians, quite contrary to the English, want to see Afghanistan divided into pieces and very weak, if not entirely cleared out of their way to India.

"The foundation stone of constitutional government has been laid by me, though the machinery of a representative government has not taken any shape as yet. . . . It is necessary that every ruler should not jump to conclusions in a hurry. . . . There are three kinds of representatives who assembled at my Court. . . . These three classes are called sirdars (aristocracy), *khawanin mulki* (commons, or representatives of the people), and mullahs (ecclesiastical heads and Church representatives). . . . This constitutional body has not yet attained the ability to qualify it for being entrusted with authority of any importance, for giving sanction to bills and acts of government. Perhaps in time they will have such authority. . . . I must strongly urge my sons and successors never to make themselves puppets in the hands of these representatives of constitutional government. . . ."

And then comes the advice to *festina lente*; the advice which grandson Amanullah has cast aside:

"My sons and successors should not try to introduce reforms of any kind in such a hurry as to set the people against their ruler, and they must bear in mind that in establishing a constitutional government, introducing more lenient laws, and modelling education upon the system of Western universities, they must adopt all these gradually as the people become accustomed to the idea of modern innovations." Then a pleasant little piece of satire: "In following the advice of any Foreign Power or courtiers of our own Durbar, they must keep before their minds the shrewd counsel given by Sadi, 'That shrewd young boy will save the purse of sovereigns in his pocket who looks upon every passer-by as a pickpocket and a robber!'" And those who have studied Persian will observe with pleasure that the Amir el Kebir adjures his son to read carefully the *Anwar-i-Suhaili*, a glorified Æsop's Fables, full of the wisdom of the Eastern world told in animal guise.

His advice on trade is replete with the wisdom of the moderns. "I have opened several canals, and several others are being cut. The trade in Astrakan skins, wool, horses, and sheep has considerably increased, and I have lent money out of the Treasury to Afghan merchants to encourage trade without charging interest on such loans. Instead of charging interest I charge import and export duties, which bring in more than the interest would, and leave a margin for the merchants themselves."

The Accession of Habibullah Khan

When Habibullah succeeded to his father's throne there were many in India who feared that he was not a strong enough character to sit where Abdurrahman had sat. But partly, no doubt, because of the preparation his father had made for him to succeed (so different from these Eastern potentates who have treated their heir with contumely), and partly, no doubt, because he had the necessary character, his reign was a great success. Slowly and steadily he followed the policy of his father, improving roads, improving trade, continuing canals. Afghanistan has never been a rich country. Vast areas can never be anything more than barren rock, and the available revenues needed careful expenditure. There was little to spend on anything but gradual development. The mullahs seemed to be content enough. Lord Curzon's coming to India as Viceroy had practically coincided with his accession. The former had once visited Abdurrahman at Kabul, and with his great knowledge of Asian matters should have been well qualified to handle those Afghan questions which were constantly bound to arise. There were a good many points to be adjusted between the two Governments—customs, border disputes, trade conventions, and the like—and Lord Curzon was anxious that the Amir should visit India. This His Highness for some reason or other was not keen to do. Lord Ronaldshay has discussed the Afghan question very fully so far as it then entered into Lord Curzon's career; but it is not difficult to see that the Foreign Department in India knew well that his lordship did not see, and could not see, the questions that arose between us from the Amir's legitimate point of view. At this time apprehension of Russia's intentions had been much revived. Lord Kitchener had been charged with bringing the whole organisation of the army up to date, and preparing its administrative organisation for a Central Asian campaign in support of Afghan integrity. But Habibullah would not come down, and probably was not sure if he was secure enough to come, or could face those who would call him *kafir* for his pains. So Inayatullah, his son, came in his stead, and in lieu of a visit of His Highness himself, Sir Louis Dane, the Foreign Secretary, was sent with a small mission to discuss matters in dispute. This mission spent six months in Kabul in 1904, six somewhat difficult months, in which the Governor-General insisted on taking up a vexatious and meticulous attitude with many of the questions that the mission was to settle.

Nevertheless the Amir was entirely friendly, and while wanting certain things that we could not agree to, was perfectly reasonable in most points.

The officers of the mission made many friends, and, as Abdurrahman has always said, "The more Afghans and British meet the better they get on," and quite repudiated the idea that the less they saw of us the more they liked us. It was not till 1906 that Habibullah paid his visit to India, when Lord Minto was Viceroy. This visit was a pleasing one, and he himself won golden opinions, and was well satisfied with all he saw. Among other things, Lord Kitchener and Sir Henry MacMahon ministered to his true spirit of friendliness by making him a master-mason in the English Rite—a pledge of fraternity and goodwill from which he never departed, though much was said by the old-fashioned mullahs at his having joined some mysterious body. But since Sirdar Nasrullah had joined the craft in England, no real harm was done and much good ensued.

During this reign especially the new Amir began to realise, as did the British frontier officers, what his father and older heads had suspected—that in extending our influence over the border tribes, and generally maintaining, as we were no doubt bound to do, our control over the trade routes, we were giving, as it were, hostages into the Amir's hand. It is perfectly true that no ruler of the past had effective authority over these hill tracts. From earliest days they had been a law unto themselves, but Dost Muhammad and Abdurrahman always claimed authority over them as Pashtu-speaking people, and they in their turn were prepared to look to the Amir when it suited them to do so. But the march of civilisation and progress had called for a delimitation of responsibility as interpreted by the Durand line, while the Sikhs in their time had long ago destroyed any claim for Kabul to control all Pashtu-speaking people.

Nevertheless the Amirs were discovering, as their rule also became more consolidated, that they, whenever they liked, could call the tune to which the Pathan tribes in the British hills, at any rate trans-Indus, would dance. This power was no doubt in the ordinary course of Eastern kingcraft duly cultivated, with the result that it had long been pretty patent that when we and the Amir were pulling the same way, that is to say the Amir's way, all was quiet on the border, and that when there was anything like an acute difference the frontier was unaccountably restless. That is the power, among other things, of Islam itself. In spite of our years of patient endeavouring to win the tribes, to help them to improve their hard life, and generally to bring them some share of the world's prosperity—endeavours in some ways much appreciated—nevertheless the fact remains that the Amir can usually call the tune! Which does not mean that the tribes may not have occasion to dislike what the Amir may be doing, and turn with double affection to the British for a while, because, as has been said, statecraft in the East means knowing when to change sides.

It always, however, pleased Abdurrahman to point to our troublous times on the border, compared with the peace of the sword, added to Islamic influence, which he could wield had we left the Khaibar, Waziristan, the Kurram, and even Miranzai in his hands!

During the early years of the twentieth century went on that struggle for a share in the development of Persia, and the great attempt of Germany to control trade in Mesopotamia, in the Persian Gulf, and generally to menace British influence in the East. As part of Great Britain's policy to stabilise matters and to limit the field of strife, appeared the Anglo-Russian Agreement of 1907. The verdict of history has yet to be recorded as to whether it was wise or whether, as Lord Curzon urged, weak and foolish. The World War tore it up, so that it perhaps matters not; but though its aims were excellently intended, it was so badly explained that it annoyed the Eastern world. It merely meant to settle spheres in which Britain and Russia should push their business activities, but it read almost like a pact for dividing other people's countries. Incidentally it annoyed the Amir Habibullah, who refused to signify his assent. The treaty included a reference to the respecting of Russian frontier between Russia and Afghanistan, as already delineated, and it also contained the remark that Great Britain had no intention of changing the political status of Afghanistan. That paragraph did contain the implication that Great Britain was the authority in such matters—a position logical enough from all that had passed from many points of view, but undoubtedly likely to raise issues that had better have been left as they were. The Russo-Afghan paragraphs were not to come into effect, and this was perhaps an afterthought, until the Amir's approval had been given. This assent he would not give, probably because he had not been suitably approached and prepared, and this was one of the points of soreness in the years before the World War. As has been told of earlier days, so in these, there were plenty of mischief-makers who would always try and misrepresent the doings of the British; in his wiser moments, however, the Amir steadfastly put them from him. There were a good many troubles on the British frontier about this time, notably with the Zakkha Khel Afridis, which did not matter, with the Mohmands, which did, as the tribe had clans on both sides of the political border, and with the Shinwaris, whom it pleased to attack the Khyber Rifle post of Landi Kotal. This, of course, was without any connivance or support from official Kabul, within whose territory the Shinwaris lie, though at the moment of its first happening the Government of India feared that an Afghan war was on them. These clouds, however, had all passed when August 1914 dawned.

Afghanistan and the World War

At the opening of the World War the East was not very directly concerned, though the British East, or all of it that mattered, took a strong enough line, Eastern troops leaving for France amid enthusiasm. When, however, Turkey joined the war, and also had the effrontery to proclaim, by reason of the Sultan's somewhat bogus claim to the caliphate, a holy war, a *jihad*, then a very different position immediately arose. The blood in the Afghan hills started a-throbbing. The cry was so well known, "Glory for all, and heaven for those who bleed"; a cry which had a pleasant background—visions of women, the comely women of India, and the loot of merchant cities. Then His Highness the Amir Habibullah sent for the Moslem gentleman who represented British India, and indeed Great Britain, at his Court, and said to him: "I shall send my official reply to the Viceroy's intimation of this war, but I want you to give him a message, a private message, which you will know how to put. I shall be true to my alliance and friendship. He is to pay no attention to what I say, for I have kittle cattle to hold; but watch what I do, and have no fear." It was the message of an Eastern gentleman who meant to abide by his word, even to his own hurt and hindrance, and he was murdered for his pains. The treatment which he and his father had received at British hands, despite the domestic quarrels and misconceptions which so often arose and which have been described, had been uniformly good, and had been supported by the best of all guarantees, hard cash. Nevertheless gratitude such as the Amir displayed is not always to be discerned in time of stress.

It was an anxious period in India. Five regiments at least had felt the bitter leaven of sedition coming from two sources. One source was German propaganda, and it is to be remembered that every prince in India received in an ornamental leather case a special letter in Urdu or Persian from the German Emperor explaining his friendship and regard for them. The second was the bitter Hindu and Bhabbar[1] Akali movement, of which Sir Michael O'Dwyer has written so clearly. The Government of India had agreed to the pick of its troops and officers going to France and Egypt. It was a time when the promptings of Belial Machiavelli in the Amir's ear were many. Had the attempt to drive the British into the sea at Shaiba made by the Turks in 1915 been successful, it is probable that the Amir could not have held his pack. Shaiba, that battle fought on the edge of the desert by some four Indo-British brigades in the growing heat of a Tigris summer, was perhaps the decisive battle of the war. But the Turks failed, the Turkish corps commander took his own life in chagrin, and the friends of England held the Moslem staunch. For two whole years the tribes on the Afghan border, the Rohillas of Ruh, were phenomenally quiet. The Amir had advised us to have no expeditions if we could avoid it, and it was not necessary. Then those misbegotten limbs of Satan, the Mahsud Waziris, could stand the inhibition no longer, and commenced not raids as we knew them in days

[1] Bhabbar=Tiger: Akali=a Sikh religious belligerent zealot.

gone by, but well-armed inroads with picketed ways of retreat, and plenty of arms and ammunition. At last the Indian Government said to the Amir, in diplomatic language, "This is a bit thick. What about it?" And His Highness sent reply, "I agree with you, you can't stand this; settle their hash, but I pray you don't send too cruel a general, lest I cannot hold the sympathisers here." And the British Government acted accordingly.

At Kabul a German mission arrived, full of plans and offerings, and the Amir sent word that he had propounded terms of alliance, so hard that they could not be accepted, for, as he hinted, there are more ways than one of killing a cat. Then a Turkish mission arrived, the green banner of Islam and all the rest of it, and the mullahs, the ecclesiastical party, were all for pouring on to the infidel, as they were in 1857. And again the Amir held the fort with diplomacy. "I am a lone man," he said to the Turks, "and fearsome of the British and the Russian allies between the upper and the nether millstone. But a good Moslem am I, and what the Kalipha [1] wills is mine to do. I await the Turkish armies on their way to India, and I shall be ready to lead the hosts of Islam by their side. *Ya Ali!*"

And so the Amir helped keep the wolves from the Indian door, and again he died for his pains. Therefore let us remember, and write it down to him and his father, that they had been staunch to their undertakings and given the lie to the old Persian saying. In India the Foreign Department had risen to the occasion. Habibullah had not drawn his allowance for some time, and now asked for the total in gold. Many said that he was but trifling; but good sense and wisdom prevailed, so with difficulty —for gold was not easy to obtain—it was sent to him, and with it also a promise of an increased allowance, for "gold shall be your master," and is well to cross the hand that helps you.

The story of the intrigue and underground hunting of that period in India and Afghanistan would make some very pretty reading, and no doubt if the old cry, "All is

[1] Kalipha—in European style caliph.

known," was sprung on many who sit smugly in various parliaments and assemblies, there would be a hurried vacating of seats.

But intrigue or no intrigue Habibullah kept the peace, and the World War came to an end without Afghanistan being numbered among the combatants. And when it ended he still sat on his father's throne, almost alone amid crumbling Eastern monarchies.

CHAPTER XVII

THE THIRD AFGHAN WAR, 1919

The Murder of the Amir · Afghan Activities in India The British Military Dispositions · The Afghans Cross the Frontier · The Trouble at Peshawar · The Second Fight at Bagh · British Advance into Afghanistan The Afghans in Kurram · The Repercussion in Chitral The Kandahar Front · The Trouble in Zhob

THE title of the Third Afghan War has been given to the attempted invasion of India by the Afghans in 1919. This Third Afghan War was staged just as the world was in the excitement of bringing its troops home and turning them back to citizenship, many of them with their fortunes to rebuild. In India the best native troops were absent in the Black Sea and in Mesopotamia, and the army, while numerous enough, was very largely composed of newly raised troops led by temporary officers, which India had been forming at the urgent request of Great Britain. The European troops were largely Territorials, due for demobilisation and repatriation, and the new Regular Army that was to follow the setting sun round the world once again had not yet come into being. India still had among its British units many of the Garrison, *i.e.* veteran European corps, invaluable for local purposes, but not available as field troops, while a considerable number of the wartime services were in process of demobilisation.

THE MURDER OF THE AMIR

The murder of the Amir Habibullah Khan, already referred to, occurred on the night of the 19th February 1919 while shooting in Laghman, in the country north of Jalalabad.

The Court, according to the usual custom, was in winter

residence in that town. Nasrullah, a whole but younger brother of the Amir, declared himself king. As Abdurrahman has pointed out, the succession in Afghanistan went by the choice of the people, but if acceptable, to the eldest son. On the other hand, by Moslem law inheritance passes to the uncles. There would be plenty of precedent for Nasrullah's action had it appealed to the people. Inayatullah, the eldest son of the murdered Amir, was also at Jalalabad, and he acquiesced in his uncle's action.

The troops in Jalalabad were much incensed at the Amir's murder, and arrested the Commander-in-Chief, Sirdar Nadir Khan.

Amanullah, the third son of Habibullah, was officiating as Governor of Kabul, and securing the support of the troops, declared himself Amir, and summoned his uncle and elder brother at Jalalabad to come to Kabul. This they did, and paid him homage as Amir. The circumstances of his father's murder have never been quite cleared up, though an Afghan colonel was executed for his share therein. The Commander-in-Chief was removed from his appointment and sent to Khost, his place being taken by Sirdar Salih Muhammad. This change with an increase of pay, and what has been described as the somewhat perfunctory steps taken to discover and punish the murderers of the late Amir, appear to have placated the army.

Afghan Activities in India

His Highness, apparently to placate the party which had so urged Habibullah to a Holy War, prepared secretly for a descent on India, to repeat, in fact, the old story which had been enacted when Zaman Shah attempted to regain the territories of Ahmad Shah. Two factors were in existence to aid him. First, the unchanging fact of the old country of Ruh from which the Rohillas had come, that long strip of fanatical tribal belt between the Durand line and the administered British provinces, which was mostly within the British political frontier, and in which the roll of the drum ecclesiastic during the long-drawn-out years of the

World War had stirred the tribes greatly.[1] The other ally was the section of the Indian politicians, varying from the vociferous lawyer who headed agitations without quite knowing what he wanted, down to that bitter, silent leaven which has always been against us, and which had been so much at work during the last few years. Those who have read the story in Sir Michael O'Dwyer's book[2] will have some idea of what was at work in this direction. Amanullah summoned the heads of the British tribesmen to Kabul and told them to prepare for war, sending emissaries with money and ammunition among the tribes themselves.

Then there was also to his hand a strange body of fanatics, who called themselves the "Provisional Government of India," who could put him in touch with Indian intrigue.

To stimulate his efforts was the knowledge that the British troops in India, European and Indian, were war-weary and were demobilising.

The first moves came from India. Riots broke out at many places, especially along the main line from Bombay to Peshawar. Excited crowds attacked and burnt railway stations, and fierce outbreaks occurred in several provinces. Fortunately the policy of indianising the railways had not then been allowed to run its foolish course, and there were enough Anglo-Indians and Europeans in the railway services to prevent them from being paralysed. The unrest in the Punjab took the form of a rebellion, where the firm hand of Sir Michael O'Dwyer and the military authorities prevented things from taking their logical way.

In this connection it is as well to remember that the controversies that raged afterwards only waged as to whether the action taken was or was not too severe, or fell on the right people. The seriousness of the situation has never been denied by responsible people.

While this very grave state of things was in progress, our young Amir, abandoning the policy of his grandfather and father, which had so conduced to the growing prosperity

[1] See Chapter XVI. The influence of the Amir over the tribesmen.

[2] Of which the Bhabbar Akali movement, p. 254, was but one of many.

and pacification of Afghanistan, now moved his troops towards the British frontier. The first moves were not very large ones, and presumably aimed at preparation and disturbing the tribes. The Commander-in-Chief came to Dakka and actually crossed himself into British territory to examine the water supply at Bagh. Some 2000 Afghan troops were moved to Dakka close to the border, 1500 to Kandahar, and about 2000 into Khost.

The Afghan postmaster at Peshawar, who was practically the Afghan consular agent at that city, was summoned to Kabul, and received copies of a proclamation from the Amir calling on all Moslems in India to aid Afghanistan in a war against the infidel, viz. the British.

It was not, however, till 3rd May, when the worst of the weather in the Punjab plains was about to begin, that hostilities commenced.

The British Military Dispositions

The actual military dispositions of the British in 1919 were those usually in force to guard the frontier in normal times, plus some extra garrisons on the Waziristan border. These cantonings were, roughly, a division and a cavalry brigade in the Peshawar area, with two other divisions behind, a division on the Kandahar front in the Quetta area, and three small forces of all arms stationed along the curtain from Kohat to the Derajat, with headquarters at Kohat, Bannu, and the Dera Ismail Khan. The last three forces consisted normally of units not detailed for the main field army. The force at Quetta and Peshawar closed the main lines of invasion from those places. That at Kohat guarded the road from the Paiwar Kotal from Afghanistan, while the force in Bannu and the Derajat kept the clans of Waziristan in some sort of order.

The troops available in the first two divisional areas on the northern line, as that of the Peshawar front was termed, were 22 battalions, 6 cavalry regiments, 66 guns. At Kohat were 4 battalions, 1 cavalry regiment, 6 guns. In the Bannu and Derajat areas, 7 battalions, 2 cavalry regiments, 12 guns, 2 militia battalions.

The Khaibar to-day

The upper and lower motor roads and the broad-gauge railway

The mail train from Peshawar to the British cantonment at Landi Kotal

Afridi tribesmen in the Khaibar (ex-soldiers of His Majesty)

Fortunately the troops immediately on the frontier were of high grade. Most of the battalions were those of the old army, British and Indian, and though full of young soldiers, had kept the cadre and a proportion of trained soldiers complete. But at that time the amount of motor transport in India was small, and the best of the animal transport was in Mesopotamia and Palestine, while the general state of preparation of the army for war naturally showed signs of the drain of the previous four years to theatres overseas.

The Afghans Cross the Frontier

On the 3rd May the first act of war occurred. The usual party of the Khyber Rifles escorting the caravan to the Afghan border was turned back by pickets of armed Afghans, then within the British border. The leader, a tribal raider, stated that he was under the orders of the Afghan Commander-in-Chief. A little later five harmless labourers working on some water-pipes were murdered. Shortly afterwards a party of Afghan infantry occupied the Kaffir Kot ridges just south of Landi Khana, and the British villages of Bagh. The next day more Afghan tribal troops arrived, followed by regulars. Farther back the tribesmen were flocking into Jalalabad to be issued with arms. On the 5th the Khyber Rifles at Landi Kotal received a small regular British reinforcement by lorry.

In the Kurram, tribesmen and regulars were erecting breastworks on the Paiwar Kotal, and the inhabitants were in some alarm. A small force from Thal was pushed up to support the Kurram Militia on 5th May, while on the 6th a general mobilisation of the field army in India was ordered.

By this date three Afghan battalions with cavalry and guns were across the border, with five more battalions behind them at Dakka. On the British side the only troops opposing them were five hundred of the men of the Khyber Rifles and a couple of guns. An attack on the post was imminent, and the Afghans then had it in their hands to achieve a local success which would have stirred the tribes round for many miles.

The next day (7th) the 2nd Somersets arrived in lorries from Peshawar with four more guns, and on the 8th the 1st Infantry Brigade under Brigadier G. F. Crocker,[1] with the 77th Field Battery (howitzers), a few cavalry, sappers, and a machine-gun company. This altered the situation, and the Afghan troops contented themselves with crossing the border in force, taking up position on the hills round Landi Kotal, and waiting for the clans to flock to their side, which they were doing in some numbers.

Brigadier Crocker at once brushed aside the enemy in his immediate vicinity and put out a line of strong outposts. On the 8th and 9th two battalions of the 2nd Brigade came in by road and lorry, and Crocker felt himself strong enough to attack the Afghans in their positions about Bagh. Fearing, however, for his northern flank, his attack was not strong enough to do more than carry the high ground on the far side of the Rangi Nullah, when large Afghan forces were seen coming down to oppose further advance. Crocker therefore decided to hold what he had gained and wait for the rest of the 1st Division, which was believed to be coming up behind him.

But the reinforcement had been delayed by amazing situations at Peshawar.

The Trouble at Peshawar

On 7th May the Criminal Investigation Department had ascertained that the Afghan postmaster, who had been left at large, though war had been declared the day before, and the Indian Revolutionary Committee in Peshawar city had arranged to burn the cantonment and civil lines, damage the railway, and destroy the mobilisation stores. For this purpose they had arranged to collect some 7000 men from among trans-border tribesmen in the city and the bad hats generally, who there abound.

By some strange reasoning the Government of India had

[1] The old title brigadier, now revived, is used for convenience instead of brig.-general.

allowed the folly of seditious volunteers and seditious strikes (*hartals*) to go on for two months. This was the fruit thereof.

The following letter, sent to the Amir by the postmaster on the 7th May, somewhat naive and disjointed though it is, clearly shows what was doing, and how deeply the Afghan action was connected with the sedition movement in India.

Translation of the Postmaster's Letter to the Amir

"Hearing that the Post Office (*i.e.* Afghan) was to be searched, I ordered armed resistance, as the whole of my correspondence went against the British Government. If necessary, I would begin a Holy War in Peshawar city. Hearing of this, 8000 Peshawaris, both Hindus and Moslems, came to help me. That night 2000 villagers from outside offered their assistance. I said that I would invite them when the time came. Sikh regiments have assured Hindus that they look on Moslems as brethren and will not fire on them. The Government (meaning India) has not sufficient troops in India, and often moves about one regiment consisting of two or three companies to make a display. In spite of many telegrams sent by the Chief Commissioner, no regiments have arrived by train. British subjects will not supply recruits. There are disturbances throughout India, and troops if sent from England will not arrive in time. It has been given out at a public meeting that the Amir and ghazis are ready to help Indians, and if the war is delayed the public (meaning Indian public) will be displeased with the Amir. The assembly cried with one voice that they would not forget the oppressions and tyrannies of the British Government. If after selected leaflets have been circulated and three Sipah Salars[1] have been appointed the Amir refrains from invading India, Hindus and Moslems will be much displeased. It is not expedient to delay and give the English time to collect troops."

Major-General Climo, who commanded the 2nd Brigade at Nowshera, which was moving up to Jamrud for the

[1] Corp commanders.

Khaibar, was detained, and with one British cavalry regiment, one British and one Gurkha battalion, was detailed to surround the city and arrest the Afghan postmaster and thirty-three leaders. He decided to do this during the hot weather afternoon siesta hour, and it was done quietly and promptly. In eleven minutes every gate was seized by cavalry, and all egress barred in thirty-three minutes by infantry when the search began. The postmaster and twenty-two out of the thirty-three leaders were secured, the bad characters of the city entirely cowed, and the movement scotched. The field army troops then hurried on to the Khaibar, those detailed for area defence taking over further watch and ward.

The Second Fight at Bagh

In the meantime the Divisional Commander, Major-General Fowler, had hurried up to Landi Kotal, and decided to remain there. As soon as his 2nd Brigade came up he intended to renew the attack on the Afghans. While this was in progress, the 1st Cavalry Brigade and an attached regiment, four in all, under Brigadier Baldwin, were got ready for a forward movement against the Afghan station of Dakka, twenty-two miles from Jamrud—a move complicated by the difficulty at that time of year of watering the horses for the major part of this distance, and therefore of getting the brigade to Dakka with any chance of being fit for severe work at once.

Early on 11th May General Fowler, with the 2nd Brigade and the best part of the 1st, attacked the Afghan forces at dawn. As the day advanced the heat grew very great, compelling the troops to halt and rest at intervals. The main attack was made by the 2nd Brigade, which, assembling behind the heights carried by Brigadier Crocker on the 9th, was directed against the Afghan right and centre, the 2nd North Staffords climbing the heights and attacking the flank of the concave Afghan position, while the two battalions of the 11th Gurkhas moved up the valley in the centre. The attack could only be supported by the

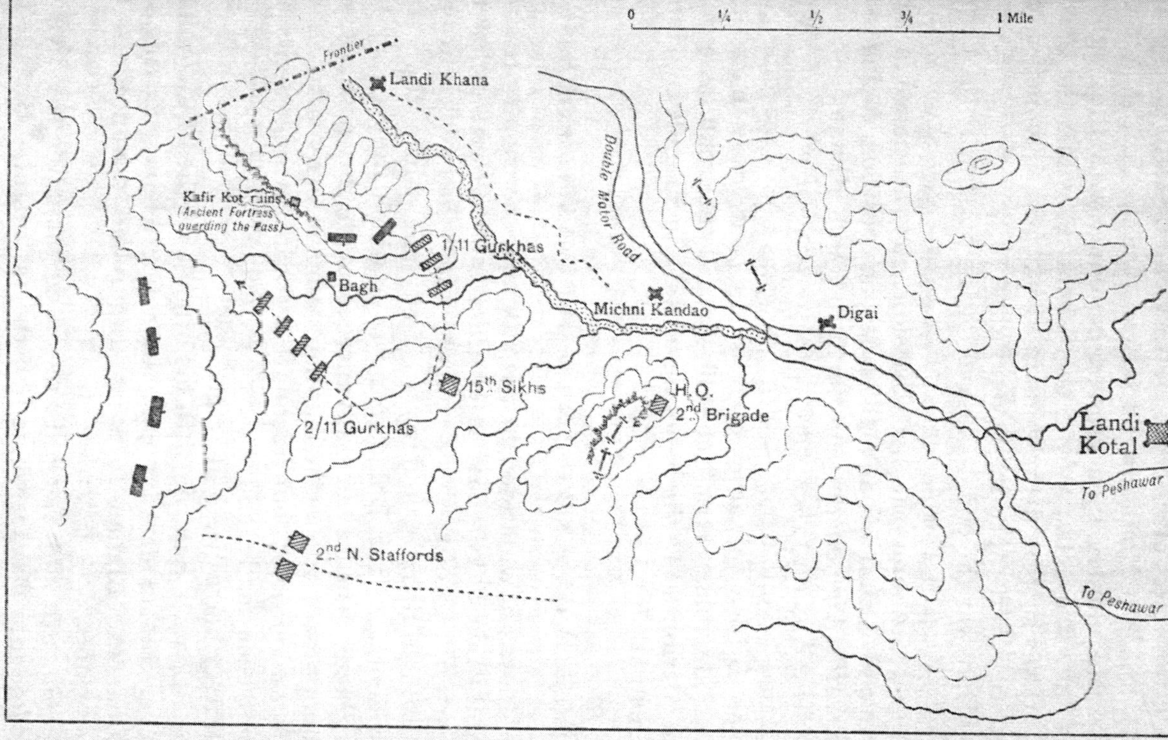

Sketch of the 2nd. engagement at Bagh on the Khaibar route

field howitzers of the 77th Battery and by eight guns of the 6th and 8th Mountain Batteries. On the British left the British infantry soon crossed bayonets with the Afghans as they drove them from their trenches, while the 2/11th Gurkhas surprised the guns in the centre, bayoneting the gunners and capturing several guns.

That was the end of it, save for the pursuit by the bombing parties. The Afghans after their sorry show were in full flight, and the 1st Division now advanced a mile beyond Landi Khana to a strong position facing east towards Afghanistan and north to Landi Khana.

The Afghan losses were perhaps 400—of whom 66 were buried by our troops—with five guns and a machine gun. The British casualties were slight, but losses from heat considerable. The Afghan flight and the small losses may be attributed to the handling of the 2nd Brigade by Major-General Climo.

The Advance into Afghanistan

It was now decided to seize Dakka, the cavalry leading, and at dawn two days later Climo moved on to picket the eastern end of the pass so as to allow the cavalry to push through thereto, and by 10 a.m. had gained the actual widening of the Dakka plain over which the cavalry had to act. The cavalry advance through the Khaibar was unopposed by any tribesmen, and it arrived at Landi Kotal by 9.30; but adequate watering arrangements had not been made, and it was past noon before the tired and thirsty horses were fit to go on.

Brigadier Baldwin with his brigade reached Dakka, however, before dark unopposed, a few Afghans having fled from the Afghan forts as Climo had advanced in the morning.

On 14th May General Fowler, commanding the division, came into Dakka, where half the 1st Infantry Brigade had now arrived, and was ordering a better camp site to be taken up, when a force under Colonel MacMullen,[1] three

[1] Part of 15th Sikhs, who were already being attacked.

miles east of Dakka, which had been carrying out a reconnaissance, reported large bodies of Afghans in front of him on the far side of the Khurd Khaibar Pass, which he had occupied. The only course was to disengage from what was evidently a force moving to recover Dakka. The steady withdrawal was closely followed by the Afghan troops and a horde of tribesmen, who were, however, charged and ridden through by a squadron of the 1st Dragoons. Some confusion was caused by tribesmen in the broken ground approaching the camp at Dakka, but the party under Colonel MacMullen succeeded in retiring in good order, but not without a good many casualties both in men and horses, covered by the 1st Somersets and 1/35th Sikhs, who had marched in during the day. By morning the Afghans were occupying a position some 4000 yards in length, which made the British camp site untenable, and Brigadier Crocker, who had now ascertained that the enemy's strength was not more than 3000 men with seven guns, decided to attack the hills with the 1st Brigade, moving out before dawn. After several hours, however, an impasse had been reached, and the long line of attacking battalions had exhausted their power of offence. At 11.30 Major-General Andrew Skeen, with the headquarters and two battalions of the 3rd Brigade from Landi Kotal, marched in and at once took charge, ordering the fresh troops to the attack at 2 p.m. But in the meantime the fire of the British howitzers had been too much for the Afghans, who had commenced to retire an hour after noon. Colonel MacMullen decided to seize the opportunity and pushed the 15th Sikhs on at once, followed by the rest of the line. That again was the end of it, and the Afghans disappeared as rapidly as they had come, leaving five of their guns behind them and losing some 600 casualties, of which 200 were killed. The British losses were 22 killed and 157 wounded, the proportion of British officers being heavy.

While this fighting was in progress the expected trouble among the Afridis came to a head. Already at Jamrud, when hurrying up from Peshawar, the 2nd Brigade had been fired on, and it was then feared that the contagion might be spreading to the Khyber Rifles, who were and are chiefly recruited from the Afridi clans.

On the 14th May, while the 1st Division was engaged beyond Landi Kotal, the 2nd Division from Rawalpindi had come into the Khaibar and taken on the defence of the communications in the nick of time. But the Afridis were up, and it was necessary to allow the Khyber Rifles to take their discharge—a disconcerting but unavoidable condition of using tribal militia for the maintenance of local order. If the tribes from which they came and with whom their women and children lived turned against us, they could not be expected to remain staunch, and arrangements to send them off had been anticipated.

Despite the inconvenience of having the tribes up all along the Khaibar, raiding and attacking at any suitable point, the military position was now much improving. More transport and more Line of Communication troops were arriving, and though some confusion, due to incomplete organisation on the communications, existed, by 26th May the British, unmolested further at Dakka, were ready to advance on Jalalabad, the summer capital of the Amir so famous in earlier British annals.

Throughout India the loyal portions of the population were declaring their allegiance, and the Princes were as usual offering all their resources, having indeed little enough sympathy with anyone who chose to attack Hindustan.

But the advance to Jalalabad did not occur, for another Afghan threat unexpectedly occurred in the Kurram. So serious might the results of this move be, and so numerous the tribes who might be disturbed by it, that it was judged wise to hold up the advance till the position in the latter area should be in hand. When that object was achieved the Afghans asked for an armistice.

The Afghan Invasion of Kurram

Mention has already been made of Afghan troops entrenching the crest of the Paiwar Kotal, of the alarm

E. N. A.

The fort at Jamrud, with its 'battleship' profile, which still bars the mouth of the Khaibar Pass

caused by the presence of a considerable body of troops in Khost, and the rumours that circulated the countryside. To understand what took place it is necessary to glance at the map and realise how the Afghan district of Khost juts into the British area, or contrariwise, how the tongue of British land that runs up the valley of the Kurram River juts into Afghanistan. The Kurram line, or the "Central line" as it is known in mobilisation parlance, is a narrow strip of partially administered country running for sixty miles north-west from Thal to the famous Paiwar Kotal, while from Thal back to the military centre of Kohat is fifty miles or so more in a north-east direction. The open valley is cultivated and inhabited by a folk now peaceful enough, while on either side are vast hills inhabited by independent tribes within the British political border. Orakzais, Zaimakhts, Chamkanis lie on the north, and variations of the Waziri group on the south, but from a point just west of Thal, the frontier line which runs parallel to the Kurram, is the actual Afghan frontier of Khost. This salient of Khost runs between the British Kurram and Tochi valleys. Looking on the flat of the map, incursion would seem possible from any point, but in reality the mountainous state of the country limits access to a few difficult routes. It was generally expected that Afghan action would commence either in the vicinity of Parachinar, the headquarters of the Kurram and Turi militia, or that sufficient incursions into the Tochi would take place to stir the tribes and unbalance the militia. Nadir Khan, the Afghan Commander-in-Chief at the time of Habibullah's murder, was now commander in Khost, with his headquarters at the governmental town of Matun. The inhabitants of Khost are chiefly the unruly clans of the Mangal tribe. The force at Nadir Khan's disposal was fourteen battalions and forty-eight guns.

The problem before the British on this front was different from that in the Khaibar. At the far end of the Kurram tongue were Turi tribesmen long intensely pro-British, whom we had taken under our protection at their own request at the time of the Second Afghan War. Being of the Shiah

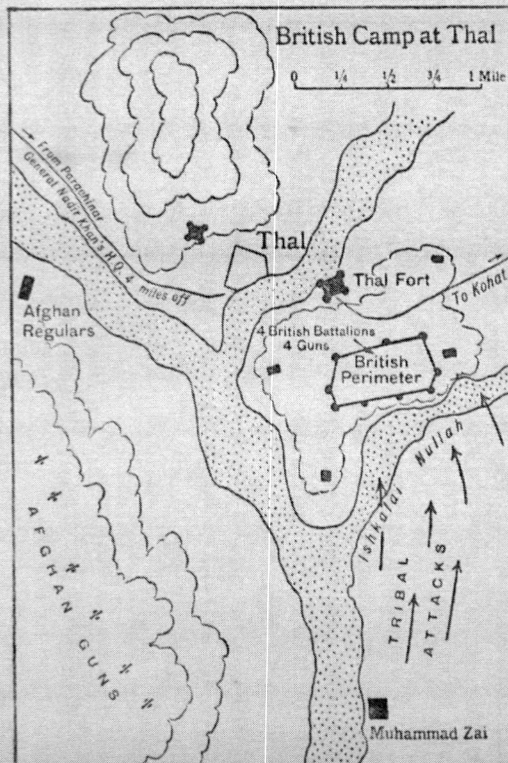

British Camp at Thal

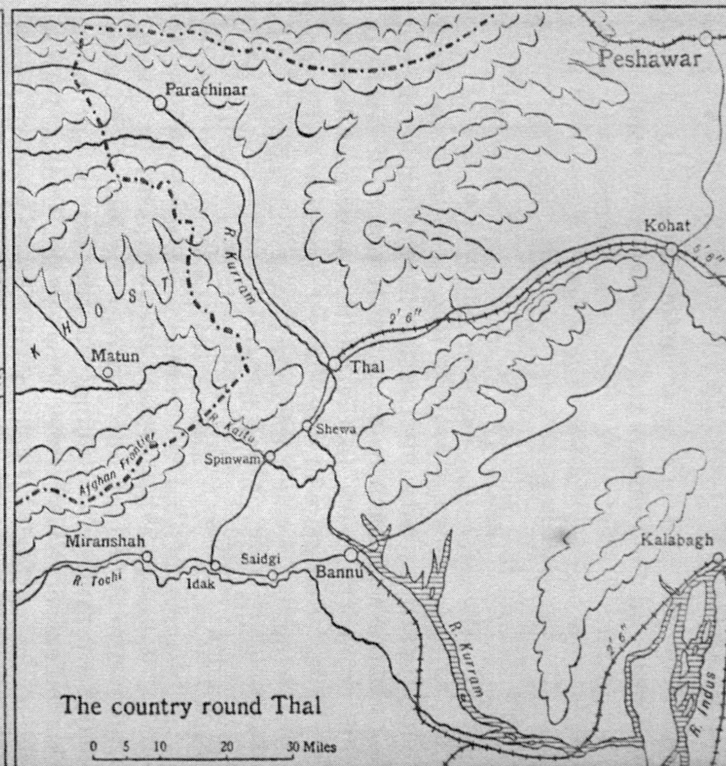

The country round Thal

branch of Islam, they had few sympathies with the ordinary Afghans or other tribes. To protect them, as already explained, Major-General Eustace, commanding at Kohat, had sent a detachment, far from support, to Parachinar. In the neighbouring Tochi valley, also threatened from Khost, there would be no great necessity to protect anyone. The Wazirs would no doubt join the Afghans, and it was intended to withdraw the militia posts rather than be at pains to rescue them.

Early in May the 60th Brigade from Ambala and the 3rd Guides were moved into the area, the brigadier being sent up with one battalion to command the force at Parachinar, now augmented to two battalions, besides the Turi Militia, with a squadron of cavalry and the four guns of the 28th Mountain Battery. By 14th May Nadir Khan was reported at Ali Khel, eleven miles west of the Paiwar, and an attack from that direction was expected.

On the 23rd May, however, Nadir Khan appeared from a totally different direction far down on the British left flank, crossing the frontier from Matun by the Kaitu gorge and moving on Spinwam, a militia post on the British frontier road between Thal and Idak. The garrison of this post and that of Shewa were withdrawn, Afghan troops entering the former almost on the heels of the northern Waziristan Militia garrison. With them were a number of Waziri tribesmen, who pursued the militia, cutting off a portion in the Tochi. The regular column at Dardoni brought in the militia garrisons in the Upper Tochi. Several of the militia, however, deserted, and it was realised that most of the Wazirs in that force and the Waziri tribes generally were thoroughly disaffected.

Shortly after the militia had moved out of Spinwam, Nadir Khan appeared there with 300 Afghan infantry, seven guns, and a horde of Waziri tribesmen. He was now but twenty miles distant from Thal, and not much more from Bannu itself, or Idak in the Tochi. A column from Bannu moved out to Kurram Garhi to hold the debouchment of the Tochi. But Thal was the strategic point. If that fell, not only would the column at Parachinar be isolated and cut off from supplies, but the whole of the Orakzai tribes, with their neighbours on the northern side, would "go." Thal, too, was the head of the little 2-feet 6-inch railway line that ran from the broad gauge railhead at Kohat. Here General Eustace had already posted two battalions and a squadron of cavalry with four mountain guns, and on 25th May he pushed up two more battalions. As related, his original force of a cavalry regiment and four Indian battalions had been strengthened by the 60th Brigade from Ambala, of which the brigadier was at Parachinar.

The general now took command of the increased force at Thal, and prepared to oppose any advance into the Kurram or adjacent Miranzai valley which leads down to Kohat. While this force was entrenching itself on the morning of the 27th, the Afghans appeared and at once proceeded to invest the British position—a course for which the tribal hordes accompanying the Afghans, slinking along every *nullah* and on to every commanding point in the vicinity, were peculiarly well suited.

General Nadir Khan established his headquarters a few miles up from Thal on the Kurram River, occupying with his regular troops a row of heights a mile from the village of Thal, and generally commanding the position taken up by the British, while his tribesmen enveloped it on the south. The British water supply was away in a *nullah* to the north, whence it was pumped into the post. On the 28th the Afghan howitzers, which far outranged the mountain guns, proceeded to shell the British camp with accuracy. The petrol dump and *bhoosa* [1] stacks outside the fort were set on fire, as also the ration dump in the railway station, while the wireless station was hit and put out of action. On the night of the 28th the Frontier Constabulary abandoned their posts on the Sanroba *nullah*, a move which imperilled the water supply. Food began to run short, and troops and animals were put on half rations, and the next night the Afghans were emboldened to attack a portion of our position, without, however, obtaining any success.

[1] Chopped straw ; *cf.* Egyptian *tibbin*.

Offensive British action which had been so effective in the Khaibar was not possible, but by the 31st both Briton and Afghan knew that reinforcements were approaching from Kohat.

The movement about to start against Jalalabad was suspended, and all energies directed to striking at Nadir Khan before the Zaimukhts and Orakzais could rise. On the 24th and 25th two battalions of the 69th Punjabis came into Kohat from down country. Among the reinforcements were the headquarters and the best part of two brigades of the 16th Division from Lahore under Major-General Beynon, with the 45th Brigade of Field Artillery and one battery also from Peshawar, all of which arrived between the 28th May and 1st June.

Early June on the frontier is intensely hot, and the movement of any troops, especially European, called for great judgment and forethought. Nevertheless a column of the 80th Battery and 1/69th, with some details of other arms, were pushed to Hangu, half-way towards Thal, at once.

Brigadier R. H. F. Dyer, commanding the 4th Brigade, was entrusted with the relief of Thal, and brought up his force, to which was joined the Hangu column, by 2-feet 6-inch rail, route march and lorry, as best he could, including four 15-pr. guns with the Punjab Garrison Artillery from the fort armament.

At the outset it looked as if the problem was to be an exceedingly difficult one in every way. The relieving force had to be got to Thal in intense heat, by road or the stuffy, crawling little railway, with water none too plentiful, and a hard fight against a difficult enemy at the end.

Brigadier Dyer determined to press on to Togh, some twenty miles from Thal, in any formation, and from there get his men into battle order. Marching from Hangu at 5.30 p.m. on the 30th May, it was an hour past midnight when the rearguard got in. The troops got food that night but little enough sleep, and at 4 a.m. started off for the eighteen-mile march, which would bring them within striking distance of Thal. In terrible dust and heat the rear column reached Darsamand, fifty-one miles from

Kohat, by the very creditable hour of 1 p.m., and communication by visual signal was opened with Thal through Fort Lockhart.

At 5 next morning the force pushed on to complete the nine miles to Thal and to fight the Afghans and their tribal allies. On reaching the aeroplane ground, two miles north-east of Thal, an officer of the General Staff from General Eustace met the brigadier with a full description of the Afghan dispositions.

Apparently some 4000 Khostwal and Waziri tribesmen under a Zadran chief, Babrak, were in the Ishkalai *nullah* south of Thal, 2000 more tribesmen were on the hills north-east of it, while on the range south-east of Thal and Yusuf Khel were the Afghan regulars and guns, with the tribesmen on both flanks. Brigadier Dyer determined to push the relief force at once against the eastern portion or right of the main Afghan position, after first attacking Babrak's tribesmen.

This was carried out by the 1/69th with the 3/150th in support, the rest of the 45th Brigade following behind. The suddenness of the attack and the heavy fire from the 18-pounders was too much for Babrak's hordes, who broke and fled in all directions, the 69th gaining the heights by 4 p.m. The 89th Battery then silenced the Afghan guns.

The tired troops now went into bivouac, while the Commander prepared his plans for a further offensive at dawn; but next morning as the sun rose the heels of the retreating Afghans could not be seen for the dust!

The Repercussion in Chitral

In an earlier chapter the policy under which the Government of India had tidied up the ragged ends of its frontier has been described. Right up to the highest passes of the Hindu Kush, the doors by which wandering Cossack officers should produce international disagreements had been closed, and the small pre-Aryan Shiah princelets and their peoples had been saved from the oppressive and quite unjustifiable claims of ambitious amirs. After years of delicate political discussion, of boundary commissions, and of armed operations in helping Kashmir to assert her authority over her feudatories, the responsibility of all and sundry from the Kabul River to the Pamirs had been defined. Among the more difficult of these lesser problems had been that of Chitral, which involved the maintenance of a British agent and British garrison in support of a tiny state, far away from reinforcement, cut off for half the year from India, and nevertheless close to a portion of Afghanistan which had a comparatively accessible way of approach on the Afghan side.

Older-fashioned political officers had always emphasised the liabilities and difficulties which isolated outposts must present in time of trouble, and Chitral afforded an excellent example of such difficulties at a time when a Chitral relief expedition would have been out of the question. At the commencement of the Third Afghan War, Shujah-ul-mulk, the princelet whom we had set up in 1895 when twelve years old, after the Chitral troubles of that year, still enjoyed his throne. The force in Chitral consisted of 450 rifles of the 1/11th Rajputs, two guns of the 23rd Mountain Battery, and a section of sappers, in addition to the frontier militia corps known as the Chitral Scouts, and a bodyguard of the Mehtar's, some 2000 strong, of whom, however, but 150 had breech-loaders. To this also had come a refugee Russian colonel with a machine gun. The Afghans had some seven battalions, twelve guns, and some machine guns in the Kunar valley at Birkot and Asmar, of whom more than half were in the upper valley. On the 5th May the political officer, Major Reilly, had become suspicious of Afghan movements, and mobilised half the Scouts. On the 8th the Mehtar received a highly inflammable proclamation from Amanullah, calling on him to rise against the British. On the 12th May the Afghans invaded Chitral territory. Major Reilly, with Scouts and the Mehtar's forces, supported by the British garrison, moved down to attack the invaders at Arnawi and Dokhalim, and, assisted by Kafir tribesmen, drove out the Afghans and occupied the Afghan village of Birkot, which was looted by the Kafirs. By this move the war was carried for the moment into the aggressor's territory. In the meantime the Afghans were assembling considerable forces, and neither the Chitralis nor the local Afghans were inclined to observe the armistice. The British advance on Jalalabad would have relieved this pressure, no doubt, had the war continued, but by the 8th of August, when peace was signed, the Afghan troops withdrew, leaving the Chitralis cock-a-hoop at their success against the formidable Afghans, and the British force more than satisfied with the sturdy part it had played in what was a threatening state of affairs, which might easily have had an untoward development.

The Kandahar Front

The position on the southern line facing towards Kandahar differed considerably from that at other parts of the Indo-Afghan frontier. Practically from the Gumal River southwards the frontier of the two states marched together, and there were no areas occupied by independent or unadministered tribes to complicate the problem, though it is true in the somewhat isolated area of Zhob there is a considerable tribal population who are only under some limited form of control. The British frontier *vis-à-vis* Kandahar, sixty odd [1] miles away, lay on the far side of the Khwaja Amran range, through which the broad gauge railway ran under the actual Khojak Pass. An invisible line drawn on a flat plain was the frontier, and while there was an open British cantonment for a battalion in New Chaman, an Afghan garrison resided in the fort of Spin Baldak, five miles within Afghan territory. Another sixty miles or so behind the frontier stood the large and healthy British cantonment of Quetta, containing the best part of a division of the army and part of a cavalry brigade, with large mobilisation reserves of stores. The Quetta plateau is some 5000 feet above sea-level, and the troops there were as fit in summer as in winter. The railway line

[1] Eighty-three by a railway alignment.

from India climbs up the passes by steep gradients, and it is therefore not so valuable a communication as it appears on the map, owing to the small load that engines can haul up at a time, and the difficulty of running frequent trains through the Shelabagh tunnel under the Khojak range.[1] Nevertheless, the various conditions are most favourable for the British, and the Afghans showed no immediate desire to run against the well-organised force commanded by Major-General Wapshare. From Spezand, a junction fifteen miles south of Quetta, the long railway line towards Seistan via Nushki took off, which had been extended into Persia during the World War to admit of the operations of the East Persian cordon. This line was also under the orders of the General commanding at Quetta, and on the 7th May the whole force was declared a field army under the name of the "Baluchistan Force."

The general organisation in the Quetta area, and especially the lay-out at New Chaman, was conceived on the basis of our entry into Afghanistan as an ally, in her support against Russian aggression, and not against Afghanistan as an enemy. The distance of Kandahar, however, and of any cantonment whence aggression on a large scale could commence without warning, minimised this defect.

The Afghan fort at Spin Baldak lay, therefore, as it were, as a gift in the event of hostilities. As a ripost to the invasion of Afghans elsewhere it was decided to capture the place. Unfortunately, the only two planes available at Quetta had been wrecked, and no information could come by air. But information by older-fashioned methods was good and complete. Troops were brought up to the frontier late on the 26th May, and at 4.30 a.m. the cavalry crossed the border to surround the fort, followed by two infantry brigades.

At 6.30 a.m. Major-General Hardy, commanding the right attack, summoned the fort to surrender. The Afghan understood not a white flag and fired on it, whereas the sending forward of a Qoran would have served the

[1] See Chapter XV, where this point is referred to at length.

purpose better. The attack commenced at 8 a.m., and by 1.45 p.m. the fort was captured, with its outlying gardens. One hundred and eighty-six prisoners were taken, 170 Afghans killed, and the remainder of the garrison of 600 escaped, owing to the failure of the cavalry to set their cordon completely.

Our own loss was about sixty all told, including three British and one Indian officer of the 22nd Punjabis, which bore the brunt of the assault. The force returned to Quetta at 3 p.m., leaving a garrison. That was the end of regular fighting on this frontier, the signing of the armistice on the 3rd June preventing any action against the Afghan troops who were beginning to gather.

The Trouble in Zhob

But far otherwise was the situation in Zhob, where the Afghan invasion had thoroughly disturbed the tribes residing therein, and those within Afghanistan adjacent thereto.

The aftermath of the needless Afghan invasion was a series of punitive expeditions, succeeding on a period of raids in the Khaibar and in the Peshawar valley, a prolonged campaign against the Wazirs, especially the Mahsud group of clans, and a definite occupation of part of their country as the only solution to the trouble. But in Zhob the aftermath, or rather the concomitant, of the invasion created a different and a very difficult situation. Since 1889 the Zhob valley has been definitely occupied. That is to say, it has been brought under a rough-and-ready administration of the patriarchal order, with the object of stopping the raids on the trade routes to India, and also covering the ancient invasion and trade routes already referred to, which converged on Multan and the Derajat from Ghuzni and Kandahar. These routes were required for movement of troops to supplement the railways in the event of a campaign to support Afghanistan against Russia, and their improvement was part of the great defence programme initiated after the Panjdeh war scare.[1] The

[1] See Chapter XV, where this point is referred to at length.

occupation but consisted of forming a strong militia to maintain order, long known as the Zhob Levy, but lately as the Zhob Militia, with supporting military cantonments at Loralai and Apozai, the latter now called Fort Sandeman, after the great frontier political officer. The usual garrison consisted of two battalions, two regiments of cavalry,[1] and a mountain battery distributed between the two, and in military posts between the rail at Harnai and Fort Sandeman; while beyond, via Mir Ali Khel and Mogul Khot, the road went on to join that down the Gumal Pass to the Derajat.

Always somewhat inaccessible, and only since the coming of the motors open to modern rapid movement, this large side-tracked district, of which the valleys themselves are over 4000 feet above sea-level, has been full of interest and fascination to those whose lot has been cast there. Its inhabitants are principally the Khakar tribes, a branch of the Duranis, and the Mando Khel, a Pathan tribe; while along the hills which separate it from the Derajat are a tiresome folk, the Sherannis, who are also possibly Durani, but more probably Pathan. Across the Afghan border are the Ghilzais, and north are the Mahsud Waziri clans.

The trouble in 1919 began with that disastrous belated order to the Southern Waziristan Militia to withdraw from Wana into Zhob. Major Russell and the loyal portion of the militia crossing the Gumal straggled dead-weary into the Zhob Militia post of Mogul Khot, after a fighting march of forty-two miles. But in Mogul Khot there was but one day's subsistence for so large a party, and after a day's rest Major Russell endeavoured before dawn to get away to Mir Ali Khel, where a larger militia garrison would give help. But large bodies of the Mahsuds had surrounded Mogul Khot, and the Waziristan Militia lost all discipline long before arriving in the friendly shelter of the Zhob Militia, who had come half-way to meet them. It was a pitiful story of men who threw their arms away or deserted, and gallant English gentlemen butchered to make a Mahsud

[1] Only one cavalry regiment at this juncture, owing to needs elsewhere.

holiday. The remnants got to Mir Ali Khel, the men mainly without arms, refusing to rally, with five British officers dead and two wounded.

This set the whole countryside aflame, and the Khakars, Mando Khel, and Sheranni were up in every direction. Some of the Zhob Militia surrendered their posts and deserted, but the bulk remained faithful. Wherever possible the smaller posts were drawn in. But the regulars in garrison were mostly young troops with young officers, and some pitiful and disastrous affairs of convoys and parties of recruits occurred before two strong columns from Quetta could be brought to relieve Fort Sandeman, which had been invested and the station burnt. The worst happening was the destruction of a convoy under Major A. W. Gooden, 3/124th Baluchistan Regiment, who was killed, and the severe loss inflicted on a column from Fort Sandeman, which tried to rescue the convoy, under Captain Copland, 3/1st Gurkha Rifles, who was also killed, in which four British officers and fifty-three men lost their lives, and many more were wounded. Several other incidents almost as serious occurred before help arrived, and it was not till the end of July that Zhob was pacified and punishment meted out to those of our own tribes who could be reached. It is to be realised that in difficult mountainous country very young soldiers, and temporary or very young British officers, were called on to meet a better armed and more elated tribal enemy than usually falls to the lot of our most experienced frontier officers and men.

With the retaming of Zhob, the disturbances that followed on the Afghan invasion, Waziristan always excepted, came to an end.

CHAPTER XVIII

THE AFGHANISTAN OF KING AMANULLAH

After the Afghan War · The Peace Treaty · The Stirring World of Islam · Pan-Turk and Basmach The Turkistan Soviets · Development and Progress The Afghan People of To-day · Women, Children, Marriage · Education, Laws, Justice · The Ingredients in the All-Blaze of Afghan Character To-day

AFTER THE AFGHAN WAR

As soon as the Third Afghan War was over, and the Amir had time to repent of his evil in suddenly turning on the allies and protector of his father and grandfather, and to turn from his folly in trying to appeal to Indian Moslems as a triumphant ruler in Islam, it was necessary to negotiate a permanent peace.

The British, tired of war, demanding rest at any cost, and with coffers empty, were not prepared to march to Kabul once again, and that being so, it was necessary to make the best peace that would attain the essential objects. Prestige, as a matter of fact, did not very much matter. Great Britain and her children had been the mainstay of the whole world in the last years of the Great War, and no one knew it better than India, while Russia at the moment was of no account. The young Amir was not all folly, and had undoubtedly aspirations that meant well for the world. His father's services to Great Britain, and enduring loyalty to his obligations, had been of very great value, and it was not too serious a matter even if the whole of Afghanistan were swelling with elation at what was in reality a complete defeat.

What was of importance was that the Afghan kingdom

should be maintained in an intact and prosperous condition to carry out its time-honoured function of *l'état tampion* between India and Russia.

The Amir had several ambitions: firstly, that he should no longer be bound to submit his foreign relationships to Great Britain; secondly, that he should be "Shah," or "King," as the Duranis were, and not "Amir"—and here it may be remarked that "Amir," or "Leader," was a title of Dost Muhammad's own choosing, as better suited to the democratic Afghan conception than "Shah"; thirdly, that he should deal direct with Great Britain and not with the Governor-General of India; and fourthly, that as a free king he should have his ministers and consuls where he liked, and receive at Kabul such ministers of other nationalities as he liked. There were other desires, but these were the main ones. He also was anxious to be recognised as having some control over the Pathan tribes within the British boundary, *i.e.* within the Durand line, or at any rate obtain from the British some guarantee that punishment would not be exacted from them in their rebellion at the time of the Afghan invasion.

None of these proposals were, under the conditions then existing, worth fighting over, save that any assurance as to our action towards our own tribes we were not prepared to give. The complete independence of Afghanistan was, it is true, a reversal of much that we had long contended for. But we had always interfered with the sole object in view of having this prosperous and self-supporting kingdom intact and definite against either Persian or Russian aggression.

The Peace Treaty

The British treaty with Afghanistan did not amount to much more than "a gentleman's agreement." That, however, also was no great matter, for there had never been any formal treaty before. Most that we had agreed to do was contained in letters rehearsing the position. Even Habibullah had not said much more than that he abided by his father's undertakings. Under the new treaty, however, we recognised the independence of Afghanistan, and we agreed to the new Amir adopting the title of "King" and being in direct communication with London and with the rest of the world. This had been denounced as a most humiliating arrangement, and a giving-away of all we had bled for in the past. In a manner of speaking it was quite true to say so. But all the old agreements were made with the idea of having this strong buffer between India and Russia, whether Imperial or Soviet. The collapse of Russia as an aggressive danger had disappeared, it was thought, for many a year. Our own Government at home had their hands more than full. As we were to see a little later in Turkey, the Empire was too tired to stir to Mr Lloyd George's call, and diplomacy as well as wisdom pointed to the advisability of a treaty with Afghanistan on the best terms available. On our side we saved the cost of the annual subsidy, and were relieved of treaty entanglements as regards the defence of Afghanistan. It was, of course, obvious that the necessity for protecting Afghanistan against aggression must always remain, not because of treaty or promise, but because of the hard facts of our geographical position and the justice of the case. The want of any promise would not in the least change the possibilities of action, but would give us a freer hand if necessity should arise. Even with the old agreement the Amir had never been able to agree to our officers coming to the frontier or studying plans on the spot, and Abdurrahman had given clearly enough his reasons for not inviting either British or Russian to train his armies. With the change of affairs in Kabul we should attain our long-needed objective of a European instead of a Moslem representative in Afghanistan, whose presence as one among the many agents of the countries of Europe would not be likely to afford pretexts for the furies of a mob.

The Stirring World of Islam

In endeavouring to follow all that promised so well in Amanullah's career, and to lend it our due sympathy and understanding, we cannot disregard the quick succession of contradictory movements in Islam itself which the war called forth. They alone have been enough to bewilder the vision of wiser heads than the young King. With this turmoil we must also take due note of that apprehension in Eastern countries which the political facts of the war seemed to indicate—facts that were interpreted in fear and apprehension. If we look at events as they appeared to the East, we must for a moment hark back to the revival of the influence of the Caliphate by clever Abdul Hamid in comparatively recent times. We have seen this astute Sultan succeed in persuading the orthodox Moslems of Turkey, India, Afghanistan, and Russian Turkistan to regard him as the Caliph—that is to say, in reviving the feeling that Islam meant a vast brotherhood, with a great Moslem potentate as its head, with the power temporal which is so essential a part of the old Islamic conception. Western Moslems—viz. those of Africa and those of Malaya—were less concerned and intrigued, while to Arabia the Turk as Caliph was something of a joke, something of a contradiction in terms, since in his heart of hearts every orthodox Moslem knew that the "Successor" must be not only Arab, but of the tribe and family of the Prophet—a thing which had not been for many a hundred year.

Then came the first happening to confuse the issues, the proclamation of *jihad*—a war of religion in aid of Turkey and the Central Powers, put forth by the Sheikh-ul-islam on behalf of the Sultan, who claimed to be the Caliph. But the writ did not run, the spell would not work! Mecca, Holy Mecca was scornful! It held aloof, and at length, after two years of waiting, proclaimed a rebellion against its accepted head, religious and temporal. Syria and Mesopotamia did not give much support; India wondered; the Moslem soldiers of King George would have none of it. The El Senussi in North Africa gave no sign for twelve months, and the deserts did not care a rap. In Afghanistan and on the mountains of Ruh, the hills of the Indian frontier alone, did the call strike and echo, "Glory for all!" But the Amir, as has been related, refused to unfold the green banner, and kept his restless enthusiasts and fanatics in some order. So thus it was that Islam lost its spell. In the jesting words of the British officer, the "Snark was a boojum" after all.

To this shock to Islam followed the coming of war to Eastern countries which were not belligerent. The breaking up of the Turkish Empire was a recognisable penalty, though looked on with much concern; but the overrunning of Persia by the belligerents and the ruthless treatment of Persians by Turk and Russian were another matter. Even the restorative treatment by Great Britain and the famine relief in 1918 seemed to indicate an unconcern for Eastern sovereignty that produced the greatest apprehension. Added to this, Persia and Afghanistan saw the running of what was called the British North Persian cordon from Baluchistan to Transcaspia, part of the precautions to prevent the spread of a Pan-Turanian conflagration in a militant form. These events but increased the forebodings which the long discussions at the Peace Conference and the issue of the Eastern mandates did little to allay. It has taken several years for the disinterestedness of Great Britain to be recognised despite the fact that she had always been the protector and cherisher of Moslem kingdoms.

The working of these apprehensions no doubt stirred those who advised Amanullah to launch his armies on India and himself declare a Holy War. Two more strange portents arose. Despite the fact that Great Britain was supporting the Sharif of Mecca and his sons and making kingdoms for them, the Moslems of India, led by a few intriguing politicians who thought to pull the Lion's tail, engineered the "Caliphate" movement, based on dissatisfaction at the exaction of peace terms from the Sultan, which dismembered the Turkish Empire. While this was in full blast, and while a Pan-Islamic movement flickered and now and again blazed in the Middle East, lo! the New Turks must needs oust their Sultan first from political and then from religious power, and must finally disendow their religious institutions and practically prohibit the outward profession of "The Submission." At one blow

Mustapha Kemal had cut the ground from below the zealots in India, many of them earnest Moslems dancing unwillingly to a politician's tune.

Akin to this we have that strange movement in 1920 when large numbers of Moslems in the Punjab suddenly decided that it was impious to reside in British India, sold up their lands and proceeded to migrate to Kabul. There the Amir refused to take them, and advised them to return. To add coals of fire, the British Government introduced special legislation to permit of these misguided simpletons recovering the land they had alienated, since when the Moslem adjacent to the border would name his mule or other beasts of burden "Amanullah," and appease his wrought-up feelings by belabouring and abusing one who bore the inhospitable name.

Owing to these strange and ill-assorted ingredients in the all-blaze pot of Islam the young King had some difficulty in steering a straight course, and was more than anxious to avoid any outward sign at least of seeking advice from his only friend, Great Britain.

Pan-Turk and Basmach

Before turning to the modern development of Afghanistan we must glance at the Soviet position in Turkistan.

Across the Oxus there had been strange changes. In the last days of the war the British had been constrained to develop a policy to check the Pan-Turk movement that was the last programme of the young Turk. Enver had planned a movement whereby all the Turk, Turkoman, and Tatar races, derived from the stock of the "Mongol fold," should combine in one confederation, on the ruins at any rate of the Russian territory. The orderly ways of Russian Turkistan, which under Imperial control had been admirably conducted, had gone. Confusion worse confounded flourished. A struggle was going on between Bolshevik and Menshevik, and Great Britain had run a railway far up into Seistan, with the consent of Persia, and thence a motor and lorry track supplied a force of Indian troops controlling part of the Transcaspian railway up to Merv. Krasnovodsk itself was in British hands. But everything was in such a hopeless state that British interference could do no permanent good, and by the end of 1920 the cordon had been rolled back. Russian Turkistan was being left to its own devices, and from this mass of Bolshevised Russians, Tzech prisoners of war, Soviet Turkomans, and the like, some form of state was evolving. To this came Enver Pasha, fugitive from Turkey, who set himself to fish in these muddy waters, and very nearly achieved his object of making a Tatar federated republic. In 1919 a Soviet mission reached Kabul; a little later a Soviet revolution had broken out in the state of Bukhara, till then a state under Russian influence, resembling to some extent the states in India. In 1921 an anti-Soviet Pan-Turanian (viz. Pan-Turkish) revolt started in Eastern Bukhara and spread all over Russian Central Asia, and is believed to have had considerable support from Afghanistan, where the Amir of Bukhara had taken refuge, and of all the mullahs, who in many places proclaimed a holy war against the enemies of Islam. Early in the revolt a Turkish staff officer from Angora had preached a Moslem league against European Imperial control. Enver Pasha, as will be remembered, had separated from Mustapha Kemal and gone in 1919 to the Moslem congress at Baku, and while there the outbreak of this revolt in Central Asia seemed to furnish him with the opportunity for which he was looking. By November 1921 he was at Bukhara, and was finally appointed by the fugitive Amir, Commander-in-Chief of the "Basmach" forces, the name by which the Moslem Pan-Turkish revolution was known. *Basmaji* is a Turkish word for bandit, but in this case was soon adopted as a synonym for a protester against unjust power, and rather similar in its accepted meaning to the arabic *mujahid*, the holy warrior who makes *jihad*.

It may be said to have been born as a movement, owing to the fact that the original Bolshevist development in Turkistan had little of equality and fraternity about it, and put Russian domination as the leading note. The period is one of very great confusion, but with the coming of Enver the movement took on an organised form and began to move towards success. Directed by Turkish officers and supported, it was said, by Afghan money and munitions, the whole thing became a grave menace to Russian control. Enver's platform included a large Pan-Turanian Empire of Persia, Bukhara, Khiva, Afghanistan, and eventually Turkey, and delivery from European influence generally. In January 1922 Enver sent an ultimatum to Moscow demanding the abandonment of Central Asia by the Russians. Then it was that the "Red" Army, which already included many of the old Russian officer class, was sent to Bukhara to cope with an Asiatic movement which seemed about to take the form of one of the old Tatar tribal waves. The Basmach forces were then defeated in a considerable battle, and Enver himself was killed in a chance rearguard action. With his death the movement collapsed.

The Turkistan Soviets

While the Basmach crisis had been developing, Russia had behaved with propriety towards Afghanistan, and in 1921 a treaty between Kabul and Moscow was duly signed, which was favourable in the direction of abandoning trade restrictions and opening the Afghan door to the Russians. Generally, Soviet consulates in Afghanistan were permitted, but as the Basmach movement prospered, Amanullah seemed to lean openly towards its support, and the treaty was suspended. With Enver's death the attitude swung back to one of amity, and in November 1922 the treaty was revived. A flight of Russian planes to Kabul produced an order for Russian planes and Russian instructors, whom we see still taking some part in the troubles of the winter of 1928–29.

From 1922 to 1925 the *entente* continued, but with some quarrels as to frontiers and islands in the Oxus, as might be expected. In the meantime, definite Sovietisation had gone steadily forward in the trans-Oxus and Transcaspian regions. The Khan of Khiva and the Khan

The Amir's Summer Palace in Paghman

The Soviet Legation, Kabul

of Bukhara had, not unnaturally, lost their thrones, and by 1924 a fairly permanent arrangement seems to have been come to. Several racial Soviets have been evolved, of which four impinge on Afghanistan. Moscow, learning by the experience of the Basmach movement to trample less severely on Asiatic view-points, after tentative shuffling and regrouping had inaugurated a series which has some prospect of finality. Once peace and order had been regained after much bloodshed, the districts have settled down to a modern and progressive way of managing their affairs, which indicate that some competent heads have gained control.

These Soviets are, beginning from the west, that of Turkmenistan, which borders Afghanistan for the whole distance between the Persian border and the Oxus, viz. that area which includes the historic names of Merv, Panjdeh, and the Kushk railhead of the Transcaspian railway, and thus faces the Perso-Turkish people of the Herat province. Across the Oxus comes the Soviet of Uzbegistan, which runs 120 miles along the river and then turns inland, and includes Bukhara, Samarqand, and Khoqand. When the frontier of this state turns inland the Soviet of Tajikistan takes up the trans-Oxus riverine land, running far up the river bordering the Afghan province of Badakhshan and those mountain regions where the Russo-Afghan collision in the nineties took place. Afghanistan is practically concerned with these three only, save that up on the Afghan Pamirs she touches the territories of the Qara Qirghiz Soviet, which marches with Kashgar. Farther away are the Soviets of Qara Qalpak (Khiva) and Qazakistan, which later is but Southern Siberia, with neither of which is she concerned at all.

The important point to notice is that the Russo-Afghan border, as has already been explained, is not a racial boundary, and there are Turkomans in the Afghan province facing Turkmenistan on the hither side of what is little more than a map-drawn line, while Uzbegs on the Afghan side face the Soviet of Uzbegistan on the other side of the Oxus, and Afghan Tajiks face Tajikistan. It also is

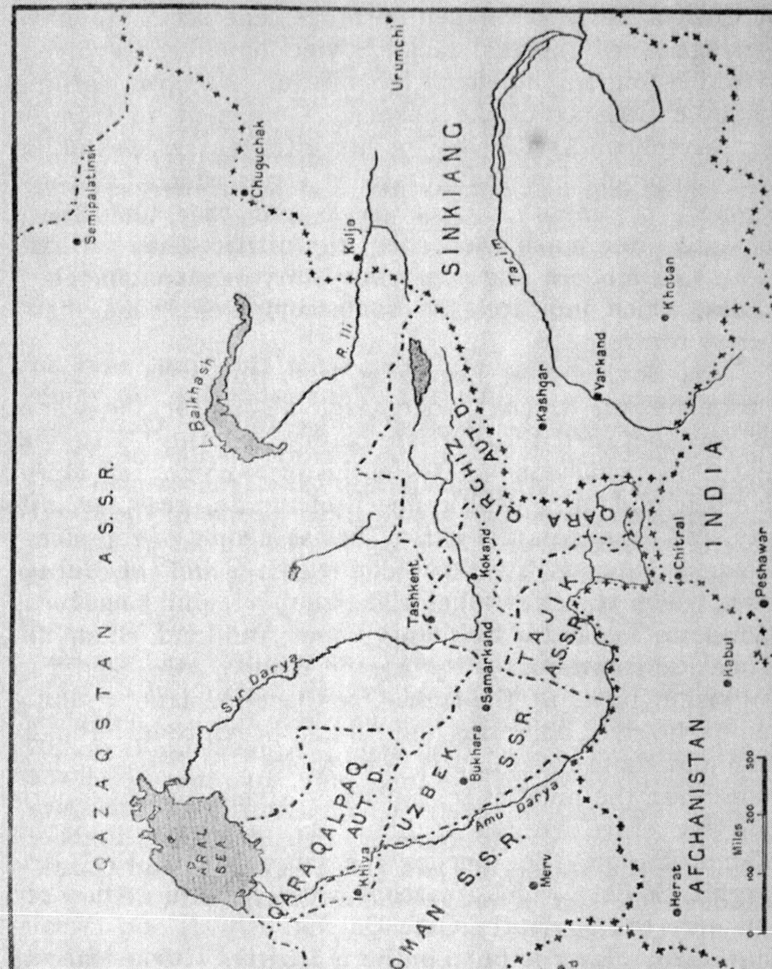
QAZAQSTAN A.S.S.R.
Semipalatinsk
Chugucḥak
Urumchi
Kulja
L. Balkhash
R. Ili
SINKIANG
Tarim
Khotan
Yarkand
Kashgar
QIRGHIZ AUT. D.
QARA
Kokand
Tashkent
Syr Darya
TAJIK A.S.S.R.
Chitral
INDIA
Peshawar
Kabul
Samarkand
Bukhara
UZBEK S.S.R.
QARAQALPAQ AUT. D.
ARAL SEA
Khiva
Amu Darya
TURKOMAN S.S.R.
Merv
Herat
AFGHANISTAN
Miles
0
100
200
300
Meshed
PERSIA
Krasnovodsk
CASPIAN SEA

pertinent to note that the Shiah branch of Islam, so despised by the Afghans themselves, is the religion of many of the tribes and races of Afghan and Soviet Turkistan.

Development and Progress

With the distractions of the Pan-Turk and Pan-Islamic movements removed and run cold, the young King was free to proceed to develop his country on the basis of the system of administration which his father and grandfather had evolved. The country had now declared itself open for Europeans, but the King was anxious that Russians and British, the two races controlling adjacent countries, should not be encouraged to enter. Under Abdurrahman, as has been recorded, a very few British did assist in developing industries and institutions, notably military munition factories; but under the new dispensation the Afghan Government deliberately adopted a policy of inviting the races of Europe, other than the British and Russian, to come to their assistance. It held that the presence of nationals of such close neighbours might innocently enough develop an influence inimical to Afghan solidarity. Abdurrahman himself recorded very similar reasons anent the policy of British or Russian instructors for his troops. In Great Britain there was little to object to in this, for it was impossible to encourage unofficial Britons to work for their living in a country where there were no capitulations, and where the ideas of law and justice were entirely divergent from those held sacred in British countries.[1] So Belgians, Italians, and Germans have worked away at motor transport, engineering construction, electrical development, and the like. Our ally, France, however, was asked to send a mission for educational and archæological direction, duties which her wide experience in Moslem countries undoubtedly well fitted her nationals to carry out. The new King also decided that a large number of young Afghans should go to Paris to study arts and sciences.

[1] As several of other nationalities have found to their cost. See *From Leipsic to Kabul*, by C. Strath-Sauer.

Much water had passed under the bridges since the British occupation of Kabul in the early eighties. The work of the British developers in Abdurrahman's time had already paved the way for much Westernisation. Bungalows and palaces after the style of British India had grown up outside the old grey city of Kabul itself, and to a lesser extent at Kandahar and the other cities. In Turkistan the Russian styles and models were more affected. The Bala Hissar of grim memory has been allowed to continue in the ruin to which it was falling, and the Amir's palace to-day lies in a fortress of more modern type, surrounded by a deep ditch, while a new palace and residential quarter is rising a few miles away. Army schools of modern type too have grown up close to Kabul, and the Amir Shere Ali's early beginnings at Sherpur are now an aerodrome.

Though born and bred, as it were, within the sound of the Bow Bells of Kabul, the King had imbibed some remarkable, shrewd, and progressive ideas. The asbestos curtain of imagination that separated India from Kabul in British eyes had not existed for the Afghans. Tens of thousands of all kinds and classes came down to India each year—traders and carriers, merchants, bankers, and the like. The banking having been done from time immemorial by Hindus with branches and relatives in India, the glories and conveniences of the *Pax Britannica* were very common knowledge, and the general influence of many of the British movements in India were well enough known, and some of them much admired. Skilled and trained hands of all kinds of Indian birth found their way to Kabul, as they had done in Abdurrahman's time. Amanullah, by instinct or by predilection, saw that he must be something of a democrat, and that he must at any rate think more of the people. But to think more of the people in the sense of "liberal" development must be to think slowly, in countries where the barons and nobles hold the cards.

Chiefs of clans meant to be chiefs of clans, and no mistake about it, and the warp and weft of the country has hitherto meant rule through, and not over, the heads of the chiefs and hereditary princelets. The dragooning ways of

E. N. A.

A typical village scene in an Afghan valley

Abdurrahman subsided soon enough when his authority was undisputed, and men were left to go their own way as lords of uplands, valleys, and fertile *kachch*; so that even in his time the developing of a people fit to follow more peaceful ways was in progress. Those ways are described by Sirdar Iqbal Ali Shah,[1] himself of Afghan descent, in a recently published book, which shows much that is of great charm in the home characters of the people, traits which have already been referred to as pleasantly shared by the British in the early days of our first venture into the country.

THE AFGHAN PEOPLE OF TO-DAY

In all this movement towards Westernisation and progress that was in the mind of the young King, it will be seen in the book referred to how little yet are the simple ways, in many respects the charming ways, of the people changed for better or for worse.

In the pages that have been written much has been said of the past, and of the appalling history of rapine and bloodshed that marks the years. But just as modern life in Europe must not be judged by the murders, motor accidents, fires, and other pleasing catastrophes that give zest to our journeys home, so must we imagine that Afghanistan is not all blindings and *coups d'état*, and the gathering of the war standards of the clans.

Life in Afghanistan varies, as in other lands, according to the status of the people and according to their avocation. As, however, it is almost exclusively a Moslem country, and one, as we have read, where the bias to the influence of religious observance in daily life is strongly marked, the religious habits of Islam are much in evidence. The daily call to prayer at regular intervals from town and village mosque is constantly to be heard. The call in the morning, "Prayer is better than sleep!"; the constant intoned call that "There is no God but God, and Muhammad is his Prophet," that "God is merciful and compassionate,"

[1] *Afghanistan of the Afghans* (Diamond Press, Ltd.).

sound beautiful and impressive, till you realise that the human himself has little desire to imitate. Nevertheless at regular hours will husbandman and trader, sojourner and traveller, prostrate themselves in prayer and lip-praise to Allah.

The towns and cities, the bazaars and the artificers, are very little different from those of Northern India. The copper- and silver-smiths hammer at and vaunt their goods, the leather-workers stain and stamp their skins with gold, and the shoemakers stud the *chaplies* with the soft iron nails that grip the mountain-side. Even yet outside the military factories there is little of industrial life as we know it in the West.

The land-owning classes have their enclosed latticed town houses built around courtyards as in any Indian city, and have their semi-fortified seats in the country valleys. Their amusements are shooting, hawking, and coursing. In Kabul the games of the West, such as lawn tennis, are affected. Outside the modern Government quarters in Kabul and Kandahar or Herat, where bungalows and offices, much as we see them in Lahore or Peshawar, have grown up in the last few years, towns and villages have changed little with the march of time. They are largely built of sun-dried brick or *pisé-de-terre*, unplanned, narrow, insanitary, and without any better water supply than well or streamlet.

The town dwellers are the merchants, the handicraftsmen, the Hindu bankers, the official classes, and their hangers on. But the Afghans proper, they for whom all the politics have seethed and among whom the invasions and uprisings had their origin, are the lesser landowners, the yeomen cultivator, the peasant, and the Ghilzai camel graziers who carry the commerce of the country, and from time immemorial spend their winters a-trading in the Indian provinces.

The highland valleys, where "the vines on the upland swell," are much as the valleys on our own frontier. There are the cluster of mud huts with a line of Lombardy poplars, and willows by the deep water cut. Here and there are outlying homesteads, each with their defensible tower, built and loopholed on a solid base that defies the petard of the underminer. Outside the hamlet may be a pomegranate grove and a group of walnut trees by a shrine, where the elders discuss village matters and mutter of doings in Kabul, which "this one knoweth and that one saith."

The water, the much-prized water, in the economy of which the villagers are singularly expert, gurgles and ripples by, edged in the spring with a fringe of narcissi. Whiles it must be brought to the surface by a *karez*, an underground channel, made from a series of connected shafts; whiles it flows in little canals along the surface. The tribesman has two tools of equal import, his rifle and his long channel spade, with which he digs and clears the channels, whence he brings the *zar-afshan obba*, the wealth-giving water, to the fields, which will grow what you will if only watered in due season: apples, peaches, and apricots, grapes of surprising sweetness, melons and pumpkins, buckwheat and millet and tall Indian corn. Hard by the shrine will be the village cemetery, which none will pass without the greeting in sonorous Arabic, "*As Salaam alaicoom, ahl-i-Kabool!*" "Peace be with you, O dwellers in the tomb." Fair over the graves grow iris and tulip, and the men's gravestones stand thin and upright by head and foot, and the women's stones broad and flat—the difference which Hindus show between *yoni* and *linga*.

By the shrine, if it be famous, will be a bunch of poles, from which the strips of rags tied by pilgrims and visitors flutter in the breeze. And if the village has no shrine, and folk make merry at the villagers' lack thereof, perhaps one day they will slay their village priest that they too may not be behind in a grave to worship come Fridays.

If you happen to find yourself riding among the tombs—for at times the burial-grounds are extensive—it is not the mound of earth that may give way below your horse's hoof. The Moslem grave is dug down some feet, and then a ledge is scooped out to the side, on which the corpse can be laid, with room to sit up at the day of resurrection, and also room for the cross-questioning *angeel* to sit and make inquiry.

Then if you know this, and know too how a corpse in the East is wrapt in its grave-clothes, you will know what that remarkable and little-understood account of a certain Grave and its Grave-clothes, the napkin folded apart, really portends. You may see it to-day in the village grave of the Afghan.

The women will be coming to the rivulet with their water-jars, and some who live afar off will drive their donkeys, carrying water-skins, and tramp many a mile each day of their life, since the water does not always rise so handily.

Women, Children, Marriage

The manner of the women, like that of the men, varies greatly in accordance with town or country. The veil in Afghanistan, apart from the innovations of King Amanullah, is, as it is in India, the privilege of the wealthier and more socially distinguished classes, and hitherto desired by women as the outward and visible sign of social standing. It is worn in the cities, though with less stubbornness than in India, and the veiled ladies of Kabul, for instance, are able to take part in social amenities in which men outside their own circles are present. The wealthier ladies can indulge in finer clothes; but in the villages adornment is not to the fore, and the women are usually in blue or grey cotton garments, with a *sari* over the head. There the lot of the women is none too light; nor does the Afghan tend to make his women's lot agreeable. Amusements are little enough, and it is the domestic festivals that provide the lighter side of life, marriages and funerals, and the ceremonies of birth and naming. In the cities, of course, there is more to see, and the conjurors, the troubadours, and the story-tellers do make some amusement even for the women in the crowd. The gramophone playing Eastern airs is popular enough, and even the cinema is now appearing. Story-telling throughout the

East is the summit of all amusement, and there was an officer not long ago who, taking part in a boundary commission, would sit round the camp-fire and tell stories, usually from the Old Testament. In the shadow outside the glare of the embers the women had drawn round to listen, and when he had finished the story, the ever-human story of the overlaid child, and the judgment of the great Sulaiman, there came to his surprise from the shadows a chorus of *Lu! Lu! Lu!* from the women, their hands on their lips in enthusiastic recognition of the dramatic truth of story and sentiment.

Marriage all the world round is a great occasion, when the women take possession, and Afghanistan does not differ from other countries. From time immemorial the go-between in better circles, the village gossip in the lesser, brings tidings of fair maids of suitable stations, and matches go forward in ceremony and rejoicing, especially the first, before additional wives are taken. The priests and mullahs are not so intimately connected with family life as in Hindu India, but in marriages and namings are naturally to the fore.

The Ghilzais and their ways are well known to the British of Northern India, as they come through the passes each autumn sept by sept and clan by clan, marching in long strings by tuck of drum, old men and maidens, the stalwart heads of families leading each his group, with their ox and their ass, their camels and their poultry, and everything that is theirs. For six months in the year several hundred thousand become British subjects, storing the arms they must carry in their own hills at the British border police posts. Magnificent folk they are too, tall of stature, aquiline of feature; and atop the camels ride bonny, soncy girls unveiled, in embroidered cotton gowns, with enamelled neck and hair ornaments, who will give the glad eye readily enough to the British frontier officer, and among whom now and again, as already stated, some bush-girl from Australia holds her own with tongue and hand if need be. On foot among the camels totter the old ladies, who cook and boil the samovars, and catch the bubbling beast that disturbs the camps o' nights. And all the while the laughing girls with the upland rosy cheeks reck little enough of the day when they must catch the loose camel and fetch and carry in the time of their wrinkles, since there be little ruth in Afghan life.

Children are happy enough, and kindly treated by high and low. Of all the jolly things of the world the Afghan children are the jolliest, from the little Carlsbad plum in embroidered velvet of the quality, to the dusty, rosy-faced village imp, who will run beside your horse and turn cart-wheels shouting "*Paisa wachawa!*" which being interpreted means, "Chuck us a copper, guv'nor!" But even here must the dourness of life at times intrude. Once the writer had an artillery orderly in far Kashmir who came from the Afghan side of an unruly borderland, whose favourite story was of a scene of his youth. Across a stream lay a village with which his village had an enmity and a feud. One summer's day, when the snows afar had all melted and that stream ran nearly dry, a toddler from the hostile village had wandered across the stream, and my friend and his little playmates had caught the wanderer. Then and there had they stretched his little wizand and slit it with a penknife, in great glee, long to be triumphantly remembered by British artilleryman Hamid Gul. In the warp and the weft, as Abdurrahman said, "I rule an iron people," of whom poor King Amanullah also said, "My people are savages and I will tame them." But they are ill-taming, these Afghans.

EDUCATION, LAWS, JUSTICE

During the short heyday of Amanullah the French Director of Education had begun to organise, as has been related, a system of education that would fit young Afghans for a place in the civilised world, but M. Foucher was hampered in this, as in other of the Europeanised advisory services, by the fact that there was never enough money to command the services of better Europeans. Even with the inferior material that was often alone to be obtained a considerable start was made, which has, however, been somewhat exaggerated.

Education in Afghanistan as elsewhere is a comparative term, and that given to those of well-to-do parentage must naturally be the better, clamour Socialists never so loudly. In Afghan circles the difference was always most marked. In the villages the peasant boys, if they could repeat the *kalima* in Arabic, it was as much as they could do, and the schools attached to the mosques taught little more than Arabic texts by rote, and a smattering of Persian. In the cities the children of the noble and merchant classes learnt something of their own tongue, Pashtu, and something of the more cultured Persian. In the towns were schools in which young men who aspired to the civil service of the pre-Amanullah days could qualify themselves for their posts; but it was not till M. Fouchet set to work that even the outline of a State system, progressive in aim and with some definite culmination, had been envisaged. Anything approaching the education of women had never been countenanced for a moment till Amanullah's attempt, and the new schemes to that end have now been dissipated for many a year.

Justice has always been *sui generis*, but in the iron days of Abdurrahman it was at any rate prompt and, where his writ ran, unbiassed. But as justice, in the British conception of the word, it was little to boast, save only that the real criminal might get his deserts promptly enough. In a land where false evidence thrives, woe betide him who did not make terms with his adversary quickly and was hauled before the judge! Justice is in the hands of the *kazi* of each district, under whom are the *kotwals* or magistrates of towns and sub-districts, who would be hard put to say where criminal cases end and civil suits begin. A year or so ago a young German professor had a whim to see the countries he was supposed to teach of, and throwing himself on a motor-bike sped away through Turkey and Azerbaijan to Tehran and Bagdad, and thence via Karachi to Peshawar. From the rail at Peshawar he hied him to Kabul on his bicycle. Nearing Kabul, a mounted Afghan in a moment of vanity essayed to race the devil carriage, whereon his pony threw him to the ground, leaving him senseless. The German stopped to aid him, and as he revived, offered compensation from his purse. The Afghan, who was armed, tried to rob his helper, and made to use his rifle. In a life-and-death struggle that ensued the German shot him dead, and then in great concern hurried on the few remaining miles to Kabul to report his mishap to the German minister. Alas! nothing availed him. He was hauled off to prison, where no efforts of the German mission could get his case heard or obtain his release. After many months of dreary detention, during which widows clamoured for his blood and bogus witnesses testified to his having robbed and then murdered his victim, and during which many of his companions left for the cannon's mouth and other methods of execution, he received a long sentence of imprisonment.[1] Not till then could the German minister interfere and obtain his pardon, when the young man's heels could not be seen for the dust of his departure for British India, with a very good notion in his head as to why capitulations are considered desirable in backward countries. From which it may be gathered that the new ways are much as the old ways. An American lady in Kabul three or four years ago wrote of the processions of Mangal heads on spears that testified to the end of the rebellion of 1924 and the taming of an "iron people."

The Ingredients in the All-Blaze of Afghan Character To-day

It is to be remembered among these quick-change atmospherics that Eastern peoples, seeing Christianity tear itself to pieces in four desperate years, have once again set themselves to examine their own alleged inferiority in the race of life. The Afghans seem to say: "Written clear in letters that all may read is our lesson of two syllables, 'JAPAN.' If anyone says Mongolian, the rest of Asia may say, 'Are not we half Mongolian even in India?' If cold climate is

[1] *From Leipsic to Kabul*, by C. Strath-Sauer (Hutchinson).

a reason, what is wrong with Afghanistan? Indians are perhaps poor things even if the British do not think so, but what of we Afghans who have conquered and colonised India whenever it suited us?" And such-like and so forth. So King Amanullah, the king with the name that means "The Peace of God," set forth with his young Afghans to dream of becoming a great people. And bravely enough, too, did they set themselves to take full measure of the opportunity which the world seemed to have given: the younger Afghans of the great families would go to France—embassies and ministries everywhere—treaties with all and sundry, foreign officers—orders and all the paraphernalia of the states of Europe. The Afghan ministers abroad, braving the derision of their own country-folk, have shaved themselves as young Europe shaves itself, though it cannot be said that the virile, often Semitic countenance of the Afghan gains dignity thereby.

There must be in the Afghan[1] character and psychology, derived from the all-blaze of races that goes to its making, from the grandeur that was Greece to the fervour that was Israel, enough to make the new kingdom a problem of infinite possibility. The French Directorate of Education has waxed more than enthusiastic over its task of nation-building. Courage, ambition, enterprise, perhaps artistic conception, certainly pride of race, broken across in many directions though it must be, are inherent in the make-up.

There were and are, obviously, immense possibilities in the people, provided always that a leader be evolved who can mould and develop the national character from the material available, and can eradicate that age-old reputation for perfidy which no doubt was but a product of times and conditions that have, it is to be hoped, gone for ever.

In the eyes of the watchers two doubts lay ahead: first, the genius of the people to accept the programme, which also implies the capacity of the leader to stimulate such genius; and secondly, the more prosaic problem of resources adequate to the ambitions.

In following the Afghan development we must see it as

[1] Using here the word in its geographical sense.

it was in the heyday of 1927 when Amanullah left for Europe, and as it appeared to be on his return, before the happenings which have revealed the flimsiness of the card-house he had built so high.

Before coming to the collapse, it is necessary to carry this story, commenced when all was fair, to the pinnacle of 1928. We shall then see what Afghanistan was promising to be, and what it must in some form on some day surely become.

Since the edifice has fallen before this book has seen the light, it is hardly necessary to dwell in detail on all the attempts to form schools, colleges, embassies, and armies on Western lines, or to refer at length to the childish pride in playing "Europe," that has now met with so severe a set-back. The more enduring prospects that lie before the country still are worthy of some description, and these will be continued with the convention that we are still writing of the blossoming dream of King Amanullah. We may accept for the moment that the two necessary ingredients to progress were present in the stew. The steps forward would take the usual course of schools, colleges, embassies, treaties, etc., added to eagerness in showing complete independence by the establishing of ministries in places where they were hardly needed, or in making treaties for the mere pleasure of making them.

CHAPTER XIX

DEVELOPMENT, PROGRESS, AND PROSPECTS

Railways in Afghanistan · Railways of the Future Motors versus Rails · Roads and Routes · Revenue and Currency · Exports and Imports · Mineral Resources The Afghan Army · Aviation and Transmission · The French Direction · Archæology

RAILWAYS IN AFGHANISTAN

THE question of railways in Afghanistan and Persia has long excited interest among all who study the development of the world and the spreading of the iron network over its surface. If we take that somewhat misleading guide a small-scale map, against which Lord Salisbury so often used to warn statesmen, we shall see that the great through systems of the world are blocked by what is the tiniest of spaces compared with that which is covered. From Bombay and Calcutta to Chaman the rail has climbed on to the Central Asian plateau on the edge of Afghanistan. At Peshawar, again, the iron road has reached to the foot of the mountains, and now, since Amanullah's excursion into British India, actually climbs the Khaibar Pass without rack, and halts within a short distance of the Afghan frontier at Landi Khana. In the direction of Persia it extends from Spezand near Quetta to Duzdab.

On the far side in Turkistan the Russian rails run to Kushk from Merv and to Termez on the Oxus, whilst on the side of Europe the rail is at Tabriz, and also coming across from the Taurus on to Iraq. It is no wonder that the railway engineer and the map enthusiast gird from time to time at this lapse in the world system.

But railways are costly things, and engineers who dream of conquering difficulties with tax-payers' or shareholders' money hold different views from Chancellors of the Exchequer and financiers.

A railway cannot be constructed unless it is going to pay dividends—in other words, give return for the money; though that dividend need not literally be measured in terms of profit in cash. A railway to be made must either serve a commercial purpose and pay a cash dividend in some form, or it must serve a definite military purpose and be part of the defensive measures of a country, regardless of remunerative traffic. Or again, it must pay its dividend in some form of political benefit in the way of amenities or civilising effect and progress, which the world needs so much that it will finance it from some other source than its inherent profits. Thus the British railway to Quetta was made as a definite measure of military protection, and it was never expected to contribute a business return. The same may be said of the extension to Landi Kotal through the Khaibar.

The making of railways in Afghanistan came up first before the world when M. Cottard, a French engineer, a collaborator of M. de Lesseps at Suez as long ago as 1873, drunk perhaps with the idea of opening up the world, urged the advantages of direct railway route to the East. Even before this General Francis Rawdon Chesney, who as a young man had taken steamers overland to the Euphrates from the Levant, and whom de Lesseps called the *Père du Canal*, was urging a Euphrates valley railway as the quickest route to India. A little later M. Cottard, now engineer to the Rumelian railways, pressed the making of East and West on de Lesseps, who took it up enthusiastically enough. Young de Lesseps and a Mr Stuart, a railway engineer, started for India to study the matter in Afghanistan from the Indian side, but could not get leave to enter the country of the Amir. Great schemes filled the air, with, incidentally, brave proposals to climb or tunnel such passes as Bamian or the Khawak to link Kabul with the Oxus; but little encouragement came from England, as the time was obviously not ripe.

When the Russians commenced the Transcaspian line

the British, immersed in the Second Afghan War and its difficulties, and much engaged in the problem of the defence of India and Afghanistan against Russia, produced their extension to Quetta, and later on to the Afghan frontier at Chaman. There were stored the materials for the eighty-three-mile [1] extension to Kandahar, not as a threat against Afghanistan, but to enable her to be supported at Herat should Russia continue her hostile policy.

By the nineties, with a Russian railway at Kushk within a very easy distance of Herat, the problem was ventilated in the European press of connecting the systems; but no answering enthusiasm was aroused in British or Afghan circles. Abdurrahman preferred that his people should remain isolated, feeling that absorption into Russia or India might easily follow any such facilities. In 1910 German writers again pressed for this junction in the interest of the world, saying frankly enough that Afghanistan as a buffer state, an *état tampion*, must go, and Russia and India march together. Again, neither Great Britain nor Afghanistan displayed any interest, and no more was, naturally, to be said.

Afghan traders have always grumbled at the want of railways. The caravans that came down the Khaibar would complain that it was more trouble to come from Kabul to Peshawar than to go from Peshawar to Australia. But again, neither politics nor the economics of those who would have to foot the bill were interested.

Again, the project had been mooted of a line from Tiflis to Tabriz–Tehran–Meshed–Herat—a line which had some considerable prospects of carrying a paying traffic. But again nothing more was heard, and possibly the World War may for the time have absorbed any cash that might otherwise have been devoted to such activities.

To the British, the situation hitherto has always seemed to indicate that the longer railway extensions were delayed, the longer would the defence of Afghanistan remain a reasonably simple problem rather than one of nightmares.

[1] The direct distance is under seventy miles.

Railways of the Future

Under the régime of Amanullah, with his desire of introducing Western ways, and with the British renunciation of any liability to control his actions, the railway question was

Sketch Map showing the Gap in the Railway System of Asia due to Afghanistan and Persia

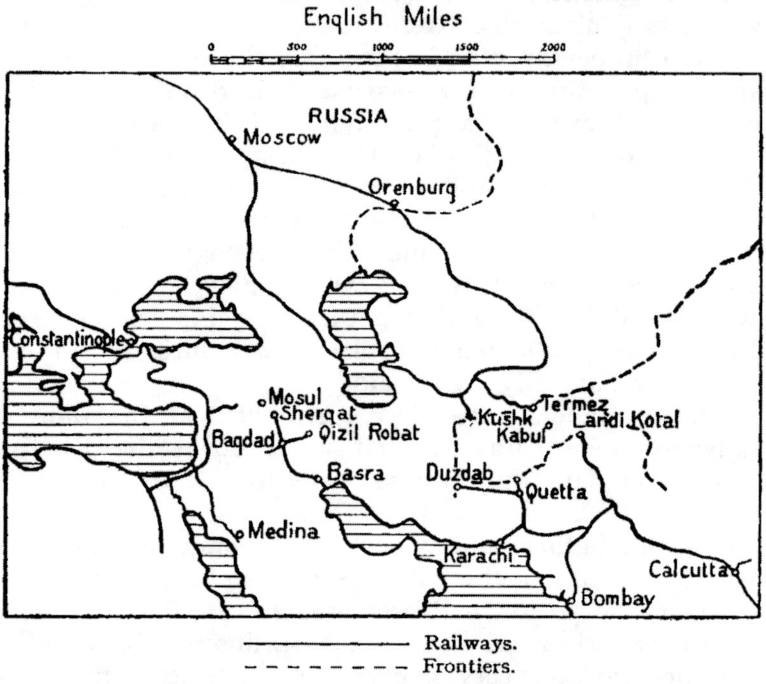

Note.—This sketch, showing how small in mileage is the gap in railways, is an excellent illustration of the late Marquis of Salisbury's remarks on the dangers of using small-scale maps. The terminus of the branch from Quetta on the Afghan frontier is at New Chaman.

bound to arise, and with continental engineers and financiers flocking into Kabul, the matter naturally enough was soon mooted once more, both French and German journals devoting some space to various phases of the problem.

The régime of hurried westernisation has for the moment

passed, but in discussing the Afghanistan of the future it must be assumed that modernisation sooner or later will return. Now that the country is better understood only two lines of rail hold the field. Those are one from Chaman to Herat and thence to Kushk, and another from Kandahar up the valley of the Tarnak to Ghuzni, and if possible to Kabul, probably of a lighter gauge. The extension of the British lines to Kandahar and Jalalabad would be simple enough, and would probably be carried out under satisfactory conditions by the British Government should the Afghans desire it. But a line from Jalalabad to Kabul would be a costly piece of engineering, and probably outside the range of practical politics.

In any case, even had the Amanullah régime remained, it is difficult to see whence would have come the money to finance the work. Afghanistan, let it be said again, is larger than France, with at most one-fifth of the population, and no one has yet seen any traffic that would pay interest on capital, though it might pay working expenses.

The following are some of the distances, both internal and those connected with the outer world, should junction ever be effected.

INTERNAL

Kabul to Dakka (near British railhead in north)	183	miles.
Kabul to Kandahar	333	,,
Kandahar to Chaman (British railhead in south) .	83	,,
Kandahar to Herat	400	,,
Herat to Kushk (the Russian railhead) . .	125	,,
Herat to the Persian border	125	,,

EXTERNAL

Kabul–Herat to Krasnovodsk (via Kandahar) .	817	,,
Kabul to Karachi (via Kandahar)	1100	,,
Herat to Karachi	1150	,,

MOTORS VERSUS RAILS

In Eastern countries short of revenue and capital, where inhabitants bury rather than bank their savings, there is now no need to struggle into railway adventures. Throughout the world, had the coming of motor traffic coincided with the spread of railways, we should have a very difficult combination of road and rail. If we turn, for instance, to the map of Persia, we shall see how costly and difficult is the railway programme just inaugurated for a line from the Caspian to the Gulf, cutting across the numerous parallel chains of mountains, which run east and west. There in a country where oil is becoming a staple was a chance to have driven motor roads down the parallel valleys. One of the great advantages of the age to a country of little State capital and credit, is that with motor roads the mercantile public find the rolling stock. Not only that, but the Asiatic is expert in tinkering with aged vehicles. Afghan and Persian merchants would find the lorries for motor ways in those countries, while it would only be necessary for the State to maintain the roads. Further, it is possible to demand a toll for the upkeep of the roads, which is not so easy to exact as a portion of the freight charges of a railway.

There is thus a good deal to be said for the creation of a motor and not a railway system in the Afghanistan of the future, and to continue the railways only by an extension of the British line to Kandahar and, possibly, a Russian line into Herat only. Oil is certain to be worked in some form in Afghanistan, while failing that, the steam-car is likely ere long to be a suitable vehicle in countries where petrol is hard to come by, where water is available.

Roads and Routes

For some few years attempts have been made in Afghanistan to make the road from the British frontier to Kabul, both via Kandahar–Ghuzni and via Jalalabad, passable for the royal and governmental motors, and since 1920 a good deal of tinkering with some actual commencements of a real roadway has taken place.

King Amanullah on his return from his European tour made great efforts to push on the construction of roads suitable for light motor traffic. None of the projected roads, apart from the two principal ones (1 and 3 in the schedule below), were completed before the rebellion (November 1928), and it is unlikely that any further work on them will be done for a considerable time.

There are many "routes" in Afghanistan, but only those so shown in the schedule may be considered as fit for motor-cars or occasional motor transport. Except in the immediate vicinity of Kabul metalling is rarely found, and still more rarely maintained. Bridges and culverts are weak, and liable to destruction by floods.

The form of transport in general use in the country is pack, *i.e.* camel, mule, pony, and donkey. The Crown also possesses several elephants.

ROADS IN AFGHANISTAN

I. From India

From—To.	Via.	Miles.	Remarks.
1. Torkham (Indo-Afghan frontier)–Kabul.	Jalalabad, Gandamak, Surkhpul, Kata Sang, Khurd Kabul, Butkhak.	175	Unmetalled, frontier to Jalalabad (46 miles), thence to Kabul has been metalled. Highest pass 8200 feet. Condition of road dependent on time of year, floods and sand presenting difficulties in places. Snow may be encountered from summit of Haft Kotal (at 140 miles) for five miles in winter, and between Surkhpul and Barikab.
2. Chaman–Kandahar.	Mal Karez.	72	Passable for motors. Obstacles, crossings of Arghastan and Tarnak Rivers, which are being improved. Open throughout the year.

II. FROM KABUL

From—To.	Via.	Miles.	Remarks.
3. KABUL–KANDAHAR. (This and No. 1 are the two principal motor roads in Afghanistan.)	Argandeh, Ghuzni, Mukur, Jaldak.	325	Metalled to Ghuzni, thence unmetalled, but passable for cars and lorries. Open throughout year, but section Kabul-Ghuzni frequently under snow in winter.
4. KABUL–GARDEZ.	Altimur Pass, Zarghan Shahr.	100	Extensions from Gardez towards Afghan military posts. Occasional motor traffic in fine weather. Some hairpin bends on the Altimur Pass.
5. KABUL–AQ ROBAT.	Charikar, Siah Gird, Bamian (Kila Sarkari).	162	Fit for light cars to top of Northern Aq Robat Kotal (and again from Haibak to Patta Kesar, being a break of about 120 miles).
6. KABUL–GULBAHAR.	Kala-Murad-Beg, Charikar.	52	Fit for passage of three-ton lorries. Almost level, except on the Khair Khaneh Kotal (first stage).
7. KABUL–JAOKUL.	Argandeh, Kot-i-Ashru, Jalrez, Sar-i-Chasma.	59	Metalled to Argandeh (15 miles). Argandeh to Kot-i-Ashru (9 miles) not possible for motors, but by alternative route (12 miles) if fit for motors. Leave Argandeh and follow Ghuzni road for seven miles, and proceed via Kala Arbab to Kot-i-Ashru.

III. OTHER ROADS

From—To.	Via.	Miles.	Remarks.
8. HAIBAK–PATTA KESAR.	Gaznigah, Tashqurghan, Mazar-i-Sharif, Siahgird.	124	Fit for light motors. Bridges too flimsy for heavy motor traffic. Impassable in winter.

From—To.	Via.	Miles.	Remarks.
9. KANDAHAR–HERAT–KUSHK POST.	Girishk Washir.	461	This road was put in order with great labour for the passage of the King's cars on his return from Europe in July 1928. Occasional light cars get through between Kandahar and Herat, but with difficulty. The section Herat–Kushk Post is on the whole more suitable to motor traffic.
10. HERAT–ISLAM KILA (KAFIR KALA) (thence to MESHED).	Aogho, Shabash, Tirpul, Kuhsan.	51	Fit for occasional light motor traffic.

REVENUE AND CURRENCY

When a country would change its scale of equipment and its standards of public life, as well as its ways of living, from Eastern to Western proportions, the revenue and the currency are the two important items which must ever be before the ministers. In trying to run out into the open world, these are the shoals to be looked for. The simple ways, mud huts, and pack beasts that graze and pick up a living on the countryside are very cheap, and to take from arid land, that only yields for short months, and scanty trade a revenue that will support a quite different scale of armies, air force, roads, foreign ministries and consulates, has produced much heart-searching. Nor does a country in which banking in the modern sense is unknown, and where savings are worn in anklets on the women, or buried deep in the corners of the farmside towers, produce capital readily. Even in India the mass of the people still hoard but do not bank, and it has been said that could those hoards be coaxed from the ground there would be more capital available for development than financiers have ever dreamed of. In this little mountain state—little in that twelve million people are not comparable with the 320 million of India—the currency of the Græco-Bactrian kings still lies buried in the cottage pots.[1]

The budget of Afghanistan for 1925–26, which is the last accessible figure in Kabuli rupees, now known as Afghans, which are quoted at about twenty to the pound sterling, is based on the following considerations:—

The sources of revenue are chiefly land tax, much as in India, viz. state land leased in perpetuity whose tax is really rent, tax on traders (which again is much the same as shop rent), and the customs. The total revenue in 1926 was about 45 million Afghans, corresponding to 2¼ million sterling, but no doubt is slightly increasing as the tax-gathering becomes more effective and trade expands.[2] It is not a great income to be a world-power on, but the country is unencumbered by national debts, and if in the future its mineral concessions and resources are worth having, the Afghans have at any rate none as yet bartered away, and therefore have a clean sheet to work on.

This revenue is about a third of that of Persia, and considerably less than that of Iraq, and it is obvious that the withdrawal of the subsidy from India—nearly three million Afghans, which was not paid since 1919, and was formally withdrawn at the peace—is a considerable loss.

The remodelling of the currency, which took place under the new régime, introduced the "Afghan" as the unit of measure as distinct from the old Kabuli rupee. An Afghan, which is a piece of 90 per cent. of silver, is divided into 100 pul, and is itself worth a shilling. The 50-pul pieces are alloy, and these are the pieces chiefly in circulation, at, of course, some considerable profit—one of the dubious courses which States in early stages of currency development have

[1] The writer has once helped to rescue a sack of Græco-Bactrians from which an Eastern mint master was coining new rupees.

[2] Written on the evidence before the *débâcle*.

to adopt. The old Kabuli rupee was to be given three years to remain as legal tender, after which a depreciation is expected. But in Eastern countries the value of currency as bullion has always been the essential factor. The "Afghans" will be in great demand for hoarding, while the half-Afghans will not. As a matter of fact, English and Russian gold is what the larger hoarders seek for, and the debasing of the half-Afghan keeps them from turning into anklets as do the British rupees.

Steady as may be the economic and revenue prospects of the country under careful and conservative administration, it is obvious that there has not been much margin on which to go large. Nor had Amanullah, as had his fathers, a store in India on which he could draw. It had been their custom not to touch their subsidy, or at any rate to let a considerable amount of it accumulate, and then if pressure, financial or political, should arise, they had a store to their private hand to serve the interests of the dynasty.

Exports and Imports

Merchants and traders the Afghans themselves have not been. From earliest days the great trade routes with India have come through the passes, and many of the people, especially the Ghilzais, have developed into expert carriers on the largest scale, breeding countless camels and dromedaries, ponies, bullocks, and donkeys to that end; but the business side of trade has always remained in other hands. Persians, Jews, Armenians, and the trading classes of Indians have done the business. Banking of all kinds has been largely in Indian hands. The tribesmen have been producers and carriers but not merchants, while chiefs and clansmen have lived on the profits of protecting caravans, which some call blackmail.

But whoever does the business, it has from time immemorial been heavy enough, and while many of the industries have flourished through the most disturbed times, the fact of their existence and continuance must point to long periods of peace in the past to enable them to gain their present prominence. Few countries live entirely by "taking in their own washing," and Afghanistan, like the others, has had its surplus and deficiencies. It is the ambition of every good commercial traveller to stimulate a desire for the goods he offers. He would stimulate an overpowering desire for motors among the people of India, for safety razors and gramophones among the clansmen of the Khaibar; he would set them trying to grow two blades of corn where one grew before to enable them to afford such luxuries. And that is the story of trade development in Eastern countries, or for the matter of that in all the world.

Afghanistan grows, of course, its own requirements in food-stuffs. It exports certain condiments, such as asafœtida, and many kinds of dried fruits; while the trade in fresh fruit with India, fruit of super-European excellence, is a remarkable development due almost entirely to the railway at Chaman and the recent provision of refrigerator rolling stock. Fruit and nuts figure as the principal exports, and then *ghi*. Skins, especially Astrakan, are an important item, and it is understood that the ex-Amir of Bukhara when driven from his state brought his flocks and stud rams with him to Kabul, and that Astrakan breeding will much improve thereby. Imports are naturally those articles which the country cannot produce. Soaps and perfumes, largely via Russia; ready-made frock coats, which has been a staple among the intelligenzia and nobility for many years, and no new thing here or in Persia, come from Europe via Calcutta. But imports can only increase as surplus wealth or exports increase, and that must be but slowly. Increase since the war is largely increase in price and not in quantity. In 1925 imports from India were 1·6 million sterling, and export much the same; those from Russia 1·1 million, and exports not more than a third of the same. The trade with Persia, chiefly via Meshed and Herat, is small. But from these scanty figures it may be seen that there is no great room for expansion of revenue through the customs.

The real increase of prosperity and in wealth will come with mineral production when minerals can be found that can be exported at a favourable rate. Here again, on the Indian side, communications with markets are long, and it is export to Russia that should give better openings. India has a long start in finding things for herself.

Mineral Resources

The potential mineral resources are considerable, but it is yet to be seen what demand there will be for them, and what the freight must be to their markets. The manufacturers of Kabul would of course gladly see coal much cheaper than their bullock-cart supply of coal from India. Householders, no doubt, would soon use it; but commerce and agriculture have got to go a long way before any of these things can be in great demand. In studying the enthusiastic outlook of the French mission we have got to realise the small purchasing power even of India compared with her population, despite tens of thousands of miles of railways and vast network of roads and numerous well-equipped ports.

It is probable that internal railways of lighter gauge or better motor roads and lorry transport, as discussed in this chapter, will allow of considerable development. Coal, copper, and lead mines exist. The mines of the Hindu Kush have been reconnoitred by Italian engineers, and coal has been found within accessible distance of Kabul. There are a good many signs of oil-bearing areas and some prospecting has been done. There seems fair prospects of oil being available on the Herat–Meshed road, where, indeed, it would be of immense value. Chrome and manganese will probably be workable, especially the former, while mica and gypsum are to be found in considerable quantity. The absence of railways and motor roads, and the difficulty of making many with the funds available, must naturally impede any rapid advance in the way of mineral exploitation. The Afghan desire to use no foreign credit and to contract no loans is creditable enough, and indeed until peace and stability is better assured there is no great prospect of such being available on reasonable terms.

In this connection it is only fair and right to remember that the much-abused foreign concessions, loans, assignments of customs, and the like, are the only means by which Eastern countries of small revenue, with the talent-burying habit irradicable, can hope to be furnished with any of the amenities of civilisation at other people's expense.

Generally speaking, it may be said that Afghanistan is rich in minerals.

Mr Onesbach, once employed by the Amir as a geological expert, has recorded his opinion in the following words: "The mountain regions of Central Afghanistan will some day become of considerable importance from the miners' point of view. . . . So far as we know at present, Afghanistan even now produces all the essentially necessary minerals, is well supplied with both iron ores and coal, and other valuable minerals are not wanting."

The various minerals so far located and the localities in which they are found are tabulated below.

Gold.—(1) Three miles north of Kandahar city. Lack of machinery at present hinders production.
(2) In hills north of Maruf.
(3) At Istalif.
(4) Alluvial gold is obtainable in many of the main rivers.

Silver.—(1) Is stated to occur in the Hazarajat.
(2) In the Panjshahr valley. The mines were formerly famous, but are not now worked.

Iron.—(1) Large deposits in the passes leading to Bamian. A geologist describes the iron ore near Bamian as "Practically a hill range of iron ore extending for many miles."
(2) Near Jabal-us-Siraj.
(3) In the Panjshahr valley and other parts of the Hindu Kush.

Coal.—(1) In the neighbourhood of the Khurd Kabul.
(2) Thin seams in the Karkacha range (about 35 miles south-east and east of Kabul).

Coal.—(3) Some of the best seams are in the valleys of the Surkhab, between Saighan and Ghori.
(4) At Ishpishta, on the left bank of the Surkhab.
(5) At Narin, 50 miles south of Kunduz.
(6) Thick seams of excellent quality at Chahil, north of Kara Koh, in Afghan Turkistan.
(7) Deposits at Shisha Walang, west of Chahil.

Copper.—(1) Five miles south of Kabul.
(2) At Khaneh Khonar, 24 miles south-west of Kabul, where it is abundant and of good quality.
(3) It is also found in many other parts of the country.

Lead.—(1) Hazarajat.
(2) Taiwara, in the Ghorat.
(3) Farinjal, where an elaborate mine exists.
(4) Lolinj, in the Ghorband valley, where there is a mine.
(The main source of supply is the Hazarajat.)

Antimony.—Shah Maksud range, within 30 miles of Kandahar, worked by the late Amir Habibullah.

Lapis.—Small quantities in Badakhshan. Mines exist south of Firgamu, on the Fyzabad–Jalalabad route.

Gypsum.—(1) Near Kandahar.
(2) Herat province.
(3) Afghan Turkistan.
(4) Dasht-i-Safed, in Kamard.

Marble.—In several parts of the country.

Rock-salt.—(1) Kataghan. The principal local source of supply. It is of inferior quality and of a bad colour.
(2) Twenty-five miles south of Kunduz, whence it is being transmitted to Kabul.

Rubies.—Jagdalak, where there is a mine.

Sulphur.—(1) Dasht-i-Safed, in Kamard, now being worked.
(2) In many other parts of Northern Afghanistan.

Slate.—Afghan Turkistan, a mine existing in the Salzar Kalan defile, Sangi Chanyak.

The Afghan Army

The army that King Amanullah had been trying to create consisted, on paper, of some eight divisions, of which two at Kabul represented the movable and disposable force, and had in some sort an army corps organisation. The military strength of Afghanistan has always lain in the fierce, hardy, well-armed tribal people, and the chiefs and their retainers. But such, while formidable in defiles and mountain passes, are of little value in the open against disciplined troops. For this reason, in 1834 Shah Shujah's two battalions of Hindustanis, commanded by the Eurasian officer Campbell, enabled that monarch to dominate Kandahar for close on a year, and for it also the Bengal Sepoys were always masters of open fight. It was not till Dost Muhammad became Amir for the second time that any attempt to raise a regular army was made—a beginning which was developed by Shere Ali, who even copied the Dragoon and Highland uniforms of the British. This army was not a force of any value except perhaps in its artillery, which so overwhelmed General Burrows at Maiwand. With the help of the Government of India Abdurrahman much improved his troops, which, however, at the time of the Panjdeh incident were little better than Shere Ali's; but in due course they certainly enabled him to suppress the serious rebellions that broke out in the earlier years of his reign.

This army has never been renowned, however, for its staunchness, largely by reason of its inferior material. In the East, as is well known in India, a man is not a man "for a' that." Men of little heart and fighting value may make good-looking, well-drilled soldiers, but cannot be induced to draw a badger. The Afghan authorities have always shirked enlisting their real fighting races, the tribesman of their hills, who apparently only the magic of the British officer can tame and lead and bring to stomach discipline and collective training. The former, therefore, have concentrated on the less warlike but more biddable Tajik of Persian and Arab origin. The result of this has been that the Afghan soldier has never done much, and when in 1919 he tried to pass the young Indian regiments and the British Territorials who stood in his way, even when aided by masses of the hill tribes, he made a poor show of it.

After the fiasco of his attempt on India, King Amanullah secured the services of a Turkish military mission under Jemal Pasha, but its ways were so unpopular that it was sent away. Later, in view of the desire to improve the schools and training, it was found necessary to recall the Turkish officers. They, however, have been no more popular than their predecessors, and the army therefore has never been quite satisfactory. In the rebellion of the Mangals in Khost in 1924, the troops took a long time to get on terms with the clans, and did not cover themselves with glory.

Nevertheless the army, before the *débâcle*, had the nominal strength of eight divisions, of the usual components, with two cavalry brigades and some unattached mounted corps. There were two military colleges of no great excellence, but a good many young Afghan officers have been sent round the armies of Europe. The cavalry are in some sense *silladar*, in that the trooper provides his own mount. They are poorly trained, and are chiefly employed as messengers and escorts. The rifle in use is the earlier pattern of the ·303. The mountain artillery is the most efficient branch of that arm, the field artillery is little trained except as gun crews, and any form of higher artillery training is in defect. In fact, as might readily be expected, the demands of a modern army, with its requirements in efficient detail and costly equipment, are not to be created in a few years in a backward and needy Central Asian state.

General Nadir Khan, who was commander-in-chief when the late King's father was murdered, who led the invasion into Kurram, and who has lately been endeavouring to raise an army and lead it against Habibullah Ghazi, has no knowledge or experience to help him in serious war. The same may be said of all the higher Afghan commanders, whom the trained Turkish instructors, not unnaturally, found wanting in basic knowledge of modern requirements.

Aviation and Transmission

Since the Basmach trouble and the appearance of Russian planes at Kabul, the "Young Afghans," to copy the phrase of Turkey, have always desired to possess them, and Russian instructors have been busy in Kabul, so that King Amanullah dreamed of an efficient force of his own while using himself the planes of the instructors. It is at present to be doubted if Eastern carelessness will ever keep the machines fit and safe, however brilliant Easterns may become as pilots.

Some Russian financial help was also forthcoming, without which a start could not have been made, and this has given a Russian influence which in later days King Amanullah would gladly have got rid of. Even, however, with this assistance the Afghan Air Force has been *pour rire*. A few Afghans were hastily passed through a school in Italy, with a good deal of damage, it was rumoured, to Italian machines; for the Afghan character does not readily lend itself to proficiency as an aviator. Repair arrangements and material are most inefficient, and, speaking generally, the Afghan Air Service can do little more than fly, and may be regarded even before the rebellion not only as innocuous, but likely to remain so.

A fairly efficient telegraph service between Kabul and the principal towns has long existed, though many of the lines would be down in the winter from snow for considerable periods on end—a condition to which British lines in the Himalaya are equally prone. Wireless, however, has now linked the country far more effectively, but is not likely to remain efficient if skilled European supervision be withdrawn.

THE FRENCH DIRECTION

For some little time the direction of the arts and sciences has been in the hands of the French, who were specially invited by King Amanullah to give a helping hand in enabling the "Young Afghan" to find himself. Education and archæology were particularly confided to their care, and it is to be premised that the French, with their experience of Orientals and their power of sympathy and fraternisation, were well qualified to undertake the task. In Paris the King was able to arrange for many of his aspirants to come to France for study, while in Afghanistan itself M. Foucher[1] aimed at an admirable school and college system for both sexes, which should also fit the brighter students for a further course in France. In archæology no nation could be better fitted to lead the work that has waited through the centuries to be done in that land which counts a thrice-storied pass, and yet is almost virgin soil.

In a special Afghan number of the *Bulletin de la Chambre de Commerce Franco-Asiatique* for January 1928 M. Foucher breaks into a pæon of joyous might over the wise, the prudent, and enthusiastic Amanullah and his glorious band of Young Afghans, who, coming with the force of a long-delayed spring, were about to burst into a wealth of the flowers of civilisation, and develop a culture suited to the gifts and psychology of this gifted race.

It is pathetic to read now, when the card-house has fallen, and some bird of ill-omen croaks the time-dishonoured croak, "*Afghan! Afghan! Be iman! Be iman!*" Poor M. Foucher, whose visions were so enthusiastic and whose Afghan garden was so lovely, but who now can see why Lyall made the Amir say in his Kabul citadel:

[1] M. Foucher was Director of Education and Archæology, and M. Fouchet who died recently on the way to Europe was the French Minister at Kabul.

"Fair are the vales well-watered,
And the vines on the upland swell,
You might think you were reigning in heaven—
I know I am ruling in hell."

And Abdurrahman saw the truth of it, and knew those verses well.

It is to be observed this chapter has been conceived when the Afghanistan of Amanullah was still full of promise, and the joyous anticipations of M. Foucher still rang true, the problems of nascent civilisation still held the field, and it is but in these last paragraphs that the fall of the card-house is taken ken of. Alas, poor Amanullah! of whom we can but say with Mark Antony, "And none so poor to do him reverence."

Before turning to the story of this ill-wind that blew, it is not unsuitable to glance at what we know of the store of buried past that M. Foucher had begun to unearth.

ARCHÆOLOGY

The rebellion in Afghanistan has for the present put an end to the bright hopes of M. Foucher as to all the treasures of the past which were to be unfolded to a delighted world through the energy of his colleagues and the archæologists of other nations who would work under his direction.

Buddhist caves, sculptures, giant figures, stupas, and temples, all that the Chinese pilgrims a millennium and a half ago had recorded so faithfully—pre-Buddhist paintings equal to the best of the Indian periods, from the rock-temples in Western India: a wealth which is yet untouched.

Round Ghuzni had arisen one of the most delicate of the early Moslem cultures, hardly yet touched since the days when ruder Moslems had destroyed them.

Among the sites to which attention has been given are especially the well-known Buddhist remains at Bamian, concerning which in the days of their glory Hiuen-tsiang, the Chinese pilgrim, had so much to say, and Balkh, where the same traveller told of a hundred monasteries and many thousand monks. At Nagrehara, at the confluence of the

Kabul and Surukh Rivers, another well-known Buddhist centre was excavated. The Hepthalite, or White Hun settlements, came under preliminary study, with their capital in Badakhshan, dating somewhere about A.D. 250.

The Alexandrine settlements naturally have had attention, and search has been made for Alexandria-ad-Caucasem at the southern foot of the Hindu Kush; while there are many important sites known to history that Hun and Mongol invaders destroyed that have been looked for or visited, such as Gulgule on the ridges near Bamian and Sohak, whose great walls still frown down on the surrounding country.

Reports on work done are appearing [1] or are eagerly awaited, all the more so that the door of exploration has been so unexpectedly slammed.[2]

But now that civilisations dating far before the coming of Arian races and religions are being explored on the Lower Indus, it may be expected that more is to be found in this connection in Afghanistan. Unfortunately the dislike of uncivilised Islam for the past, especially if that past is connected in their imagination with idols and carvings of figures, is intense, and relics of the cult of the *but-parast* [3] but rouse the zeal of the *but-shikast*.[4] Already in the recent troubles the finds of the German mission in the Hindu Kush have been destroyed by zealots.

[1] E.g. *Mémoires des Missions Archæologiques Françaises en Afghanistan* (Godard & Hackin).

[2] A collection of the finds of the French explorers is to be seen in the Musée Guimet in Paris.

[3] Idol-worshipper.

[4] Idol-breaker.

CHAPTER XX

THE END OF THE DURANI DYNASTY

The Last of the House of Cards · King Amanullah's Trip to Europe · The Return from Europe · The Coming of Bacha-i-Saqao · The Last of the Barakzais Amanullah in Southern Afghanistan · The Attitude of the British Government · Looking Forward

THE LAST OF THE HOUSE OF CARDS

THIS book was commenced and largely written when King Amanullah was still in Europe, and there was fair reason to believe that the modern Afghanistan might win through without abysmal trouble on the Western course that the young ruler had planned for it. It had for its object to show how close and intimate from earliest times had been the connection between Afghanistan and India, and how British policy, even when failing in its practice, had always aimed at maintaining that connection. It has tried to explain how, after forty years of groping for the best way of intercoupling the countries, we had achieved a considerable measure of success, and how an ordered Afghanistan had existed for another forty years. It has also endeavoured to show how, supported by British prestige in her outer relations, directed therein by British advice, and strengthened by a financial subsidy that was by no means unwelcome, the mountain kingdom had attained a stability and prosperity never yet reached in its history. It has also tried to trace the trend of affairs which induced Amanullah, caught in the whirl of the false inferiority complex which seized Eastern countries after the World War, to tear up the mutually satisfactory relationship which had so long existed. It has essayed to show how we had acquiesced in the new situation that had followed on the unprovoked attack on India in 1919, in the hope that good might come therefrom, and the old object of a strong and prosperous

E. N. A.

Sir Francis Humphrys, the British Minister at Kabul, and his Staff

Afghanistan be still achieved by this new road. All the while has the book been conceived in the aspect of the Afghanistan of 1927 and 1928, and though in the last two chapters it has not been possible to ignore what has happened, it is only now that the collapse of the young King's card-house has been taken ken of and described in such outline as the scanty facts at present in possession of the public permit of. The inner history of what happened, the secrets of the Foreign Offices of Simla and Whitehall, and the share in advising all parties taken, and to what extent taken by the very capable British Minister, Sir Francis Humphrys, cannot yet be estimated or divulged. The facts in outline, the humiliating and pathetic accounts of the return of the ex-King and Queen in humbleness where a few months before they lorded it bravely, we have before us. Furthermore, it is almost imperative for a book that ends in cataclysm to indulge and end in a note of prophecy, however much events may condemn the vision even as the pages leave the press.

King Amanullah's Trip to Europe

In the winter of 1927–28 the Afghan King started down through British India on his trip to Europe. It is not clear if this was the emanation of his own brain or if anyone else was behind him. It was obvious that so zealous a Westerniser should himself desire to see more of the civilisation and progress he wished to introduce, and learn something of proportion in the great places of the world. But there were many wise heads in Afghanistan and in India who looked askance and wondered. Never before had an Amir of Kabul felt secure enough on his throne to leave it. Time and again internal doubts prevented his predecessors even coming as far afield as India. Money indeed was none too plentiful, and the expensive legations in irrelevant Courts of Europe had already put a severe strain on the exchequer. Could the card-house stand this added story? The King thought it could, and bravely enough he and his Queen came down the passes and sailed to the fairylands of the

West. The Moslems of all India, especially in the North, had their eyes fixed on this young prodigy. The inherent spirit of Islam demands a power temporal. Shrewd observers at Chaman and Quetta noted with what scarce concealed satisfaction the Moslems revelled in the outward signs of his might. In Lahore and the Punjab the dread of any parliamentary control by a Hindu majority was stirring men's minds a good deal. The spiritual home of Northern India was with Kabul, failing the British, rather than with a Hindu Delhi, and this point of view should always be before a British statesman who would follow Indian problems.

But the observers also could not fail to see that Amanullah was becoming what is expressed in the Persian phrase *dunya-dar*, "world-possessing," and to become *dunya-dar* is a very bad thing for young Eastern heads. Here in England we call it "being too big for your boots," and it is a condition that goes before a fall. The first symptoms were a tendency to be somewhat jaunty and impertinent to the representatives of the Great Power that was paving the way of his tour, paving it, too, with gold. At Bombay, when the Viceroy was too unwell to receive the King, his want of manners was most marked. However, that passed, and the King sailed for Egypt, where he saw and learned much of the modern relaxations from the laws and rules of Islam that modern Moslems deem permissible. There, no doubt, he heard much of the desire of Muhammadan folk to break free of any control by Europe, and no doubt his modernising tendencies became more and more confirmed.

We need not follow him through his tour. He went to Paris, and Paris commended his desire that Frenchmen should lead his country in its development. Here in England, as we can remember, his welcome was genuine and distinguished, and he saw much that pleased him greatly. Berlin, Rome, and Moscow continued his European experiences, and then he was to take a fresh infection of his disease by going to Angora and thence home through Persia. At Angora he saw Mustapha Ghazi driving from

Photo by Central Press Photos Ltd.

King Amanullah arriving at the Grand National, 1928

his State machinery [1] all connection with Islam. Worship and faith in the Deity were being eradicated, and the Turks were apparently enjoying their apostasy and the discomfiture of the ecclesiastic. It has been remarked in this book that the Mongol nature in the Turk was more pagan than monotheistic, and Amanullah forgot that the part of his people who counted were largely Semite, with hearts of a different beat. At Angora it was believed that everything that was Eastern and national in appearance and dress produced an inferiority complex and must be abolished, and Amanullah took note thereof. Then, leaving Angora, came another dose at Tehran. Shah Riza was busy, too, trying his cantrips and downing into due proportion his turbulent priesthood, and Amanullah saw that it was good. In the autumn of 1928 he was back in Kabul, full of reforming zeal and ill-digested impressions.

And here for a moment we may turn aside to dwell on the genuineness of the patriotism and the desire for the good of his people that animated this unfortunate young man. He believed, and he often remarked to those with whom he conversed on the subject, that his people were steeped in savagery which only drastic remedies could cure. He was determined to lose no time in bringing in his educational and sartorial reforms, and his edicts and example, and the freedom that his Queen had adopted, were to be the pattern for the nation. It was all admirable in intention, genuine in the belief that by this road alone could salvation lie, and all the while his French advisers forgot to impress on him the saying of their wise countryman, the *cordon bleu*, "*Surtout ne pousse pas le poivre jusqu'au fanatisme.*"

The Return from Europe

In the early autumn of 1928 King Amanullah and his Queen returned by way of Meshed and Herat, and they returned to an Afghanistan to outward appearance much

[1] To whom the epithet "Ghazi," Warrior for the Faith, *Fidei Defensor*, is now somewhat misapplied.

as they had left it. By sea via the ports of British India had come the acquisitions of their tour, and especially the gowns of London and Paris which were to inaugurate the emancipation of the women of Afghanistan. Their doings in Europe had, of course, been much canvassed. The eager writers of the young Afghan press had described with gusto their freedom from the trammels of old-world Islam. And all the while the underground dissatisfaction from which all Eastern lands suffer had been spreading. Taxes were heavy, money was short; the outlandish goings-on in the capitals of Europe, so lusciously dwelt on by the telegrams and letters from the West, were magnified and bandied about. And folly piled on folly. Rumour had it that army pay, already in arrears, was likely to be withheld to meet other drains. How far this was really so we shall no doubt hear, but an army based on little national sentiment or tradition and on no great personal draw cannot be expected to stand such a strain. Again M. Fouchet might have emphasised the truth of *pas d'argent pas de Suisse.*

The fact that, despite the underground workings of the mullahs and malcontents, nothing had occurred to prevent the King's return to his capital does, however, show that the latter's confidence in the wisdom of leaving it for many months was not actually misplaced. The crop of discontent need not have borne fruit even in the autumn of 1928 had His Majesty left well alone.

As late as the end of October the fascinating game of "Europe" still continued, and a whole series of treaties on the subject of extradition were announced with Persia, Turkey, Egypt, Finland, Switzerland, and Bolivia. But already were the fatal proclamations and orders launched that were to blow the smouldering discontent into flames. In September Government officials were forbidden to practice polygamy, despite the Islamic sanctions. In October European dress was imposed on the people of Kabul, even as a like edict has debased the beauties and dignity of Constantinople. But European dress must postulate European habits. You cannot sit cross-legged or squat on your hunkers, which Eastern calves are especially shaped to do, in trousers. Yet chairs exist not. While wearers of Western sleeves cannot eat by dipping their hands in the cinnamon stew, and such unthinking edicts postulate knives and forks and mean expenditure. The capital of Kabul was very naturally annoyed, and showed it. In this connection we may imagine the hurried passage to the nearest lamp-post that would await a Home Secretary who issued an edict ordering the men of London to wear the reformed dress, or the business young ladies to lengthen their skirts and sleeves, with penalties for disobedience, accompanied by a stoppage of police salaries.

In late October or early November the flame burst out among the Shinwari tribes who live round the winter capital of Jalalabad. The King hurried off to see what the trouble was about and to open the road to India. After the tribesmen had attacked the city without success for some days, parleys and armistices took place, and while these were in progress an apparently different and unconnected revolt broke out in the hills round Kabul, among that horde of fanatical tribes who had flocked in their tens of thousands to attack Sir Frederick Roberts in 1879. It was the mullahs of Eastern Afghanistan who had fanned this flame by issuing an edict that the King was an infidel.

Even Abdurrahman with all his ruthless ways had to bow at times to the mullahs and all they stood for, while they in their turn took care not to oppose him beyond bearing. But the changes that the young King had introduced were insupportable. Priestly revenues were being sequestrated, endowments confiscated, and now an order had been published forbidding asylum to all refugee priests evicted from the Sovietised khanates of Russian Turkistan.

So, to add to the Royal troubles, the priesthood went out wholeheartedly against him. But the army, the army said to be short of pay, what of them? There were several factors here to be reckoned with. In the first place, the troops were largely Tajik, from those more biddable and easier disciplined folk of Persian or Perso-Arab descent from the neighbourhood of the Oxus.

The second Turkish military mission charged with training the army was no more popular than the first, and this fact has not conduced to content. With an army drawn largely from the races other than those dominating the country, with military schools and colleges full of young men wedded possibly to the alluring prospects of an Afghan future, but with no pronounced loyalty to the Durani throne, there was ample room for dissatisfaction to grow apace. Standing armies, unless animated by a carefully cultivated loyalty of long standing, can be hot-beds of propaganda when their serenity is upset, and this is what happened with the army of Amanullah with all its imitation of Balkan ways.

The Coming of Bacha-i-Saqao

While the risings of the tribes in the Kabul Kohistan went on apace, the King for the moment had succeeded in coming to a *modus vivendi* with the Shinwari tribes round Jalalabad, and returned to Kabul. The tribes were already beginning to surround that city, and with them were revolted troops. This trouble seems to have been distinct from those at Jalalabad, but they were definite and increasing. By the 17th December 1928 hostilities were in progress round the city, with cannon on both sides, and the foreign residents in Kabul took asylum in their respective legations.

Now arose a leader and a spokesman, the man of grit and character, one Habibullah, leader of bandits, an outlaw and a wolf's head, who with a following of some four hundred, it is said, attacked the suburbs and gained many to his side. Habibullah was at first said to have been a Mohmand, that is to say, a Pathan from the country north of the Kabul River; but was soon known to be a Tajik, a Robin Hood, among that normally simple folk, and one who, strange to say, had always commanded a following.

The King proclaimed martial law, and summoned levies from tribes that were still loyal to come to his assistance. Communication between Kabul and India had now been interrupted, though a wireless message said that all was well with the legations. Nevertheless, on the 20th, British planes from Peshawar flew over Kabul and reported all quiet, but the British Government sent for the heavy troop-carrying planes from Iraq to be at hand to evacuate the British subjects and Europeans of other states.

The King's call for levies met with apparent success, and those who came were armed from the arsenals; but a large number of rebels succeeded in entering the city dressed in Government uniforms, and the situation went from bad to worse in spite of many arrests and summary executions. The belligerents, rebel tribesmen and loyal tribesmen, mutinous troops and loyal troops, continued to fight in the outskirts of Kabul and in the surrounding gardens, during which, though in the middle of it all, the British legation remained unharmed and respected, so great apparently was both the prestige of the British Government and that of Sir Francis Humphrys himself.

Nevertheless, the neighbourhood was too hot to be pleasant, and the chance of the restoration of order more remote, so that on the 23rd December it was decided to remove all the women and children sheltering in the legation, the carrier planes from Peshawar making most successful flights to that end. On the 24th, twenty-eight women and children were removed, and on the two following days a good many more. By the end of December the immediate environs of Kabul had taken on a quieter aspect and the rebels had drawn off from the city. News, however, from Jalalabad showed that the arrangements with the Shinwaris would not hold, in view, apparently, of developments at Kabul. The age-long Afghan view of good diplomacy, which meant changing sides at the right moment, was not to be in abeyance. The royal garrison at Nimla surrendered, and the evacuation of foreign families by British planes continued over the snowy ranges, while all the world applauded.

King Amanullah, still in authority, commenced in the opening days of January 1929 to give way to popular demands, agreeing to close down the girls' schools and to create a controlling council on which priests and sirdars should preponderate. On 7th January, this was followed by a proclamation withdrawing decrees about conscription and dress and forming a council of fifty. Such concessions, however, were too late, and fighting round Kabul recommenced. The evacuations of Europeans and Indian subjects by plane were continued, one hundred and thirty-two more persons getting away. A serious set-back to the King's cause now took place in the assassination of an important supporter of the dynasty, one Mirzaman Shah, a leading chief of the Afghan Mohmands who dominate the country north of the Kabul River and Jalalabad.

By the middle of January the unfortunate young King had realised that fate was too strong for him, that he had been deserted by his army, and, like the Dost his ancestor, must leave his capital. To add to this, his Queen was expecting her confinement in a country where there was little ruth for those who were down. He managed to get his wife and family, however, flown away to Kandahar in his Russian planes, and then accepted the representations made to him by his advisers that the country would have no more of him, and that the only hope of saving even the dynasty lay in letting his elder brother Inayatullah take the throne. Any attempt to resist could but mean a hopeless attempt to defend the modern fortified palace outside Kabul that had long taken the place of the Bala Hissar, and would only result in bloodshed harmful to Afghanistan and injurious to the dynasty.

Amanullah then formally abdicated in favour of Inayatullah, the legal heir, from whom he had indirectly snatched the power, when with the help of the army he deposed his uncle Nasrullah,[1] after their father's murder in 1919. On this being settled, arrangements were made that got the King out of the palace and into planes for Kandahar.

[1] Who had proclaimed himself Amir in 1919 with Inayatullah's consent. See Chapter XVII.

Inayatullah then sat on the throne that he might have occupied before.

The Last of the Barakzais

But the good Inayatullah was not the man to sit on that throne of uneasiness even in the way of peaceful succession. Stout, amiable, lethargic, not even, so far as was known, wise in council, the situation was far beyond his control or the group of king-making sirdars who hoped to save the dynasty and secure continuity. Bacha-i-Saqao was on the top of a wave of Islamic fervour, which was for the moment almost reaching the height of Wahabism in its clamour for the dour tenets of the desert and the old, simple ways of "The Submission." He had denounced Amanullah and all his ways, and those of his house and his entourage, his laws, his proclamations, and his iniquities, and the drum ecclesiastic throbbed and rolled on the mountain-sides and poured forth warriors from the glens and gorges. "Howl! Son of Man, howl!" shouted the Isaiahs. "Glory for all and heaven for those who bleed!" screamed the mullahs, as they howled it round the British in Sherpur. The Government post of Jagdalak fell, and Kabul was cut off from the outside world. The hearts of the Barakzai sirdars turned to water within the palace, and the good Inayatullah realised that that throne was no place for him. In five days he too abdicated, and his withdrawal by plane to Peshawar was arranged.

During all this period the British minister appears to have stood for reason and for moderation before all parties, and became strangely enough the counsellor of each. Above all was he able to impress on them that the civilised world was looking on, and that no one's purpose would be served by an orgy of dynastic or vengeful bloodshed.

On 17th January the water-carrier's son proclaimed himself Amir of the Afghan people, or such as would follow him, until such time as the people should elect their own Amir, vowing that he sought not aggrandisement but only the will of God, under the style and title of Habibullah

Ghazi, "The Beloved of God and the Defender of the Faith."

But the disappearance of "the crown" was the signal for the old fissiparous tendency, against which Abdurrahman had so long fought, to reappear. Amirs began to spring up all round. At Jalalabad, Sirdar Ali Ahmad Khan Jan, a cousin of Amanullah and for some years Governor of Kabul, persuaded the Shinwari chiefs to proclaim him Amir, though, in face of the Puritan tendencies, his predilections for strong waters were soon to procure his ejection. At Kandahar itself Amanullah found many sympathisers, and as his abdication was in favour of his brother, he not unfairly declared that it now no longer bound him. There was every precedent for an attempt to restore his position from the chief city of Southern Afghanistan as a base, or at worst to establish that separate principality which had existed prior to 1839, and which the British themselves had set up for a while in 1880.

While these movements were endeavouring to orient themselves, the British minister and his relieving planes continued their work of what was practically the rescue of a stranded and possibly starving colony. By the first week in February no less than three hundred and eight souls had flown away, of whom fifty-five belonged to the British legation, European and Indian, and one hundred and nine were of Indian race. But by now even those nationalities who had aspired to weather the storm were anxious to get away, and two more batches of fifty-eight each followed in quick succession, and by the 26th February the numbers had risen to five hundred and eighty-six. And then with his humane task done and with Afghanistan in tatters, the pilot left the ship. Sir Francis Humphrys listened to the voice of wisdom and the wishes of his own Government, and at last swung himself with his remaining assistants into the last plane and shook off for a while the romantic and exciting dust of the tragic city of Kabul. But though the British minister has left, British prestige and reputation for disinterested dealing stands there higher than it has ever stood before, and many there be of standing who mourn

The empty British Legation outside Kabul

The mud walls and bastions of an Afghan town

the day when a young fool left the established friends of his fathers and spurned their liberal and helpful coffers.

Amanullah in Southern Afghanistan

It has already been explained that he who would rule at Kabul must make his peace with the Ghilzais, and make it to a great extent on their terms. This it would appear that neither the Ghazi at Kabul nor Amanullah Barakzai was able to do. Amirs all and sundry had sprung into power in every direction, and during this spring no fewer than seven held the field—no very great number, however, when we reflect on the size of the country, and its divergent races and variant faith be considered. Malik Ghaus-ud-din, chief of the Ahmadzai section of the Ghilzais, proclaimed himself Amir of Ghuzni, and those who have read the earlier chapters of this book will agree that Ghuzni has no mean claim to headship. How far all the Ghilzais will follow him is not yet clear, but as they hold the hills between Kabul and Kandahar and between Kabul and India, they can bide their time and cultivate the highest bidder.

In Turkistan there are many aspirants, and at the moment Herat and Maimana and Tashqurghan have all something to say. Amanullah at Kandahar found many supporters of a Durani against a Tajik claimant. Somewhat reluctantly Inayatullah, murmuring the Persian equivalent for *nolo episcopari*, was rushed in a State train by the British from his rest at Peshawar when he landed from his aeroplane to the frontier at New Chaman, whence he drove to Kandahar. There the King was gathering together as much of the garrison as would support him, and endeavouring to enlist the support of the Duranis of Zamindawar. Unfortunately the King's kinship was not enough to counterbalance, in their zealot minds, his modern practices, had not Amanullah had a brain-wave. Outside Kandahar was the famous shrine of the Khirqa-i-Sharif, "The Holy Cloak." For two hundred years this genuine and thrice-holy relic of the Prophet had lain locked in a brass-bound chest. No infidel, no wavering and uncertain follower of the Prophet, could unlock the chest. It was in this shrine that the mullah had taken refuge who had so far forgot himself as to call Abdurrahman *kafir*, and where that man of blood and iron, as already told, had him brought forth and slew him with his own hand "that so impious a dog should not defile the earth."

King Amanullah established his orthodoxy by opening the box with ease and drawing forth the relic in the presence of many thousands of excited populace. For a while his influence was restored and he was able to push up the road to Ghuzni, reoccupying Kelat-i-Ghilzie and getting as far as Mukkur, whence incidentally had come that mysterious British mullah whom men used to talk of as "the Buster's double." [1]

But though he reached Mukkur, Ghuzni was not to be attained. Whether or no the King's personality was at fault it is not yet possible to say. The hard school that bred the *Bacha* is probably a better start when kingdoms are in the balance than the luxury of an Eastern palace. We have yet to know if Amanullah could really draw a badger. But whether he could or whether he could not, it is certain that he was short of money, short of the needful to pay his soldiers, buy his petrol, which meant ready cash, and short of the large sums necessary to buy those faithless ones whose natural home is on the fence.

By May Amanullah made his unsuccessful advance on Ghuzni, and then in despair returned towards Kandahar; but avoiding that city threw up the sponge, appearing with his delicate Queen and family at New Chaman, craving hospitality. And then we see him and his brother waiting at Bombay for their ladies' pleasure ere making for their resting-places in Europe and in Persia.

During the attempts of Amanullah to rebuild his fortunes from Kandahar, the world was treated to a series of proclamations aimed at each other from Habibullah and

[1] The famous Sir James Browne, the frontier soldier-political, whose uncanny influence over Afghans was partly due to the existence of this holy double. See his *Life*.

the King which were not particularly edifying. Sirdar Ghulam Nabi, formerly the Afghan agent at Moscow, arrived at Herat in April to work in the interest of Amanullah, with no great success; while as early as 24th February General Nadir Khan arrived at Peshawar from his residence on the Riviera and proceeded to Khost, anxious to see what the situation really was, and if possible to save at any rate Afghanistan from itself, and to preserve the organised kingdom as a state in being. His efforts have been backed by some of the Mangals, who have long been at loggerheads with the Government both of Amanullah and his predecessors, and the Jedrans and the Jajis, none of them very important politically. He had advanced into Logar from Gardez via the Altimur Pass, apparently hoping to come to some arrangement with Malik Ghaus-ud-din and the Ahmadzai Ghilzais, but has now been beaten by Kabul troops, with whom are said to be the lashkars of the Sulaiman Khel group of the Ghilzai clans, which means that the Ghilzai influence itself is split. Nadir Khan is also said to have joined the ranks of the soi-disant Amirs, but is credited by the better informed to be anxious to put forward Asadullah Khan, Amanullah's nephew, for election as Amir. The latter is or has been in durance in Kabul.[1]

It is to be remembered, in struggling with the multitude of names that now come before the news-reader, that the number of Barakzai sirdars all closely interrelated to one another and to Amanullah is legion. The twenty influential brothers of Fath Khan, who ruled almost every Afghan province and district from Kashmir to Herat ninety years ago, left an immense progeny; while there are many scions of the Saduzai family also extant. As many of them have the same name, a "Who's Who in Afghanistan," which exists in the archives, would drive any but the highly initiated to distraction. Among the many looking out for opportunity is a son of Ayub Khan, the son of Shere Ali who escaped from his residence in India, one Muhammad Omar Khan.

Since the flight of Amanullah after the failure of his

[1] But see p. 343.

move on Ghuzni, Ali Ahmad Khan Jan, the ubiquitous and ambitious, having come round to Kandahar to make his peace with Amanullah, had himself proclaimed Amir of the South. He was not to enjoy the position long, for Sirdar Abdul Qayyum shortly after took Kandahar on behalf of Habibullah and sent the bagman Amir a prisoner to Kabul.[1]

And while the country is refinding itself, trade is beginning to move again by leave of the tribes who hold the passes, overjoyed that the stern rule which protected the caravan has gone, and they are free to do so once again on their own terms and at their own price; for they agree heartily with one Falstaff that "young men must live, and gorbellied knaves with fat purses are fair game."

The Attitude of the British Government

Those who have some acquaintance with Afghan problems are somewhat intrigued to know what has been the precise attitude and inclination of the British and Indian Governments during the upheaval. That, however, cannot well be divulged to us for some time yet. Undoubtedly the Indian Government did look very askance at the tearing up of their work of many years, and must naturally enough have cast a thought towards the possibility of supporting the King. It was pretty well known, however, that the King's influence had been much undermined in his absence, and that his mad series of edicts would make his position very precarious. Fortunately, he had forfeited his right to say with Shere Ali that our friendship was a word written on ice, in that it was he who so wantonly broke it in 1919. Nor is it possible yet to say what attitude we can take towards Habibullah, who at the present moment is keenly anxious to be recognised. Our policy is, as before and as always, that of a friendly and strong Afghanistan. We cannot but be secretly amused that the man who crowed so loud should now sing so small, were it not that British interests were so intermingled with that of his edifice.

[1] But see p. 343.

Fortunately our own frontier has stood the excitement well, and has not reacted seriously to the disturbances. In fact, at present we with our uniform support of all the reasonable aspirations of the Moslem peoples in the world, and our liberal attitude to all Moslem religious viewpoints, are far more acceptable to the ecclesiastics of Islam generally, and of wild frontier mullahs in particular, than usual. The only frontier disturbance in progress is the recrudescence of the ancient quarrel between the Shiah and Sunni factions among the tribes of the Orakzai Tirah, and the attitude of the Afridi neighbours in the matter. It was at one time thought that Amanullah might have been playing an unauthorised hand in this, but he had too many Shiah subjects of his own to handle to get a reputation for preferring the orthodox to them. Our frontier officials, who have had the Amir or King of Afghanistan thrown up in their faces by impertinent chiefs, are perhaps not sorry to be able to say, "Where's yer friend the Amir the noo?"

The descendants of the sons of Shere Ali, both of Yakub Khan the Amir and Ayub his brother, have long lived in India supported by the Indian revenues as one of the measures of securing the dynasty of Abdurrahman. When Sirdar Muhammad Omar Khan, without the consent of the Government, slipped away to Afghanistan a few months back to try his luck, the remaining refugees of the family, of likely age, were removed for a while to a safer residential site in Burma, lest they too should hurry to take part in the dog-fight.

Looking Forward

Since India's affairs are so deeply connected with Afghanistan, we cannot look on with equanimity at the present turmoil, nor can we, as in the safe days of John Lawrence, wait unconcerned for order to evolve itself. He, it will be remembered, did actually accord recognition to an Amir in Kabul and another in Kandahar, and even a third in Herat, when the succession to Dost Muhammad was in dispute. But now far worse than ambitious Imperial Russia approaching the Oxus, we have the group of Soviets, behind whom is this bitter, restless, relentless desire to tear up all the prosperity that the *Pax Britannica* stands for. Hence before us now is the double anxiety, that of the warring centre of disturbance on our border and that of the Soviets on the other side.

For years, as has been explained, Great Britain has resisted the desire of Russia to absorb Afghan Turkistan, and has turned a deaf ear to the not unattractive suggestion that we should share the kingdom, with the Hindu Kush between us. Allusion has already been made to the network of Soviet intrigue which has been at work in Afghanistan, not only to upset the natural order, but more especially to get through it to the disturbance of India. In the disintegration of Afghanistan lies the hope of Soviet success.

For long it has been known that the Soviet aspirations lay in the direction of stirring the non-Afghan races on the cis-Oxus to demand political affinity with their kinsmen in the Soviets, and if necessary to demonstrate to that effect. When the Afghan Government proceeded to suppress any such demonstrations, then Soviet troops in the name of freedom and self-expression would intervene. Indeed, for some years the General Staff in India have had before them the problem of how to give military support in such a dilemma to the Afghan throne.

The position in Turkistan has always been complicated by the fact that Afghan overlordship has never been too popular. Hitherto their rule has always had behind it a tinge of thoughtless want of ruth, so entirely different from the methods of the Ottoman Turk over his subject peoples. In Turkey, for instance, you might be as Christian and as foreign as you liked so long as you did not make a song and dance about it. Squeeze and let live was the Turkish motto. Nor for them to kill the goose that laid the golden egg. *Continuez, mes enfants, continuez !* The Afghan was never so wise; "strip bare" was his way, and come again to-morrow lest he had left something over. This fault, translated into terms of government, has never made Afghan rule beloved, and it is possible that the Turki and Tajik population would be quite prepared to Sovietise.

The question that may at any moment come before this country is whether it is prepared to let its policy of a century go overboard and accept not an Imperial Russian answering in some sort to the methods of diplomacy, but a raw-red, mad-dog Russian neighbour on the Hindu Kush. If it is, does it realise the implications and the military expenditure and anxiety that such a change must involve? It would be disastrous if such a situation be sprung on us while mentally unprepared.

From these reflections we may turn to the state of affairs in Afghanistan with a pretty clear conception of what we need. It is obvious that we want the kingdom restored. It is also clear that we have no use for a restoration that does not appeal to the general sense of the more dominant and virile races. We saw one that did not, and burnt our fingers in the process with the ill-fated Shah Shujah, though that may have been more in our action than in our policy. We have seen Dost Muhammad, Shere Ali, Abdurrahman, Habibullah his son, all fill the rôle with varying success, and we have seen a young, too modern man gamble his heritage away. What now? A Tajik has the power for a moment. Nadir Shah was a Turk and an upstart. We who hold by William, the son of a tanner's daughter, need not worry about the water-carrier's son if he can deliver the goods to his people's satisfaction. We want him to make good, or we want General Nadir Khan, or someone of goodwill who can make an all-round settlement that the factions will accept. We emphatically do not want a heptarchy, since, though such would relieve us of any menace of another Afghan invasion, it would not hold the Oxus fords, nor could its states ever lie together in peace and amity.

It is perfectly possible now for Afghanistan, with its trained officials, to restart on its road to progress, while maintaining the character of a theocratic state with a Moslem establishment, and be infinitely the better therefor. This done, we shall see the gradual rather than the forced development of those resources which have just been described. Whether or no Habibullah Ghazi can continue to fulfil the rôle no man can yet say. Apart from his origin, the discovery of which shortly after his first success came as a shock to the Afghans of other than Turkish or Tajik descent, he has at his command some of the factors required besides his personal character. He has in his possession, for instance, the arsenals; but, unfortunately, the hitherto jealously guarded stocks of ammunition have been scattered far and wide among tribal followers, both by Amanullah and himself, and that does not make for order or power. Money in the form of hard cash is his real need. In pursuance of the eternal Eastern desire for a personal superscription as an outward and visible sign, he has restruck the coinage; but that does not fill his coffers. Hard cash is the rock on which he is likely to split.

It is not unamusing to learn that Persia, if you please, has intimated "hands off Herat" to the Soviets; while the Afridis, who are little concerned, mindful of their own old predilection for the Saduzais, have said that they will only favour some Amir of the "Royal" clans, though they can hardly mean the former—both indications of the direction of the breezes. It is, too, of interest to reflect how the old anti-British influence of the Moslem party is now instinctively on the British side, while all along the Oxus the refugee ecclesiastics from Russian Turkistan are among the best bulwarks against Soviet penetration.

The British Government is only too anxious to learn that the country has made a decision and can agree about it. Recognition, and recognition in practical form, will very soon follow in the interests of civilisation and trade. Habibullah Ghazi, or whoever may be chosen, will find better advice and support from a Government which still considers revealed religion the proper basis on which to build a state, and which, moreover, has ever been cognisant of the power for good that dwells in the discipline and teaching of "The Submission."

However that may be, the young Afghan in all his

bravery has the sympathy of many who hope that he may win through to a realisation of at least a good deal of what King Amanullah, patriot but *dunya-dar*, dreamed for them. But for the nonce it would seem that the country must pass through that condition once again of which Lyall sang:

"And far from the Suleiman heights come the sounds of the stirring of tribes,
Afreedi, Hazara, and Ghilzi, they clamour for plunder or bribes;
And Herat is but held by a thread; and the Usbeg has raised Badukshan;
And the chief may sleep sound, in his grave, who would rule the unruly Afghan."

. . . .

ENVOI

Even since these last words were written, the sword, the noose, and the platoon have been at work in this sad land of ill omen. Debonnair, pleasure-loving Ali Ahmad Khan Jan, the late King's cousin, has been dragged in contumely to execution through the streets of Kabul.[1]

Asadullah Khan, the nephew of Amanullah, in whom the dynasty had hopes, and four of his associates, have been, it is believed, dispatched by the noose, and before these pages leave the press the tally of past pretenders may have mounted sadly, since Afghanistan even in these days stands by the saw that "stone-dead hath no fellow."

[1] Which, according to accounts that have reached India, was carried out in an unspeakably barbarous manner.

APPENDIX I

THE DYNASTY OF THE DURANI EMPIRE

(The Saduzai Family)

- Ahmad Shah (1747)
  - Timur Shah
    - Humayun (blinded)
    - Shah Zaman (blinded)
    - Shah Mahmud
      - Shah Kamran
    - Shah Shujah (murdered 1742)
      - Timur [1]
      - Fath Jang [2]
      - Safdar Jang [3]
      - Shapur [4]
    - Firoz
    - Abbas

[1] Governor of Kandahar Province till the British left in 1842.
[2] Shah in name after murder of Shah Shujah.
[3] Governor of Kandahar when the British left in 1842.
[4] Shah for a while after the British left in 1842. There were other less prominent sons.

APPENDIX II

GENEALOGICAL TABLE OF THE BARAKZAIS

(Showing descent of King Amanullah)

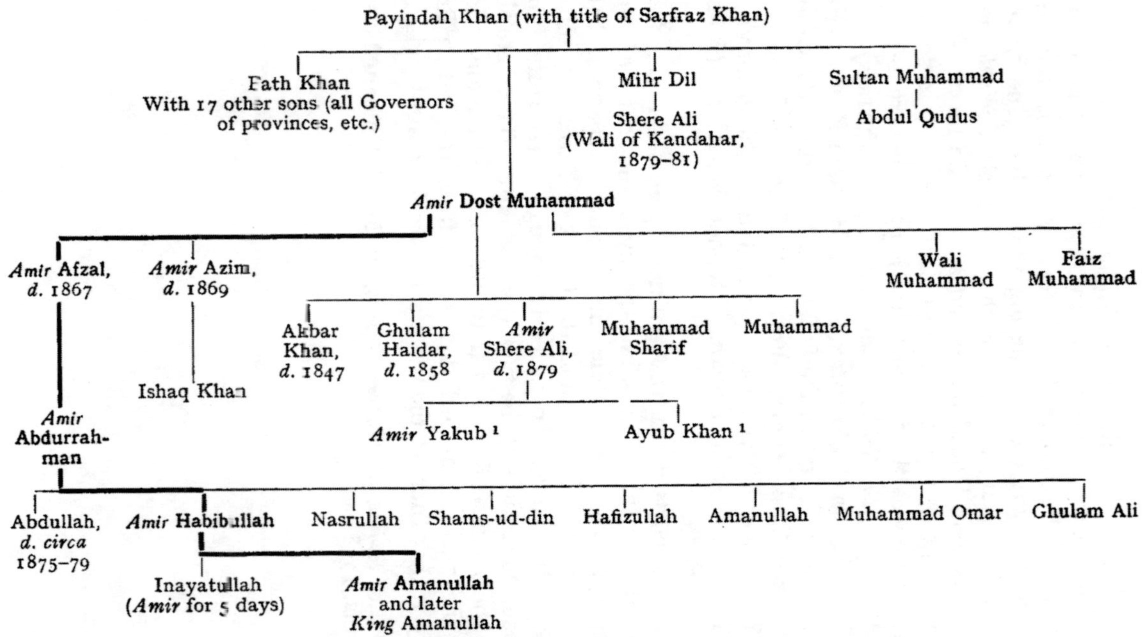

[1] Sons of Yakub and Ayub are pensioned guests of the Indian Government.

BIBLIOGRAPHY

THE books that deal with Afghanistan in one form or another are almost too numerous to catalogue, but it is not too much to say that the *Cambridge History of India* is the last word in summarising and co-ordinating all that has gone before, and that for the ordinary student neither the basic *Ferishta* nor the *Sair-ul-Mutaqerin* [1] need be opened again. So far as the nineteenth century goes, the following present the story in some detail and with more wealth of colour than is possible here :—

History of the Sikhs. Cunninghame. (Murray.)

The War in Afghanistan. John William Kaye. (Bentley.)

Forty-one Years in India. Lord Roberts. (Macmillan.)

Neville Chamberlain. Forrest. (Blackwood.)

The Life of Abdurrahman (an edited autobiography). (Murray.)

The Amir Abdurrahman. Stephen Wheeler. (Bliss, Sands & Foster.)

The reports from the political agents on the frontiers are valuable as showing what the eyes and ears of Government conveyed to them, while the dispatches passing between the Government of India and the Court of Directors, and later with the India Office, show clearly enough what from time to time was in the minds of the two Governments. These are all available at the India Office, and it would seem that many of the critics of the period imbibed their views from the Indian Press of the day rather than at the more accurate fountain-heads.

[1] I.e. *Review of Modern Times*, by M. M. Ghulam Hussain, 1782. Trans. 1798.

INDEX